THE SCIENCE OF MAGIC

THE SCIENCE OF MAGIC

How the Mind Weaves the Fabric of Reality

DEAN RADIN, PhD

HARMONY
NEW YORK

To my charming wife Susie and a small dog named Mr. Scrappy,
who was a good boy who never bit anyone and barked only at other dogs.
He occasionally poked his head out of the dog door and peed in
the house, but for that minor transgression he was always forgiven.

CONTENTS

PREFACE

There. Did you feel the ground shake?

No, it wasn't an earthquake. What you just experienced is a radical paradigm shift—a scientific reconsideration of the role of consciousness in the physical world. Major paradigms in science don't change very often; they prefer to sit around like curmudgeonly custodians of conventional wisdom, scoffing at new ideas. But when those ideas do start to slide, confusion erupts, experts bicker, and skeptics start to sweat. When the dust settles, a new paradigm takes shape. Then what?

Then we live in a new world.

One of the consequences of this new world is that the esoteric practice of *magic* will emerge from the shadows, where it has been quietly simmering for about five hundred years. But this time magic, sometimes spelled *magick* to distinguish it from magic tricks, will be seen through the lens of science. Societal taboos that long suppressed this natural capacity will begin to dissolve, and new light will shine on who we are and what we're capable of.

This worldview shift is so radical that when a stranger asks me what I do for a living, I've learned that there's some risk in admitting that I study magic. So I just say I'm a scientist. If asked what kind of scientist, I'll say it's a little complicated and offer them an answer via a puzzle. I'll describe where I've published articles, and then they can guess what I do. It's like a game show, but without the fabulous prizes.

If they're open to this game, I'll say that I've published a few hundred articles in scientific journals, including *Foundations of Physics, Frontiers in Human Neuroscience,* and *Nature Translational Psychiatry.* I've also served as a referee for two dozen other journals, including *Psychological Bulletin, Integrative Cancer Therapies,* and *Nature Scientific Reports.*

If they haven't stifled a yawn yet, I'll add that I've given about eight hundred invited presentations around the world, including at universities like Harvard, Stanford, Princeton, Columbia, and Cambridge; for US government organizations like the Naval War College, the Naval Postgraduate School, the Army Special Operations Command, and the National Academy of Sciences; for companies like Google and Merck; and for government programs and agencies in Australia, India, and Malaysia. At this point, the listener thinks I'm either a genius or completely full of it.

If they're not backing away slowly, I'll add that for over two decades I've worked at a research institute founded by the sixth man to walk on the moon. Yes, the actual moon, not a soundstage in Hollywood. I also worked on a formerly classified program charged with investigating exotic methods for gathering intelligence data. Then I'll ask, What do you think I do? The trick is, whatever they say, I'll say Yes, that's it! They feel satisfied because everyone likes to solve a puzzle, and I feel relieved because I can avoid explaining what I do.

I'm reluctant to say that I study magic and its close cousin, psychic phenomena (*psi* for short), because I know that these topics conjure Hollywood stereotypes. Paranormal-themed horror films have so thoroughly enchanted the modern mind that it's practically inconceivable that a scientist would take such phenomena seriously.

And yet a majority of the general population, including a surprisingly large percentage of scientists, have had personal experiences that can best be described as magical or psi. Unfortunately, the taboo about these topics is so powerful that we quickly learn to not talk about them. And we certainly don't chat about magic in the academic world, unless it's about stage magic or why people believe in silly superstitions.

As of this writing, I've been studying psi and magical phenomena for about forty-five years, mostly full time as a scientist in major university, industrial, and private research institutions. I've also served five terms as the president of the Parapsychological Association, an international organization for scientists and scholars engaged in the serious study of psi phenomena. Since 1969 the Parapsychological Association has been an elected affiliate of the American Association for the Advancement of Science (AAAS), the largest and most prestigious scientific society in the world. For an organization to become an affiliate, the AAAS council, some 30 representatives of mainstream science, must elect it. As of 2025, the Parapsychological Association is one of 273 AAAS affiliates.

Perhaps in recognition of parapsychology's scientific status, in April 2024 one of my books was included in a feature article by the *Times of India* news service. The article listed eight books the *Times* selected that would "change the way you look at the universe."[1] It included works by the authors Albert Camus, Friedrich Nietzsche, Fyodor Dostoyevsky, and Franz Kafka, and by physicists David Deutsch and Stephen Hawking. My book on that list was *Entangled Minds*, which focuses on the physics of psi.

As I was writing that last sentence, something caught my eye. I looked out the window just as a blue commercial van drove by with the word MAGIC emblazoned on the side. The van was part of a fleet for a plumbing company whose motto is "Service so good *you'll believe in magic*." One of its core values is "Get shit done," which seems apt given its area of expertise.

The synchronicity of writing about magic as the word *magic* appears outside your window is a sign that we've entered a zone where the laws of physics turn into mere suggestions. One of the more celebrated physicists of the twentieth century, John Archibald Wheeler, put it this way: "Useful as it is under everyday circumstances to say that the world exists 'out there' independent of us, that view can no longer be upheld. There is a strange sense in which this is a 'participatory universe.'"[2] In such a universe, Wheeler emphasized that physical laws are not fixed but rather are, as he put it, malleable. In his famously pithy style, he noted, "There is no law except the law that there is no law."[3]

Wheeler's quip was strangely similar to the catchphrase of the notorious occultist Aleister Crowley, who said: "Do what thou wilt shall be the whole of the Law." This is not to say that Wheeler and Crowley were bosom buddies, because they barely existed in the same universe. On the other hand, is it a meaningful synchronicity?

Let's get shit done and find out.

PART I

A REVOLUTION IS BREWING

Some say magic is a legendary power that can bend destiny at will.

Modern minds are naturally skeptical about such claims. Science tells us that magic is wishful thinking. It violates the laws of physics. It's fantasy. No educated person could take it seriously.

But it turns out that magic is quite real and has been hiding in plain sight. Today, through the bright light of science, we can see and begin to understand magic in new ways.

Part I of this book provides an overview of the magical revolution that's actively brewing in science. Part II reviews a small but relevant selection of the scientific evidence supporting the reality of magic. Part III discusses how to understand magic from a modern perspective. And Part IV explains how to do magic.

CHAPTER 1

INTRODUCTION

There may be no such thing as the "glittering central mechanism of the universe" to be seen behind a glass wall at the end of the trail. Not machinery but magic may be the better description of the treasure that is waiting.

—JOHN ARCHIBALD WHEELER[1]

In a series of invited lectures to a special study group at the Naval War College, one of the topics I discussed was the scientific evidence for telepathy—direct mind-to-mind communication. During a break, two submarine commanders approached me and described a strange episode they had independently experienced. While under maneuvers and submerged at classified depths, a crew member in each commander's sub urgently requested that they surface so they could call home. They were certain that something bad was happening in their family. The commanders replied that after their undersea exercises were completed, then they could contact their families.

Each sub surfaced days to weeks later, and in both cases, it turned out that something upsetting had indeed happened in their family at the time that each crew member made their request. Importantly, both commanders noted there were no false positives; that is, these were the only times any crew member had asked to surface early.

A typical operational depth for a submarine is 150 to 300 meters, and based on the commanders' remarks, these subs were likely at the deeper end of that range. At such depths, the only way to receive a signal from the surface world is through extremely low-frequency electromagnetic transmissions, which require antennas tens to hundreds of kilometers long. The rate of these transmissions is only about one letter per minute. Even if a human brain could detect and decode such messages (which is exceedingly unlikely), those transmissions are used solely for military purposes. They aren't used to send personal messages to crew members about their families. Moreover, submariners are carefully selected for their exceptional mental toughness, resilience, and emotional flexibility—not the type of person you'd expect to report a fanciful telepathic experience while deep underwater.

But they do.

You may have experienced something similar—a time when you just knew that something unexpected was happening to a loved one at a distance, and later you discovered you were right. Or you found yourself thinking about an old friend and soon received a call or an email from them. In fact, two nights before writing this passage, I had a dream about a friend from summer camp, over fifty years ago. Out of the blue, "Joan" showed up in my dream. I hadn't thought about her in years.

The next morning I received a blind-copied email from Joan, which prompted me to write back and ask why I was suddenly included in her mailing list. She explained that her realtor had mentioned Edgar Mitchell—an Apollo 14 astronaut—and that Edgar had talked about the noetic sciences. Because I work at the Institute of Noetic Sciences, which Mitchell founded in 1973, Joan thought of me. That night I dreamed about her.

Because of commonly reported experiences like this, most people, including scientists, quietly maintain some belief in psychic and magical phenomena. At the same time, mainstream science insists that these phenomena *can't exist* because the mind is solely a product of brain activity, so everything having to do with mental activity, including consciousness, is locked inside our skulls. End of story.

But there's a problem with that story.

Psychic and magical experiences are frequently reported, and they *require* that consciousness somehow transcends the brain and extends into the physical world. Until about five hundred years ago, most people believed that consciousness was fundamentally interconnected with the physical world, and from that perspective the existence of psychic effects like telepathy and magical effects like divination was taken for granted. Then, as science became the dominant way of understanding reality, magic fell out of favor, and generations of students were trained to see reality solely through the lens of *materialism*, the philosophical assumption that everything, including consciousness, is made of matter and energy. That worldview has become so entrenched in our way of thinking about reality that science textbooks don't bother to mention that nearly all the physicists who developed quantum mechanics believed that consciousness played a key role in the physical world.[2] Some, like Max Planck, believed that consciousness was the *only* primary reality.

But science marches on, and we are now in the midst of a remarkable period of remembering what our forebears knew. Science is rediscovering magic.

ABOUT THIS BOOK

This book is about the science, theory, and practice of real magic. These practices come in three flavors: *enchantment, divination,* and *theurgy.* Enchantment is the ability to mentally modulate aspects of the physical world and shape destiny. Divination involves perceptions that transcend the everyday limits of space and time. Theurgy is about spirits and spiritual development.

Magic, like meditation or mathematics, is a mental skill. Anyone can learn some of the key elements, but true mastery requires practice and natural talent. Magical practices can be found throughout history and in all cultures.[3] Among the thousands of books about magic, only a small percentage discuss this topic from a scientific perspective. And most of those address magic in terms of tricks and illusions, or mistaken beliefs about magic, or the malleable brain-body relationship.[4] Only a handful of books about *real* magic have been written by scientists.[5]

WHO IS THIS BOOK FOR?

This book's subtitle, "How the Mind Weaves the Fabric of Reality," refers to the emerging scientific recognition of the role that consciousness plays in the behavior of the physical world. This perspective transforms psychic, mystical, spiritual, and magical experiences from weird and rare brain-centric hallucinations into predictable and commonly reported mind-oriented experiences.

I am confident that we'll eventually have a rational, scientifically satisfying explanation for magic. The most prominent physicists of the nineteenth century couldn't have imagined how much the laws of physics would be revised by the turn of the twentieth century. Nor could the most accomplished scientists at the beginning of the twentieth century have anticipated how much the meaning of the term *reality* would be transformed by the early decades of the twenty-first century. History provides endless examples of leading intellectuals whose prognostications about future discoveries were laughably wrong in hindsight. Each new generation insists that *now* we're finally modern and sophisticated, and so *now* we're absolutely positive that this or that is impossible.[6]

I believe it is likely that by the dawn of the twenty-second century, our scientific understanding about mind and its relationship to matter will have evolved to the point where what we currently call "magic" will be accepted as self-evident.[7] Today's leading edge in physics already proposes that spacetime is an emergent property of quantum entanglement, which is "outside" space and time.[8] In the future we may discover that mind, matter, energy, space, and time—concepts once thought to be entirely separate features of reality—actually emerge from a single source that is none of those concepts but somehow all of them and more. At that point a scientific theory of everything will begin to catch up with the esoteric worldview, in which the physical world emerges from a primordial form of consciousness and its two primary qualities: *awareness*, meaning first-person subjective experience, and *agency*, the ability to freely choose and act.

WHAT THIS BOOK IS NOT ABOUT

Many experiences might seem like magic, but they're not. With 8 billion people on this planet, and each of us having a thousand or more unique experiences every day, a few extremely unlikely coincidences will always occur by chance. Some of those coincidences will be told and retold, giving the impression that we're awash in magic and miracles. Other amazing experiences will be told in hushed tones, but some of them will be mistakes of memory, wishful thinking, or fabricated to gain attention. It would be foolish to believe that all tales of magic are true, and just as foolish to believe that none of them are true. As the mathematician and physicist Henri Poincaré put it: "Doubt everything or believe everything: These are two equally convenient strategies. With either we dispense with the need for reflection."

How do we know, then, what's true *in principle* about magic? The approach my colleagues and I have taken is to test the claims of psi and magic using the tools of science. Science is not perfect, but it is the most powerful way we currently have for sifting the magical wheat from the mundane chaff. For ethical reasons, scientific methods also impose constraints on the ways we can safely study human abilities, so what we observe in controlled laboratory studies is typically much weaker than magic as it's expressed in the everyday world. But scientific tests also give us greater confidence that the effects we do see are not due to a dozen ordinary things that might seem like magic.

After you finish reading this book, it's important to take a step back and take a deep breath. If you start to hear dark omens issued by every raven that happens to fly by, then stop listening to the birds for a while. Challenging your worldview is healthy, but it can take time to reintegrate your belief system with the knowledge that magic is quite real. So before you quit your job, sell all your belongings, don the leathers and feathers of a shaman, and retreat to a bunker in the woods, relax with your newfound knowledge that magic was always here. It's not something brand-new that just dropped out of the sky. If after a few months the forest and the ravens are still calling you, then go for it. But it might be prudent to put your belongings in storage and get a satellite phone.

Shortly after I wrote the above passage, my wife and I took a walk around our neighborhood and encountered two ravens. One made a strange wooden knocking sound, like the wood block instrument you'd find in a percussion section of an orchestra. Both ravens were clearly watching us. Years before, I'd spotted a wild raven, but I hadn't seen any in recent memory. In mythology, ravens are messengers between the earthly and spiritual realms. What this raven's message was, I don't know. Maybe it was recommending a satellite phone.

NORMALIZING THE PARANORMAL

If you wanted to find out about near-death experiences, you had to go to the back of the bookstore. You know, where they have witchcraft and magic and other esoteric things. But now, over the last ten to fifteen years, many of these things are beginning to be mainstreamed and normalized.

—NEUROSCIENTIST CHRISTOF KOCH, DURING
A PLENARY TALK AT THE SCIENCE OF CONSCIOUSNESS
CONFERENCE, TUCSON, ARIZONA, APRIL 2024

Entrenched prejudices that have long relegated real magic to the metaphysical permafrost are slowly melting. The emerging world-view is known in the esoteric traditions as the "perennial philosophy." It's the idea that reality is fundamentally mental. Philosophers call this worldview *idealism*. Idealism is at the core of Western esoteric traditions like Hermeticism and Neoplatonism and of Eastern eso-teric traditions like Advaita Vedanta. It is also increasingly found across a broad array of scientific and scholarly disciplines.[9]

In idealism, the physical world is regarded as a mere appearance created by consciousness. A common critique about this idea is that it suggests the moon isn't there if nobody looks at it.[10] But idealism doesn't insist that reality is created only by human consciousness. There may be a cosmic or universal consciousness that is always "looking" at everything.

The shift toward taking consciousness seriously in science was sparked and then accelerated by advances in the neurosciences, the renaissance of psychedelics research, the mainstreaming of medita-tion, and an unresolved enigma about the role of the observer in phys-ics. As the neuroscientist Christof Koch put it,

The wheel is turning back to much more ancient understandings of experience, including *idealism*, the proposition that ultimately even matter and energy are mental manifestations, and *panpsychism*, the school of thought that all creatures, and perhaps even matter itself, are ensouled, that it feels-like-something to be anything, not just a human or even a bat. Modern science is supporting aspects of this remarkable turn of events.[11]

Such ideas are no longer found in obscure journals and starry-eyed New Age magazines. They're found in practically every issue of the popular science press, including *New Scientist, Discover,* and *Scientific American.* Even intensely fierce critics of the paranormal are changing their tune, perhaps without realizing it.

For example, Richard Dawkins is an evolutionary biologist and crusading atheist who coined the term *meme* and authored books like *The God Delusion.* He is also a fellow of the Committee for Skeptical Inquiry, which for decades has enthusiastically vilified parapsychology as a pseudoscience. With that background, Dawkins said something quite unexpected in a 2020 podcast interview with popular podcaster Lex Fridman:

> I have thought about using Nick Bostrom's idea [that we are living in a simulation] to solve the riddle of how the human brain [can] achieve so much. I thought of this when my then hundred-year-old mother was marveling at what I could do with a smartphone. I could look up anything in the encyclopedia, I could play her music she liked, and so she said is all that in that tiny little phone? No, it's out there. It's in the cloud, and maybe what we do is in the cloud. . . . [We] interface with something else, like what Roger Penrose [proposes] with panpsychism, that consciousness is somehow a fundamental part of physics, that it doesn't have to actually all reside inside the brain. But Roger thinks it does reside inside the skull, *whereas I'm suggesting that it doesn't.*[12] (emphasis added)

The implications of the mind not residing inside the brain seem to have escaped Dawkins's attention, because it's exactly what the philosopher and 1927 Nobel laureate Henri Bergson proposed as the "filter theory" of consciousness. Bergson said the brain doesn't create or store memories; rather, memories are nonmaterial and are retrieved only when they're required, *from elsewhere*. Incidentally, in 1913 Bergson was the president of the London-based Society for Psychical Research (SPR). Founded in 1882, the SPR was the first professional organization devoted to the systematic scientific study of psi (psychic) phenomena.

Prominent philosopher David Chalmers described the renewed interest in consciousness as follows: "One starts as a materialist, then one becomes a dualist, then a panpsychist, and one ends up as an idealist." He explained this sequence by noting that graduate students interested in the relationship between mind and matter evolve through four phases. First, the student is

> impressed by the successes of science, endorsing materialism about everything and [also] about the mind. Second, one is moved by the problem of consciousness to see a gap between physics and consciousness, thereby endorsing dualism, where both matter and consciousness are fundamental. Third, one is moved by the inscrutability of matter to realize that science reveals at most the structure of matter and not its underlying nature, and to speculate that this nature may involve consciousness, thereby endorsing panpsychism. Fourth, one comes to think that there is little reason to believe in anything beyond consciousness and that the physical world is wholly constituted by consciousness, thereby endorsing idealism.[13]

MAGIC AND PSI

You've noticed by now that I use the terms *magic* and *psi* interchangeably. That's because these words are reflections of the same phenomenon. We might think that *telepathy* (mind-to-mind connections) is entirely different from *clairvoyance* (perceiving through space and time), but both are just different ways we experience—jargon alert—

nonlocal consciousness. Nonlocal consciousness is a euphemism that's gaining traction in academia. It refers to an aspect of awareness that is not constrained by ordinary space or time, and through which focused intention can directly interact with properties of the physical world. In other words, magic.

While magic and psi are facets of the same phenomenon, the history and methods of these two realms differ. Magical beliefs and practices are deeply entwined with indigenous spiritual and orthodox religious traditions. The history, methods, and culture of psi research are more limited, partly because as a discipline it is relatively new, and partly because psi research is a secular academic pursuit that intentionally strips away any occult, spiritual, religious, and supernatural connotations.

Viewed from the earthy, hot, and wild perspective of magic, psi research is impossibly cold and stuffy, like magic for nerds. Magic promises leather-bound cosplay with world-shattering sex and drugs. Psi offers a glimpse at statistical peculiarities that excite subversive academics who may have read about sex and drugs in a journal article but are otherwise unfamiliar with those concepts.

While these traditions may be wildly divergent, magicians (meaning those who seriously practice magical techniques) largely agree with psi researchers that magic rarely produces "big" effects, like those in magic-themed action or horror films. Psi effects observed in the laboratory and magical outcomes in the real world are often subtle and manifest as meaningful synchronicities. On the flip side, some spontaneous psi effects, like poltergeist episodes, can be quite impressively "big," and occasionally even a controlled laboratory outcome will raise eyebrows.

That magic and psi point at the same phenomena is not a new idea. Jane Roberts, the channeler for the entity known as Seth, wrote: "We were immersed in 'magic' no matter what we called it . . . manifestations of telepathy, and so forth, were just places where our magic 'showed.'"[14] Magicians, too, have noted the connection. Isaac Bonewits, in his book *Real Magic*, wrote that "almost any phenomenon in magic can be given a name that can be fitted into the field of parapsychology, regardless of whether the parapsychologists or magicians appreciate the fact."[15] The chaos magic pioneer Peter J. Carroll, in presenting his "Equations of Magic" in *Liber Kaos*, described his equations as "three formulae which describe the necessary ingredients of any spell or ritual designed to have parapsychological effect."[16]

One of the differences between psi and magic was noted by Carroll, who wrote: "I always caution against trying to 'prove' the existence of magic by participating in laboratory parapsychology experiments. They will almost certainly fail anyway because the experimenters set the conditions to strongly favour failure."[17] The occultist Julian Vayne agreed: "Psychic ability has been demonstrated time and again in parapsychological laboratories all over the world. . . . Go and read some of the (generally rather dull) experiments if you don't believe me—yes, people are psychic. So that's magick. . . . Well, yes and no! Yes, this kind of effect is part of what magick is but no, that's not the whole story."[18]

The magician J. Finley Hurley, in his book *Sorcery*, devoted many pages to psi research.[19] But again echoing Carroll's and Vayne's comments, he noted that the psychiatrist Jan Ehrenwald, who had extensively studied how psi is expressed in the everyday world, said that in the laboratory "psi phenomena are in effect derivatives of magic that have been dehydrated, de-boned, and filleted to make them digestible for scientific consumption."[20]

What magicians and those who study "psi in the wild" are referring to are the ethical constraints placed on the methods that researchers are allowed to use. If we gave participants powerful psychedelic drugs and then did the laboratory equivalent of pushing them off a cliff, we'd probably see some pretty impressive psi. But, of course, we can't do that, so we're limited to studying weak magic. Still, factors said to enhance magical efficacy—like *belief, motivation, desire,* and *imagination*—are also found in psi research, so we know we're studying the same underlying phenomena.

Incidentally, these same factors are also found in the core teachings of all New Thought practices, including methods called manifestation, affirmation, and the law of attraction. For example, in *Think and Grow Rich*, one of the best-selling self-help books of all time, Napoleon Hill said that success depends on

> desire, the subconscious mind, the sixth sense, and the master mind. . . . But this desire has to be more than just a vague wish. It must be an intense, burning desire so strong that in our mind the goal is already attained and no obstacle can prevent it becoming physical reality.[21]

Motivational speaker Claude Bristol described his approach in the influential book *The Magic of Believing*:

> I discovered that a golden thread runs through all the teachings . . . and that thread can be named in the single word—*belief*. . . . It is essential that your desire be an all-obsessing one, your thoughts and aims be coordinated, and your energy be concentrated and applied without letup. . . . That kind of belief has the magic touch.[22]

Similarly, Neville Goddard, a prominent teacher and mystic, wrote in his book *Imagination*: "Your imagination is unlimited in what it can accomplish. If you can imagine something, you can achieve it. . . . You must be persistent in attaining your desire. Continue to imagine what you want until you have actually obtained it."[23]

In Part II, we'll review some of the scientific evidence that supports the existence of magic. Understanding this evidence is important for fledgling magicians because magic works best when you *believe that it exists*. So, unless you're already a firm believer thanks to personal experience, the best way to boost your confidence is to explore how scientific studies have investigated psi phenomena, and what they've found.

PART II

SCIENCE OF MAGIC

Yesterday's magic is now called biology, medicine, chemistry, and astronomy.

Today's magic is called genetics, quantum weirdness, and cosmology.

Tomorrow's magic? Stay tuned.

CHAPTER 2

SCIENCE OF ENCHANTMENT

Science is always discovering odd scraps of magical wisdom and making a tremendous fuss about its cleverness.

—ALEISTER CROWLEY

Enchantment is the magical practice of influencing the physical world through focused intention. Mind-matter interaction effects have been studied in a broad range of increasingly rigorous scientific experiments for over ninety years. In the lab these effects are called *psychokinesis* (PK). Most of the earliest PK studies were proof-oriented and focused on one question: Does PK exist? More recently, these experiments study factors thought to modulate the effectiveness of PK, or they're designed to explore ideas about the underlying mechanisms.

For most scientists, conducting a single successful PK experiment would not be sufficient to overcome doubt that this phenomenon exists. After years of being told that mental "powers" are fantasies because they supposedly violate the laws of physics, or that experiments reporting positive PK effects can only be due to fraud or flaws, strong skepticism is to be expected. In my case, it took years of conducting experiments before I was persuaded by the data to accept that PK is real. What convinced me requires a bit of backstory.

BACKGROUND

Like many children, I was fascinated with fairy tales and folktales. In my teens, I graduated to science fiction and amazing stories about mystic masters, like Paramahansa Yogananda's tales in *Autobiography of a Yogi*. Many of these books included themes that assumed the reality of psychic, mystical, or magical powers. I was also attracted to scientific wonders, and from that perspective, these amazing powers were rarely mentioned. If they were touched upon at all, it was only to explain away such silliness as infantile delusions. I found the awe-inspiring stories about special powers more interesting than dry and often smug scientific denials. But I was a kid. What did I know?

One day an astute librarian noticed my fascination with all things mystical and scientific, so she introduced me to a section of the library I hadn't wandered into yet. There I found books on parapsychology, the scientific discipline that studies powers of the mind, just like those in my favorite stories. I was thrilled to learn that professors like the botanist-turned-psychologist-turned-parapsychologist Joseph Banks Rhine, at Duke University, were using scientific methods to provide evidence of psychic abilities like telepathy and clairvoyance.[1]

I also read books by scientists who were skeptical of these abilities, like the curmudgeonly psychologist Charles Edward Mark Hansel. I was impressed with Rhine's methods and results because he based his conclusions on experimental data. I was less impressed with Hansel's critiques because he assumed that virtually every success that Rhine and others had reported was due to flaws or fraud. He often based his assumptions on imaginary scenarios that purportedly showed how the subjects in the experiments cheated, but without providing any evidence that they actually did cheat. This is not to say that strong pushbacks on controversial claims are unworthy. Doubt is an essential corrective element in science, and constructive criticism helps to sharpen methods and interpretations. But when critiques descend into denialism and wailing, that's not useful.

By the time I was in college, I was dabbling with simple psychic experiments. Throughout graduate school, I continued this interest as a hobby, eventually writing what was probably the first online precognition experiment in 1975, using the educational computer network PLATO (Programmed Logic for Automated Teaching Operations) at the University of Illinois.[2] That system was a forerunner of the Internet, and by the time I was programming my experiment, PLATO already had more than a thousand networked computers.

After I earned my doctorate, I started working at Bell Labs, the research and development arm of the Bell Telephone System. At the time Bell Labs was one of the largest industrial labs in the world. It's where the transistor, the laser, the communications satellite, and much of the infrastructure of the modern information age were developed. Given my academic background in both engineering and psychology, I was assigned to a group focused on the design of the human-computer interface. This topic was of prime interest to the Bell System because thousands of its employees were involved in computer operations centers around the world, and they were responsible for making sure that when you picked up a phone and dialed any other phone anywhere in the world, the connection would go through in a matter of seconds.

To achieve that goal reliably, these telephone network computers were designed to be triple-redundant, meaning one or two might fail—possible but rare—but then a third computer would immediately take over. Disaster avoided.

Except sometimes the third computer would also fail. The question was why? Failure analysis was able to identify plausible reasons about 95 percent of the time, but that last 5 percent was frustratingly evasive. That's what attracted my interest.

Every technical environment eventually develops its own version of Murphy's Law, also known as "lab lore." These quasi-serious "laws" arise from anecdotes repeatedly reported over the years. Murphy's Law states that "if anything can go wrong, it will." There are many variations, like "if anything can go wrong, it will, and at the worst possible time." Anyone who has anxiously rushed to a copy machine holding a piece of paper that just *has* to be copied *right now* will be familiar with the experience of having the machine decide to break the instant they press the start button. There's even a Murphy's Law story that's well known in physics. The Pauli Effect is named after the eminent quantum physicist Wolfgang Pauli, who gained a reputation for causing laboratory equipment to break or go missing whenever he was in the vicinity.[3]

The lab lore hints that there might be a connection between a person's anxiety and the behavior of machines. At Bell Labs we would occasionally give a demonstration of a complex software system to visiting dignitaries. When the person performing the demonstration was the lead software developer—let's call him Bob—the demo would invariably fail. If Bob wasn't present, the demo would work just fine. After Bob broke the system a few times, we banned him from being present when we performed important demos. This and other examples led me to think that maybe Bob's anxiety, when he had to run an important demonstration, had evoked a mind-matter interaction effect similar to what I had been reading about in the parapsychology literature.

To pursue this idea, I took advantage of a business trip to visit Dr. Helmut Schmidt, a physicist at the Mind Science Foundation in San Antonio, Texas. Schmidt had pioneered the design and use of truly random number generators (RNGs) for testing mind-matter interaction effects. Again, the psi jargon for these effects is psychokinesis, or PK.

One of Schmidt's RNG designs was an electronic circuit where the source of randomness was the timing of when a piece of pitchblende (an ore also called uraninite, the primary source of uranium) would emit charged particles. Pitchblende is radioactive, which means it contains unstable atoms that release their excess energy every so often as particles, typically positively charged alpha particles.

Schmidt used pitchblende because *when* a radioactive substance emits a particle is considered to be fundamentally random. That is, absolutely nothing known *causes* these particles to be released. It just happens unpredictably, which is one of the many strange things about the quantum world. But while the precise timing of each emission is random and cannot be known, if you measure the time between emissions (called latencies), the probabilistic *distribution* of the latencies is predictable. The latencies fall nicely into an exponential distribution, where shorter intervals are more common than longer intervals.

Schmidt used this random timing effect to design a physical system to test if the mind could influence matter, not with a kind of physical force but by modulating the probabilities related to the radioactive emission latencies. He did this because previous experiments had been conducted to see if PK could move or levitate physical objects (like we see in the movies). If that kind of PK were possible, then one or more of the basic forces already known to physics, like electromagnetism, would almost certainly be detected. But so far macroscopic PK effects have proven to be exceptionally evasive under laboratory controls. Thus more sensitive methods were developed, like seeing if the mind could modulate the *probabilities* of events. In that way, one wouldn't need to levitate a building to study PK. Just nudging the behavior of elementary particles would do the trick.

The device Schmidt made was a rectangular metal box about the size of a magazine, two inches thick, with a circle of small lamps embedded on one side. When the box was turned on, each lamp lit up in sequence for about a half-second, creating a pattern of light that appeared to move in a clockwise direction. When a Geiger counter detected a particle emitted by the pitchblende, the direction of the lights reversed, and they began to light up counterclockwise. The participant's task was to mentally intend that the number of steps that the lights moved clockwise would be more than counterclockwise. This required the mind to first "hold back" radioactive particles from being emitted so the lights would keep moving clockwise. Then, as soon as a particle was emitted, the lights would reverse their apparent direction, and the mental task would be to "encourage" another particle to be emitted quickly so the lights would reverse again. And so on. Using this built-in counterbalanced design, mental intention was tasked with alternatively pushing and pulling against the latencies involved in radioactive emissions. Most physicists would consider it impossible that mental intention would have any noticeable effect at all on radioactive latencies. Among other things, it would imply that our understanding of quantum mechanics was incomplete.

The experimental task continued until the clockwise and counterclockwise movements each occurred ten times. Then in a new run, the task was reversed, and now the intention was to make the lights move more counterclockwise than clockwise. This ensured that if there happened to be some sort of bias in the radioactive emission rates that favored the hypothesis, it would be balanced out. The machine was programmed to automatically count all steps in each direction, so that once a run began, if the participant wasn't doing well and decided to quit, the data would still be recorded. This flagged "optional stopping" biases, which if not taken into account could make the results of an experiment appear to be better than they actually were.

I admired the simplicity of this device as a way to test for PK, and to my delight, Schmidt kindly loaned it to me. I took it back to Bell Labs to see if I could replicate the results he reported. I used myself, my friends, and my colleagues as participants in a total of twenty-seven experiments. Then I ran eight control studies, where the machine was allowed to run by itself with no one present. To evaluate the results, I invited a statistician friend, Jessica Utts (who years later would be elected the president of the American Statistical Association), to check my analysis to make sure that the results I calculated were correct. She confirmed that the experiments yielded odds against chance of 27,000 to 1, and the controls resulted in odds of 2 to 1.[4] I'm fairly sure that if I had not obtained that result, I'd have followed a much easier and more conventional career path.

But after seeing the results of the studies that I ran myself, on a machine that I had thoroughly inspected, I was hooked. I was pleased that I was able to witness the PK effects I had been reading about in the literature, but I was also shocked because the results violated everything I thought I knew about the way the world worked. The mind directly influencing the physical world was, well, *magic*. And magic is just wishful thinking. Right?

Thus began my *ontological crisis*. Those words refer to the mind-boggling discomfort that can arise when something challenges your expectations about reality. Nearly twenty years of my education were suddenly thrown into doubt. My way of dealing with the crisis was to immediately conduct more experiments to see what other psi effects I could repeat. I eventually presented some of that work in 1981 at the annual conference of the Parapsychological Association. That I was allowed to do this must have involved some sort of magical intervention, because I also obtained permission to use the Bell Labs imprimatur for one of my presentations (about a precognition experiment).[5]

Even though I was able to successfully repeat psi effects in the lab, a recurrent refrain ran through my mind that I couldn't shake: *I can't imagine how this can be.* It was disturbing because it felt like a core component of my identity as a scientist was being attacked, and I was the assailant! Ontological shock has been discussed by many other scientists and scholars who encountered evidence, or personal experiences, that shattered their worldviews.[6]

One day I complained about my unresolved angst to a friend who was more metaphysically oriented than me. He suggested that the problem was with my imagination, not with reality. A lightbulb lit up when I suddenly realized that years of education had caused me to unwittingly adopt a thoroughly materialistic worldview as the *only possible way* to understand reality. You mean there are other ways to think about reality? But isn't that just philosophy? What does philosophy have to do with science? Nothing, I thought. Stupidly.

I eventually reconciled that science and magic could comfortably coexist. And after four decades of conducting over a hundred controlled laboratory experiments on nearly every type of psi effect that can be studied, I began to understand how science could accommodate magic.

In this chapter, we'll explore what scientific experiments reveal about factors that are said to enhance the efficacy of magical enchantment, including *belief, motivation,* and *intention.* Magical lore also assumes that group rituals, or *collective consciousness,* may be more effective than magic performed by individuals, perhaps because closely aligned group efforts can go a long way in supporting focused attention and increasing motivation, and also because if something radically magical happens, it can be less frightening to attribute the effect to the group than to oneself.

We'll also review the evidence for *glamouring,* a shape-shifting enchantment used to make oneself irresistibly fascinating. Charismatic politicians use glamouring to powerfully hypnotize others to perceive them as archetypes of the savior, martyr, wise man, or king. Incidentally, the word *fascination* is derived from the Latin word *fascinum,* referring to a magic spell that's intended to mesmerize another person's attention. Other words with magical origins permeate the beauty and perfume industries, where product advertising explicitly invokes magic through words like *charm, allure, bewitch,* and *spellbound.* Consider the text for an oddly seductive ad for red perfume sold by Christian Dior:

> You don't wear Hypnotic Poison perfume, it wears you: that is
> the credo of this magnetic eau de toilette. The sultry fragrance
> bathes the skin in a mysterious and irresistible scent, like a
> bewitching elixir.

Maybe it's just me, but the idea of bathing in poisonous red magnetic toilet water doesn't seem all that appealing. And that this poison also somehow "wears me" seems especially alarming. But there's no accounting for taste (or scent), so if hypnotic poison sounds good to you, go for it.

BELIEF

When a belief is widely held in the face of overwhelming evidence to the contrary, we call it a superstition. By that criterion, the most egregious superstition of modern times, perhaps of all time, is the "scientific" belief in the non-existence of psi.

—THOMAS ETTER

Beyond the Placebo

Does belief modify psi and magical efficacy? Magical lore assumes so. In the lab, scientific studies of this effect are called sheep-goat experiments, where psi believers are the sheep and psi skeptics are the goats.

In the early 1940s, the psychologist Gertrude Schmeidler of the City College of New York asked a group of participants to fill out a questionnaire about their beliefs in psi. Based on their responses, individuals were categorized as sheep or goats. Then everyone took the same simple extrasensory perception (ESP, a common term for clairvoyance or perceptual psi) test using a special deck of cards sometimes referred to as Zener cards (after psychologist Karl Zener, who helped to develop the method). This technique was popularized by J. B. Rhine in the early 1930s. It consists of a deck of cards composed of five groups, where each card in a group had one of five symbols: circle, cross, wavy lines, square, and star, as shown in Figure 1.

Figure 1. Classic ESP card symbols

The design of this test is called "forced choice" because you are asked to select one of five symbols that another person is attempting to mentally send to you (in a telepathy test), or guess the symbol on a face-down card on top of the desk (in a clairvoyance test), or guess the card that will be randomly pulled from the deck after you make your choice (in a precognition test).

The ESP card test is simple to take, easy to administer, and straightforward to evaluate. The disadvantage is that you can't help but be influenced by your previous guesses, because surely—you'd think— there wouldn't be four cards with the same symbol in a row (even though that could certainly happen by chance). The unavoidable statistical counter in your head can overcome your intuitive impressions, which introduces unwanted noise into the test results. The test can also become stupendously boring after you've done it a few times. Still, it was one of the most popular methods for testing ESP over many decades and remains useful today.

Schmeidler found that with this test, sheep tended to score above chance and goats generally scored at or below chance. Oftentimes the difference in the two groups was statistically significant. Dozens of variations have examined this effect of belief in psi. It's one of the most replicated experiments in psi research.

The sheep-goat design can also be used to show how fragile the psi-belief factor can be. In 2007, a University of Colorado student, Kevin Walsh, and the photonics and quantum engineering professor Garret Moddel conducted an experiment to explore this interaction.

Students were classified as sheep or goats based on their prior beliefs, then were randomly assigned to read either a passage that was supportive of psi or one that criticized psi.[7] Then the students all ran the same psi test. The results fell into four groups: believers or skeptics who read the pro-psi or anti-psi passage. The results were as you might expect: The sheep/pro-psi group obtained a significantly positive hit rate; the sheep/anti-psi group performed positively but not significantly; the goat/pro-psi group performed positively, like the sheep/anti-psi group; and the goat/anti-psi group performed at chance.

Walsh and Moddel concluded: "Innate psi ability alone cannot explain why some subjects perform better. *Belief in psi is required.*" The study demonstrated that beliefs can be modulated surprisingly easily. The lesson for budding magicians is that if you tell everyone you know that you're doing magic, and a skeptic loudly snorts that you're nuts, then it's a good bet that your magical efforts will be diminished and possibly even extinguished.

How robust is this sheep-goat effect? Over the long haul, very.

The first meta-analysis of sheep-goat psi experiments with ESP cards was reported in 1993 by the psychologist Tony Lawrence, at the time at the University of Edinburgh. He was able to find seventy-three reports by thirty-seven different investigators, involving more than 685,000 guesses contributed by 4,500 participants. The combined result supported the sheep-goat effect, with odds against chance of over a trillion to one. In 2017, psychologists Lance Storm of the University of Adelaide, Australia, and Patrizio Tressoldi of the University of Padua, Italy, searched for all published sheep-goat forced choice experiments conducted after Lawrence's analysis. They found forty-nine additional studies reported by forty-three investigators. The new results again supported the sheep-goat effect with odds against chance of 12 million to 1.

Their conclusion: "A belief-moderated communications anomaly in the forced-choice ESP domain . . . has been effectively uninterrupted and consistent for almost 70 years."[8] In other words, for optimal performance, *you must believe*.

Note that if an experimenter maintains a strong belief in psi, that bias might cause her to influence the participants or the data analysts to produce her desired results. Fortunately, a well-designed experiment can overcome such biases using methods like double-blind protocols. In a sheep-goat test, that protocol might specify that anyone who interacts with the participants (the first blind) or analyzes the data (the second blind) would not be allowed to know the purpose of the study. In this way, any biases that the experimenter may have are less likely to influence the outcome.

Sort of.

An astute reader will eventually notice that the use of double-blind methods, or shielding a target by distance or time, is assumed to adequately prevent a participant from gaining information about the target. But if psi is true, it means that any experiment in any scientific discipline, regardless of how strictly controlled it may be, has a serious and unavoidable loophole: Our minds do not appear to be constrained by commonsense assumptions about the nature of space and time. Everyday experience constantly reminds us that we live in a world where objects like minds and bodies are strictly separate. But psi reveals that this sense of isolation is actually an illusion. We are far more interconnected than we know.

Odds Against Chance

Let's pause a bit so I can explain what the phrase "odds against chance" means, because I'll be using it a lot in this chapter. It expresses how *unusual* a result is as compared to chance, or how much *confidence* we can have in the results. In the "soft sciences" like psychology, an odds figure above 20 to 1 suggests the results of an experiment may not be due to chance and can be called "significant" (assuming of course that the study is well designed). Obtaining odds of 1,000 to 1 would be considered impressive. In psi research, skeptics may demand odds of 100,000 to 1 to be considered impressive, and odds of a million to one for a meta-analysis (combined results of many repeated experiments using exactly or conceptually similar designs).

In the "hard sciences" like physics, an experiment that results in odds above chance of 1,000 to 1 would be seen as interesting, but odds above 3.5 million might be impressive enough to win you the Nobel Prize (as it did for the discovery of the Higgs boson at CERN in 2012). Importantly, these odds figures do not tell you how "big" the results are in terms of absolute magnitude.

For example, let's say Bob claims that he can mentally cause a flipped coin to land heads more often than tails. You can test this claim by having Bob flip a coin one hundred times, and let's say he got sixty heads, for a 60 percent hit rate. That's pretty good, 10 percent higher than expected by chance. But is that difference meaningful, or could it just be due to chance?

To find out, you can calculate the probability of getting 60 percent heads when chance would predict 50 percent. That turns out to be associated with a probability of $p = 0.028$. To calculate the odds against chance from p, you use the formula odds $= (1-p)/p$, so in this case the odds against chance are 34 to 1. So we can call Bob's "hit rate" a *significant* effect.

Odds against chance of 34 to 1 are interesting, but you're not going to change your worldview based on that outcome. You will need truly extraordinary evidence to seriously consider Bob's extraordinary claim. So the next thing you'll do is test whether Bob was using a biased coin. To do this, you ask ten other people to each flip the same coin Bob was using one hundred times. Say they get a combined total of 515 heads out of a thousand flips. Odds against chance for that are only 4.5 to 1, so it looks like Bob's coin was not biased. Now you ask Bob to toss the coin a thousand times. He again gets a 60 percent hit rate, so you calculate the odds of a 60 percent hit rate after one thousand coin flips, and that turns out to be 7 *billion* to 1. How can that be? He got the same 10 percent over chance hit rate as before, so why are the odds now so wildly significant? The answer is that the more data you get, the more confidence you can have in the results. The technical term is *statistical power*.

Now, are you convinced that Bob has amazing psychokinetic skills? After all, odds against chance for his demonstration were 7 billion to 1, so you know that Bob's outcome was *not due to chance*. That's good, but it's not the whole story.

The reason you should be cautious is that certain conjuring techniques can cause a fair coin flip to be biased, and also because even completely fair coin flips can be biased a bit because of the physics involved. In one study involving more than 350,000 flipped coins, the coins tended to land on the side that they started from more often than expected by chance.[9] There are many ways that an experimental effect may not be due to chance, so you'll need a more rigorous way to test Bob's claim to exclude explanations other than psi. And then you'll need to test those methods repeatedly, and then get feedback from your colleagues to see if they agree, and get them to independently run replication studies, and so on.

This test, evaluate, reconsider, and test again cycle has been repeated in psi research for over a century. Dozens of subtle and not-so-subtle loopholes have been found over the years and then closed. After many iterations, several classes of psi experiments have been developed that, when followed correctly, take into account all known flaws. And these revised experiments *still show significant evidence for psi*. That justifies high confidence that psi exists.

An "Intuition Placebo"

The Italian psychologists Riccardo Boscariol and Patrizio Tressoldi from the University of Padua conducted a simple twenty-five-card ESP test.[10] Participants in their test were invited to guess the ESP symbol that would be drawn from the top of the deck *after* it was shuffled, so this was a test for precognition. The investigators asked 150 participants to each complete fifty trials where the card was presented on a computer. One hundred people were assigned to an experimental group and fifty to a control group. The participants were mostly students and were not selected for having special claims about psi abilities.

So far this study was like hundreds of others using ESP cards and published since the 1930s. But this introduced a new twist by including a placebo variation. Each person first completed twenty-five trials in a no-placebo condition, and then they did twenty-five more trials in a placebo condition. In both cases, they listened to a one-minute audio clip before each condition. In the no-placebo trials, the audio clip was a sound that was simply intended to be relaxing. In the placebo trials, the sound was described to the participants as follows:

> This sound has been created by the researchers to enhance people's intuition, and its effectiveness has already been demonstrated. It has no side effects. It will temporarily increase your intuitive abilities and your ability to guess in tasks of this type, both during and for the fifteen minutes following the listening period.

This statement was a placebo because it was designed to modify participants' beliefs and expectations about their psi abilities, even though the claim *wasn't true*. The audio sound wasn't created to enhance intuition; nor had it been previously demonstrated to work.

Meanwhile the control group followed the same procedures as those in the experimental group, except before the first twenty-five and second twenty-five trials, they didn't listen to any audio clips. This group was included to see if the design used in the experimental group might have created a learning effect over the course of conducting fifty trials.

The results showed that in the experimental group during the first, no-placebo condition, the hit rate was a nonsignificant 21.04 percent (20 percent was chance expectation). But during the second, placebo-enhanced condition, the hit rate was 22.8 percent, associated with odds against chance of about 200 to 1. In the control group, the hit rates in their first and second sessions were both at chance, with 20.8 percent and 19.0 percent.

In other words, this was a sheep-goat study where sheep were created simply by telling them that they were hearing a special psi-enhancing sound. The implication for magical practices is that if you believe that a certain amulet or talisman, or ritual, or spell, will enhance your abilities, then there's a good chance that it will.

Willis Harman, president of the Institute of Noetic Sciences (IONS) from 1978 to 1997, once said, after reviewing everything known at that time about human potentials, "Perhaps the only limits to the human mind are those we believe in."[11] After forty-five years of conducting psi experiments, I've come to agree.

MOTIVATION

Spontaneous Remission

In 1993 the Institute of Noetic Sciences published a book entitled *Spontaneous Remission: An Annotated Bibliography.*[12] Spontaneous remission was defined as "the disappearance, complete or incomplete, of a disease or cancer without medical treatment or treatment that is considered inadequate to produce the resulting disappearance of disease symptoms or tumor."

These were cases not of mild viruses or sniffles that resolved in a few days, but of cancer and other serious diseases that are invariably fatal, except—oddly enough—sometimes they're not. In such cases, not only was there a return to permanent health, but it often occurred much faster than was thought to be medically possible. The term *spontaneous* means that there were no known reasons why the person recovered to full health, and that the recovery involved four characteristics: It was *sudden, total, definitive,* and *inexplicable* according to today's knowledge.

The data IONS assembled for that book included 3,500 case studies from more than eight hundred medical journals in twenty languages. The annotated bibliography that formed the core of the book is available for free on the IONS website,[13] and the database is being updated to include hundreds of cancer subtypes as well as new cases involving HIV, hepatitis, and eighteen other medical categories.

Spontaneous remission cases are not as rare as one might think. A search for this term on the US government's medical bibliography (PubMed.gov) as of early 2025 retrieved over nineteen thousand citations. Fears of losing one's credibility that may have once limited reports of remarkable remissions—a repeated refrain when it comes to talking about any sort of controversial phenomena—may be dissipating as more reports appear in the medical literature.

Spontaneous remissions are also not new. Methods for spontaneously curing infections were described by the Egyptian physician Imhotep in 1550 BC. Today it is known that certain bacterial and viral infections can stimulate immune responses that evoke spontaneous reductions of cancerous tumors.[14] As research continues, medical researchers will undoubtedly find triggers that spark some types of spontaneous remissions, in which case they will no longer be considered so mysterious.

The Nearly Permanent Paranormal Object

In her book *Radical Remission,* Kelly Turner identified nine factors frequently mentioned by patients who survived cancer.[15] One of the factors was having an immensely strong motivation to live. I observed the power of such motivation in a friend named Alexander Imich. Alex was acknowledged to be the oldest man on Earth in 2014. He was profiled in *The New York Times* on May 4 of that year in an article entitled, "An Ever-Curious Spirit, Unbeaten After 111 Years." Alex was interested in the powers of the mind for decades longer than the average person's lifetime. One of his obsessions was to discover a "permanent paranormal object." This refers to a physical object that had been manipulated in some inexplicable psychic way to create a permanent record of the miracle. An example might be an ordinary wooden pencil bent into the shape of a pretzel, or the bowl of a heavy soup spoon bent in half with a gentle touch.

Alex had examples of these objects in his collection, but it was not possible to tell by casual inspection if they were genuine. And even if they could be established as legitimate, the artifacts were so strange— like the glass stem of a wine goblet bent in half without breaking— that most people would find it hard to believe that they were created solely via mental power.

While Alex did not discover the permanent paranormal object he had been searching for, through his iron will and lifelong motivation, he ended up creating that very object *in himself*, by becoming the world's oldest living man.

Metal Bending

One portion of Alex's collection of paranormal objects was a pile of bent spoons and forks that were supposedly bent with the mind. The idea of psychic metal bending had been popularized by the Israeli psychic Uri Geller in the 1970s. For a decade or so it was quite a popular pastime, but after skeptical stage magicians showed how similar effects could be mimicked through sleight of hand, and some cases of fraud were brought to light, interest waned.

Less known today is that during the 1970s and '80s there were serious scientific attempts to study psychic metal bending, some with remarkable outcomes. Unlike better-known experiments focusing on mind-matter interactions at the microscopic scale, which require statistical analyses to extract the "signal" from the noise, when a piece of metal bends, it's an in-your-face phenomenon that cannot be ignored. No special expertise is required to appreciate that something remarkable happened.

The history of scientific studies investigating this phenomenon is recorded in several books and technical articles. A comprehensive review of this fascinating tale would require a book of its own, but I will briefly discuss this portion of history for two reasons. First, it is relevant to our discussion about the importance of *motivation* in modulating magical efficacy. And second, metal bending became a worldwide sensation largely because of the efforts of Edgar Mitchell, the astronaut founder of IONS. I knew Edgar, and after many discussions with him over the years, I had confidence that his metal-bending experiences with Geller and others were trustworthy. Astronauts do not become among the most storied explorers in human history by being credulous, inaccurate, or irresponsible.

I recommend the following books for the serious student who would like to dive deeper into this topic.

- University of London physicist and mathematician John Taylor, *Superminds*, 1975.
- Science editor at *Newsweek* Charles Panati, ed., *The Geller Papers*, 1976.
- The same John Taylor, *Science and the Supernatural*, 1980.
- University of London physicist John B. Hasted, *The Metal-Benders*, 1981.
- Professor of economics Walter Uphoff and Mary Jo Uphoff, *Mind over Matter*, 1980.
- Cardiff University sociologist Harry Collins and Cornell University sociologist Trevor Pinch, *Frames of Meaning*, 1982.

The first book by Taylor and the works by Panati, Uphoff, and Hasted were unabashedly positive. The second book by Taylor thoroughly reversed his initial position; and the book by Collins and Pinch was more neutral. Short quotes from each book will serve to illustrate their positions. In his first book, Taylor wrote about his ontological shock:

> One clear observation of Geller in action had an overpowering
> effect on me. I felt as if the whole framework with which I
> viewed the world had suddenly been destroyed. I seemed
> very naked and vulnerable, surrounded by a hostile,
> incomprehensible universe. It was many days before I was able
> to come to terms with this sensation. (from an opening blurb in
> the paperback edition)

In Taylor's second book, he concluded:

> We have searched for the supernatural and not found it. . . .
> Everything that I investigated turned out either to have a
> scientific exploration, such as the electrical explanation of
> certain psychokinetic results, or did not occur at all under careful
> test conditions. The earlier results of others in these latter cases
> were found to be explicable under the headings of mischief,
> fraud, credulity, fantasy, memory, cues and fear of death. With
> this evidence and the fact that all of these phenomena disagreed
> completely with scientific results, we have to conclude that the
> paranormal has "disappeared." (164–65)

To drive the stake deeper and leave no question about his revised opinion, Taylor added: "The supernatural has thus become completely natural. *The paranormal is now totally normal. ESP is dead"* (emphasis in the original). One reason for Taylor's change of heart is that he was thoroughly convinced that the only thing that could possibly explain the metal-bending phenomenon was electromagnetism.

After conducting tests to look for such forces and not finding them, he concluded that the results had to be impossible, and thus any apparent instances of metal bending could be due only, as he put it, to mischief. The physicist John Hasted found Taylor's insistence that electromagnetism was the *only* possible explanation frustratingly stubborn.

Like Taylor, Hasted described numerous firsthand observations of metal bending followed by controlled laboratory experiments that produced intriguing results. Taylor probably retreated from his earlier endorsement of metal bending after he received scathing attacks from colleagues; Hasted, too, endured such critiques. With some exasperation, he wrote that "such attacks are more familiar in party politics than in scientific investigations," and to his credit, he did not bow to that pressure.

But Hasted did add a comment that's directly pertinent to magical practice: "A criticism I have often heard is that 'we all wanted the events to happen.' This is in some degree true, *and it may be that this is why they did happen*" (emphasis in the original). He continued: "There is an unmeasured parameter in the experiments, namely the attitude of the observers."

Panati's book is a collection of twenty-three articles about metal bending written by scientists and, in a few cases, by stage magicians. The authors hailed from the United States, Canada, England, France, Denmark, and South Africa. Panati wrote:

> Geller has been tested in seventeen laboratories in eight different countries. The scientists who have worked with him have watched him deform solid steel rods without touching them, cause part of an exotic crystal to vanish from within a sealed container, alter the memory of a rare metal alloy, erase information from computer tapes, set Geiger counters ticking with only his thoughts, and read the thoughts of others while he

is sealed in a room that blocks out all types of radio waves. They are men and women of probity, affiliated with major universities and research centers throughout the world. . . . Four [stage] magicians have worked closely with Geller, applied their own standards to prevent any sleight of hand, and have observed inexplicable events. It is their unanimous opinion that Geller either has paranormal abilities or is acquainted with a form of magic unknown to the entire brotherhood of [stage] magicians.

The book by the Uphoffs is primarily about their experiences investigating a Japanese teenager who could purportedly bend metal. The teenager was also said to perform "thought photography," in which images would anomalously appear on unexposed film. That book is more like a travelogue than a technical report, although it does contain many photos of what the authors observed.

Perhaps the most interesting book is by Collins and Pinch, because it is less about the scientific story than about the sociology of what they call "extraordinary science." It may seem strange that what is taken as "known" in science is a social construction, but the reality is that science is a human enterprise, and as such, what it takes to be true, and what science considers to be mainstream, is based on opinions (hopefully, expert opinions). The extraordinary claims of psychic metal bending brought the effects of this social process into high relief, with some experts insisting that metal bending was a hoax, while other experts claiming it was real. No firm consensus could be reached.

This ambiguity is not satisfying, but from a sociological perspective, whether metal bending is real or illusory isn't important. The fact is that if *any case* of genuine psychic metal bending actually occurred, it would be of immense importance, and not only for scientific reasons. It would also have huge implications for society because mind-matter interactions would no longer be an easily ignored microscopic anomaly. It would be the equivalent of UFOs landing on the White House lawn (which was reported in many newspapers in July 1952, including on the front page of *The New York Times*). It would also have had obvious national security implications, which may be why this topic seems to have faded from public discourse.

One might think that sociologists would want to get to the bottom of this issue. On the other hand, whenever large-scale psychic effects are claimed, the pushback from skeptics is usually so fast and furious that claiming neutrality is understandably easier, especially for academics who wish to retain their jobs and credibility.

As I write this, we are some fifty years after the spoon-bending craze. But the denouement of this story did not go in the direction one might have predicted. In July 2023 *The New York Times* published an article about Geller entitled "The End of the Magic World's 50-Year Grudge." The story reported, "In 1973, Uri Geller claimed to bend metal with his mind on live television. Skeptics couldn't beat him. Now they've joined him." It continued:

> Mr. Geller was long shadowed by a handful of professional magicians appalled that someone was fobbing off what they said were expertly finessed magic tricks as acts of telekinesis. Like well-matched heavyweights, they pummeled one another in the '70s and '80s in televised contests that elevated them all. . . . Mr. Geller ultimately emerged the victor in this war, and proof of his triumph is now on display in the museum: a coffee-table book titled "Bend It Like Geller," which was written by the Australian magician Ben Harris . . . who was once among Mr. Geller's most avid debunkers.

An Impossible Bend

Here I describe my own take on metal bending and its relevance to understanding magic. As background, when I visited my friend Alexander Imich in his apartment in New York City, I noticed that one of his paranormal objects was a heavy soup spoon with the bowl bent in half. Alex said this had been accomplished with a gentle touch. My feeling at the time was that even though I had conducted many successful *micro*-PK studies in the lab (meaning with elementary particles or random events), and I had trusted colleagues who claimed to have bent quarter-inch metal rods with a light touch, I remained very skeptical that large-scale PK effects like metal bending were possible.

I was skeptical because even if someone was physically strong enough to bend the bowl of a soup spoon in half, the effort would have damaged their fingers. And yet my colleagues did not report finger injuries. Their claims didn't make any sense to me, but I didn't share my doubts with Alex because he was showing me these objects with such obvious pride. I figured his paranormal objects were just tricks that he failed to detect.

Seven years later I attended a lighthearted workshop offered as an evening event at a conference where I was scheduled to give a talk. In the workshop, which included about fifty people, we were going to bend spoons and other cutlery. I had heard about such events for years, and some of my friends and colleagues who had attended such workshops later excitedly showed me their bent or twisted spoons. This would be the first time I had a chance to personally participate.

At the party, I was determined to see someone in the group do the impossible—bend the bowl of a large, heavy soup spoon in half. I wanted to see it happen right in front of me, inches away. I chose that as my goal because it's virtually impossible for a normal person to do, and even with the use of a hidden conjurer's gimmick, it's not trivial if you're being closely watched and you know how such tricks and gimmicks work. I was also aware of standard techniques like misdirection and sleight of hand as ways of surreptitiously bending spoons, so I was on the lookout for such maneuvers.

The workshop participants were advised that anyone who was able to bend the bowl of a heavy soup spoon with a gentle touch would receive a big yellow button with the words WARM FORMER printed on it. That strange term referred to the idea that somehow the mind could make the metal *warm,* and then you could easily *form* it into shapes. People who said they could do this typically reported that the metal momentarily felt like soft putty, but paradoxically it was always cool, and not warm, to the touch.

For reasons I do not understand, when I learned that it was possible to earn a big yellow button, I desperately wanted it. No—I *obsessively needed* that button, perhaps because the next day I knew I would be giving a talk at the conference, and I visualized myself at the podium wearing the yellow button. I normally shy away from any form of self-aggrandizement, but at that moment the thought of showing off the prized yellow button was alluring in a most peculiar way. It wasn't an idle moment of ego-inflation. It was a crazed fascination, quite out of the ordinary for me. Without hyperbole, I felt at that instant that the fate of the entire universe depended on my getting that button. I clearly remember that odd, senseless feeling of hypermotivation.

Fortunately, the manic moment soon faded into the background, and I found a woman at the party who claimed that she had bent the bowl of a spoon in a previous workshop. I stood about two feet in front of her, holding my own spoon, mimicking what she was doing with her spoon. She held the stem in her right hand and the (unbent) bowl pinched lightly between her left thumb and forefinger. I did the same.

After a few minutes nothing was happening, and I was getting tired because my full attention was focused on her and her spoon, and I was tightly holding on to mine. Then someone in the room suddenly shouted with delight, indicating that they had probably bent a spoon or fork. A second later someone behind me yelled, "Look what you've done!" I looked around to see what the commotion was, and the person said, "No, you. Dean! Look at your spoon!" I did, and to my astonishment I had bent the bowl of my spoon about 90 degrees. I know that no one surreptitiously switched my spoon while I was distracted because I was holding it tightly the whole time, and I had the presence of mind to immediately examine my fingers to see if there were indentations or any other signs of force on my fingers. There weren't.

The person behind me then shouted, "Keep going! Bend it all the way!" So I touched the bowl of my spoon with a finger, and it felt soft like putty. I pinched it with my finger and thumb, and the bowl easily folded all the way over and immediately hardened again. It was cool to the touch throughout this episode. Figure 2 is a photo of that spoon, which sits on my desk to this day as a reminder to avoid limiting my imagination of what psi is capable of.

Figure 2. Bowl of a heavy soup spoon bent over after a light pinch

The spoon has remained this way ever since. As soon as I returned to my lab, I checked to see if it might have been a trick spoon, like one made out of nitinol (also called memory metal). That metal alloy adopts a different shape if subjected to heat or cold and is a common gimmick that stage magicians use to fake metal bending. It wasn't nitinol. The bend itself is shiny and smooth, unlike what a spoon bent by force would typically look like. Using a torque wrench on the same kind of spoon from the same manufacturer, I measured the amount of force required to make that bend, and it was far beyond what I, and I'd guess anyone, could accomplish using only two fingers.

The day after this workshop I gave my talk onstage while wearing that big yellow button, and while doing so I felt that the universe had returned to its proper state, and the crazed sense of motivation that I had had vanished. If I had not experienced this episode firsthand, I would probably have remained highly skeptical that this type of mind-matter interaction was possible. That experience taught me that extreme forms of motivation, with suspended disbelief, can accomplish powerful magic. I recall what that remarkable state of consciousness felt like, and I have been able to evoke weaker versions of it on demand but with comparably weaker outcomes. I sometimes imagine what might have happened to that poor spoon if I had been able to sustain both unlimited motivation *and* absolute belief.

This episode serves as an example of the role of motivation in magical effectiveness. Intention and belief are key factors, but super-strong motivation can amplify those effects to push beyond the limits of what is normally considered possible. One wonders what magical marvels might be achievable by optimizing all those factors. As the chaos magician Peter Carroll has pointed out with his magical equations, discussed in Chapter 6, the answer in principle is *anything*.

ATTENTION AND INTENTION

We have the power to analyze and explore the world. Yet, we
panic when data threaten to contradict our expectations.

— FRANS DE WAAL

Another important factor in enchantment is clear *intention:* desire,
focused like a laser, to effect a specific change in the physical world.
Regardless of the method used, whether crafting a sigil or using knots,
candles, words, or any other form of enchantment as discussed in
Part IV, it is the intention behind the craft, as well as the clarity of the
desire and how much the universe would have to bend to accomplish
that desire, that determines effectiveness.

Enchantment on Elementary Physical Targets

ENCHANTED DICE

The first systematic scientific studies exploring the reality of enchantment began in the 1930s, when J. B. Rhine and his colleagues at
Duke University investigated a gambler's claim that he could toss dice
and mentally influence the outcome.[16] Those tests began a category
of PK experiments that were designed to investigate if the mind could
shift the probabilities of random events. Incidentally, the idea of using
random events like the toss of a die to study PK was first proposed
some three hundred years ago by Sir Francis Bacon, one of the founders of modern empirical science.[17]

Over the next five decades, some fifty-two investigators published
148 dice-tossing experiments in English-language journals. These
studies, which were conducted in increasingly rigorous ways, suggested the presence of a genuine mind-matter interaction effect. In
1989 the psychologist Diane Ferrari and I reviewed the overall evidence for PK in dice experiments using meta-analysis. I reviewed the
results in my 2006 book, *Entangled Minds,* and in more detail in a

journal article,[18] but for convenience I'll briefly repeat our findings here.

We found seventy-three publications describing dice-tossing experiments. From 1935 to 1987 some 2,500 people attempted to mentally influence 2.6 million dice throws in 148 different experiments, and just over 150,000 dice throws in thirty-one control studies where no mental influence was applied. The results showed that the odds that the dice falls were due to chance alone were a duotrigintillion (that's a 10 with ninety-six zeros after it) to 1. By contrast, the results of control experiments were within chance expectation. Something interesting seemed to be going on.

Maybe these results were due to just a few investigators who reported most of the studies, raising suspicions about possible sloppy work or fraud. To test that possibility, we tallied the number of studies conducted by each investigator, which ranged from one to twenty-one, with most of the investigators (64 percent) reporting three or fewer studies. So we calculated the overall odds against chance just for that subset of investigators. That resulted in odds against chance of over a billion to one, so the results weren't due to just a few possibly suspect investigators.

Maybe the results were due to experiments with impossibly good results, again suggesting flaws or fraud. To test this idea, we discarded 35 percent of the studies with the largest effects, but the remaining ninety-six studies still resulted in odds against chance of more than 3 million to 1. Maybe the results were due to a selective reporting problem, whereby only positive studies were reported and the rest were left behind in a file drawer somewhere. To test that idea, we used an analytical method that estimated "missing" studies. That procedure estimated twenty-one missing studies, all of which were assumed to have negative outcomes. When those studies were added to the known studies, the overall effect was adjusted downward, but odds against chance were still a septenvigintillion (a 10 followed by seventy-six zeros) to 1.

We continued to investigate ways that one or more mundane explanations might account for these results. After consideration of all the usual criticisms, we concluded that chance, poor methods, selective reporting, suspect investigators, and so on could not explain away these results. Dice could be enchanted.

ENCHANTED ELECTRONS

Dice studies began to fade from the literature by the 1970s, when Helmut Schmidt, a physicist at Boeing Aerospace Labs at the time, created a binary random number generator (RNG) based on the random timing between emission of natural radioactive particles. When such particles are emitted is called quantum indeterminate, which means the emission is completely and fundamentally unpredictable.

The quantum random nature of RNGs used in psi research makes these devices a perfect target for PK, because if the experiment shows that the distribution of 1s and 0s is not expected by chance when a person intentionally tries to influence the device, then that indicates the mind is somehow involved in influencing probabilities. That in turn might suggest that the mechanisms underlying mind-matter interactions operate at the quantum scale, and thus quantum theory might provide an explanation for the role of the mind in the physical world. That is, quantum theory tells us not what will happen to any specific random event, but rather what happens to groups or *distributions* of events. As it turns out, there are reasons (we'll discuss them in Chapter 6) that quantum theory may indeed be relevant to understanding PK.

Helmut Schmidt ran many PK experiments with RNGs, often with outstanding results far beyond chance. His work inspired many others to try to replicate these studies, including the Princeton University Anomalies Research Laboratory (known as the PEAR Lab).[19] To date, four meta-analyses of this body of research, involving hundreds of published replications, have been conducted. Two of those meta-analyses were conducted by my Princeton University colleague, psychologist Roger Nelson, and me, a third was also by me, and the fourth was reported by researchers from the Institute for Frontier Areas of Psychology and Mental Health in Freiburg, Germany.[20]

The bottom line is that all four meta-analyses found highly significant evidence for PK effects in RNGs. (They are referred to as PK-RNG studies, for short.) Each publication sparked vigorous debates about whether the observed effects in these hundreds of studies might be explained by selective reporting practices or some other bias or flaw. Such critiques have been analyzed and discussed for years and have been found to be unlikely explanations. But a more recent contribution to this debate has made a much tighter argument in favor of genuine PK-RNG.

QUESTIONABLE RESEARCH PRACTICES

The new approach rests on measuring the biasing effect of possible flaws, which in academic-speak is known by the fancy phrase "questionable research practices" (QRPs). These practices come about because of enormous pressure in science, especially academic science, to produce successful and novel results. That's what gets you noticed, promoted, and maybe even a prize. You gain little by carefully conducting a very expensive study that takes years of diligent work and ends up with nothing interesting. Horror at the thought of wasting time and money can motivate an investigator to make decisions like "That participant smelled bad, so I'll just drop him from the study," or "If I round these numbers up just a tad, the results will look better." Each time one of these QRPs is used, interpretation of the results becomes muddled. If enough QRPs are used, then the critic's lament is valid—the results are unreliable.

QRPs are not a trivial problem, and they can be found in all scientific disciplines. For example, one analysis studied all experiments published from 1996 to 2017 that used the gold-standard methodology in medical studies, the randomized controlled trial. Some 163,000 publications were examined using a specialized software application to look for possible QRPs.[21] The analysis found that between 43 and 63 percent of the studies had one or more QRPs.

This is critically important to know because medical studies inform what practices, therapies, and medications are ultimately deemed to be effective. Fortunately, because it is now becoming better recognized that flaws and biases can creep into any experiment, methods have been developed to reduce their impact. This includes publicly pre-registering methods and analyses to be used in an experiment, then making all the data from a study publicly available.

But the question remains about already published work. In particular, are psi studies rife with QRPs?

The physicist Peter Bancel of the Institut Métapsychique International in Paris, France, developed a way to test how QRPs might have influenced evaluation of psi experiments.[22] To do this, he calculated what would happen if all of these experiments were contaminated by one or more QRPs. He found that after throwing the equivalent of the kitchen sink of QRPs at the PK-RNG studies, they still showed overall odds against chance of 10,000 to 1. This means assertions that the results of these studies must have been due to flaws *aren't valid*. Some form of mind-matter interaction really does occur in PK-RNG experiments.

A comprehensive review of PK-RNG research was published by psychologist Bryan Williams in 2022.[23] His review confirmed something long suspected by psi researchers: PK-RNG does not operate like any known physical force. That is, the RNGs aren't being influenced by electromagnetic "force beams" emitted by the brain or by any of the other known forces. We know this because shielding and distance between the RNG and the participant don't matter and the effect isn't even tightly constrained in time. This shows that PK does not behave like any conventional causal effect.

Instead, the effect appears to be goal-oriented.[24] That is, when intention is focused on a certain outcome, like making the output of an RNG deviate from chance expectation in a certain way, the mind does whatever is necessary to achieve that goal. If it requires ESP to scan the past, present, and future to help make decisions on when to interact with the device, or PK to help tweak the probability that certain events will unfold, then that is what will happen. This is part of an integrative theory of psi, which we'll discuss in Chapter 6.

ENCHANTED BRAINS

A recent development in PK-RNG research was based on Henri Bergson's "filter theory" (mentioned in Chapter 1). It's the idea that normal brain functioning gets in the way of psi. To test Bergson's theory, neurologist Morris Freedman from the University of Toronto and his colleagues conducted several experiments. They asked participants to try to mentally influence an electronic random number generator so its output would cause an arrow displayed on a computer screen to move to the right or to the left.

The idea was that if the filter theory is correct, and the brain gets in the way of psi, then perhaps patients with certain kinds of brain damage might perform better on a psi task than people without brain damage. In an initial test with several brain-damaged patients, Freedman found that two patients with left frontal brain damage could repeatedly demonstrate a significant PK-RNG effect when they were attempting to mentally move the arrow to the right.[25]

Based on that outcome, his team recruited 108 healthy people and used a technique called repetitive transcranial magnetic stimulation (rTMS) to temporarily inhibit the left or right frontal regions of their brain.[26] In rTMS, a magnetic coil is placed on or near the scalp. When the coil is repeatedly pulsed electrically, it generates a magnetic field that induces electrical currents in brain tissue below the coil. That in turn inhibits neuronal activity in that region. As a control, Freedman used a "sham" rTMS that looked like the real one, and it was handled in the same way during the experiment, but it didn't produce a magnetic field.

The results of this experiment, which showed improved PK performance when the rTMS device was used, suggested that Henri Bergson was on the right track: The normally operating conscious brain seems to block psi. By comparison, a brain that is forced out of its normal operating mode, in this case by interfering with neuronal behavior, is less effective at blocking psi.

From an evolutionary perspective, the idea that the normally operating brain blocks extrasensory perceptions makes a lot of sense. If we were *consciously* aware of everything, everywhere, all at once, we'd be overwhelmed. A brief moment of mental paralysis in the wild, where we didn't know where or even *when* we were, would be bad. Your mind might enjoy psychically admiring the pretty rings around Saturn as they were forming 100 million years ago, but if you weren't paying attention to the tiger in front of you, right here and now, then your branch of the family tree would be quickly pruned out of existence.

ENCHANTED LIGHT

Particles of light—photons—are an especially interesting target for PK studies because if the mind can influence photons, that means it can influence *energy*. That is, it would demonstrate not just a mind-matter interaction but also a *mind-energy* interaction.

The equipment often used in these studies is an optical system designed to generate photon interference. By analogy, you can think of interference as what happens when you toss pebbles into a still pond. The ripples created by the pebbles hitting the water will interpenetrate, with some of the ripples combining to create wave crest peaks, while others cancel them out. The peaks that emerge tend to momentarily behave in a *particle-like* manner, while those that flatten out behave in a *wave-like* manner. Note that this does not mean photons *are* particles or *are* waves. In fact, while the analogy is useful as a way to visualize photons, it's not quite right, because while the energies we're discussing behave mathematically like water waves, according to quantum theory they're not physical waves. They're wave-like *possibilities*.

If this makes your brain hurt, that's okay. No one understands why the electromagnetic energies we call photons behave this way. Nevertheless, in physics it's very well accepted that they do, because both the equations and endless experiments demonstrate that this is so.

Photons also exhibit a much stranger property that is relevant to our understanding of magic. Photons behave like waves or particles *depending on whether you're observing them or not*. This is called the *quantum observer effect*. This effect offers a straightforward way to study mind-energy interactions. A rough analogy for the quantum observer effect in the everyday world can be experienced by smiling pleasantly at a stranger and noting their reaction. Then intently stare at another stranger like a deranged maniac and see how they respond. (I disavow any responsibility for unfortunate outcomes when trying this second experiment.)

If you were a participant in a photon staring experiment, you might be asked to look at a graph on a computer screen that's displaying an ongoing squiggly line. Sometimes the line would meander upward, sometimes downward. Your task would be to mentally urge the line, purely through your intention, to move upward. You'd do this for thirty seconds, and then the screen would go blank and nothing would be displayed. That's a signal to withdraw your attention from the experiment and think about something else, or just relax with an empty mind. The computer running this study would automatically provide instructions to direct your attention toward or away from the graph, alternating each time for thirty seconds. This sequence would repeat multiple times, and one test session might last twenty minutes.

Meanwhile a camera or light sensor inside the optical apparatus would continuously record the amount of light at various locations according to the type of interference pattern the apparatus produces. When all the test sessions are completed by multiple participants, the investigator will compare interference measures between the observing and not observing periods. The "nothing interesting happening" hypothesis (the jargon is "null hypothesis") is that the act of observation makes no difference in the interference pattern. The PK hypothesis is that it does.

As of 2025, thirty-one experiments using photon interference patterns have been reported by five laboratories.[27] Of them, fifteen studies described statistically significant results with odds in each case of at least 20 to 1.[28] The likelihood of obtaining fifteen significant results out of thirty-one experiments, each with odds of 20 to 1 or better, is associated with odds against chance of over 200 billion to 1. This figure is not the result of a formal meta-analysis for several reasons: Many of these studies were exploratory, and they used different kinds of equipment and experimental protocols, so as a group they were not a sufficiently uniform set of replications. Nevertheless, these results so far provide support for the idea that consciousness does interact with photons in unexpected ways.

But wait, there's more.

Double-Slit Review

In 2023 the psychophysics researchers Teodora Milojević and Mark A. Elliott from the National University of Ireland, in Galway, published an extended review of this line of research in *Progress in Brain Research*. They concluded that:

> The well-known, quantum physics "double-slit" experiment was the first demonstration of wave-particle duality of light— photons naturally behave like waves, but once they are registered by a conscious observer they switch to behaving like

particles. In recent years, a new avenue of research has reported a psychophysical interaction occurring when focused attention was employed in the double-slit experiment. . . . *These studies suggest that mental activities are capable of influencing physical systems.*[29] (emphasis added)

One of the factors examined in these studies as a predictor of performance was competence in the ability to focus one's attention. Experienced meditators were found on average to produce larger effects than nonmeditators. In our own studies, we tended to select meditators for the simple reason that the experimental task requires participants to maintain some control over their attention, and meditation is all about training attention.

Consciousness as Causal

In 2021, my colleagues and I published the results of a double-slit study designed to test if consciousness can be said to *cause* a change in the behavior of photons.[30] As in our other studies, participants were asked to repeatedly focus their attention toward and away from the optical system for thirty seconds each. To simplify the discussion, let's call the attention toward condition **O,** for "observed," and attention away **U,** for "unobserved." The new element introduced into this study was that, rather than just alternating **O** and **U** periods, we used condition pairs, like **OO,** which meant that for thirty seconds one would observe the optical system, followed immediately by observing for another thirty seconds. Likewise, **OU** would mean an observed period followed by an unobserved period, and so on. The four possible pairs, **OO, UU, OU,** and **UO,** were presented in a random order.

We invited twenty-five participants to each contribute ten test sessions, and each session was matched with a "sham" session run exactly the same way, except that no one was present and we used a lightbulb in place of the participant to simulate body heat (because optical interferometers are sensitive to small changes in ambient temperature). The results showed that none of the planned comparisons were statistically significant.

Bummer.

But then we thought maybe there was a simpler way to measure changes in photon interference. As an exploratory analysis it wouldn't provide the same level of confidence as a planned analysis, but given how little we understand about these effects, we figured it would still be a useful exercise. I won't bore you with the technical details; if you're interested, it's described in our published article.

With the new interference measure in hand, the first thing we did was compare all the experimental samples collected in the observed condition versus all samples in the unobserved conditions. That resulted in odds against chance of 500 to 1. Then, using the same method applied to the sham data, odds against chance were a measly 5 to 1. So far, so good.

Next we examined each pair of conditions (that is, **OO, UU, OU,** and **UO**) along with several other measures to see if the results conformed to the expected outcomes. They did, with odds against chance of 10,000 to 1. For the matched sham data, the same analysis resulted in odds of a mere 3 to 1. The bottom line was that this study provided additional support for the idea that consciousness interacts with the wave-like nature of light in a way that looks like a causal influence.[31]

Polarization and Scattering

Light plays an important role in the history of psi research. Experiences involving light include luminous auras perceived by sensitive people around magnets, gems, and the human body, points of light reported during séances, mental and physical effects associated with exposure to "transforming lights," cases of psychic photography, tests of differences in psychokinetic effects performed in light versus dark environments, and so on.

Light continues to be an interesting object of study because photons are the quintessential quantum mechanical "objects," and as already discussed, experiments involving photon interference might help to inform the numerous interpretations of quantum theory. In a study led by my colleague Loren Carpenter, we investigated properties of light called polarization and scattering.[32] Polarization refers to the way the electromagnetic components of light vibrate, analogous to the way vibrations behave in a plucked string. Scattering refers to how a beam of photons that collide with charged particles would disrupt the direction that the photons were originally traveling. This experiment tested if focused intention might act as a kind of "charge" that would affect the trajectory of photons.

The polarization experiment design was conceptually simple. If you shine light through a linear polarizer, the only light that can pass through will be aligned with the direction of the polarization. This type of optical filter is commonly used in sunglasses to reduce glare. If you take another linear polarizer and place it on top of the first polarizer but turn it 90 degrees, then the light passing through the first polarizer will be completely blocked by the second, and no light will pass through both filters.

Our experiment measured how much light would get through two crossed polarizers if the mind could intentionally "twist" a laser beam as it passed *between* the two polarizers. If that happened, then the polarization of the photons would be modified slightly and more light would be allowed to pass through the second filter. The experiment involved fifteen sessions of twenty alternating intentional twisting and no intention periods, and fifteen additional sessions as a control without anyone present. We predicted that during the focused intention periods, we'd see more light passing through the two filters as compared to the no intention rest periods.

To our surprise, the results showed a significant *decrease* in light amplitude, with odds against chance of about 5,000 to 1. Control data, analyzed the same way, showed chance results. We guessed that maybe the process of focusing intention toward a laser beam interfered with the beam in some way and caused it to scatter. That speculation led to the second experiment.

In the scattering experiment, we passed a laser beam through a highly reflective sphere. The task was to mentally block or deflect the beam inside the sphere. That would, we guessed, reduce the light beam intensity observed by a camera positioned outside the sphere. This study involved thirty alternating periods of intention focused toward and away, and we ran a total of forty sessions, each with a different participant. We also ran the same number of control sessions where the participants sat in the same location as during the experiment but were asked to read a book and not pay attention to the apparatus.

The results were again *opposite* to what we expected. In the experimental condition, the amount of light passing through the sphere significantly *increased* during the mental "blocking" task, with modest odds against chance of about 175 to 1. In the control condition, the results were close to chance expectation.

There were two outcomes of interest in these puzzling experiments. First, they indicated that focused mental intention could influence the behavior of light, even if not as we expected it to. And second, the fact that the outcomes were unexpected was important because it indicated that the results were not due to "psi experimenter" effects. That is, it is well known in psi research, as in many experimental domains, that some investigators have "golden hands." They tend to get experimental results that conform to what they *want* to get. This is fine for them, but it complicates how to interpret the findings, because if others can't easily repeat the same effect, then it raises all sorts of questions. Like, why are some effects so difficult to repeat? Why can only some people replicate these studies? One answer is that experiments often involve *tacit knowledge*, meaning aspects of practices or methods that are difficult to articulate or are even unknown to the investigators.[33]

We do know that how investigators interact with participants, and how they personally exercise their attention and intention, are important factors. We also suspect that because of a sprinkling of "magical talent," some researchers are highly adept at getting experiments to work. From a conventional perspective, the difference between successful and unsuccessful experimenters is often attributed to subconscious cues, variations in how data are analyzed, experimental bias, and so on.

But some psi studies were specifically designed to explore the "golden hands" concept. They used the same equipment and participant populations, and they were conducted at the same time and in the same location, but they were performed by investigators with successful versus unsuccessful track records. The results obtained in those studies conformed to the investigators' prior histories.[34] This says there really is something like "magic hands" for conducting psi studies, just like the "green thumb" in gardening and the "greasy thumb" in auto repair.

The next experiment we'll discuss requires unpacking a few new concepts, but it's worth it because among other things, the experiment investigated the efficacy of magic in a new way.

The SIGIL Experiment

As my team and I continued to conduct studies involving mind-photon interference, we tended to select meditators because they have practice in maintaining focused attention. But after thinking about the practice of magic, I realized that meditation generally involves focusing attention *inward*, while the task in our studies involved focusing attention and intention *outward*.

To test if the direction of attention mattered, we conducted a photon interference experiment comparing performance in meditators versus people practiced in focusing intentions outward, namely *magicians* familiar with enchantment techniques. This led to an acronym I used for this study: SIGIL—Scientific Investigation of Gazing with Intention at Light.[35]

As far as I know, this was the first scientific experiment to explicitly test magical efficacy in a mind-matter interaction task. Such experiments are directly relevant for studying fundamental questions in quantum physics, but this study added a new twist by seeing if magicians might be especially appropriate for exploring these types of issues. It turned out that they were.

The experiment also explored an aspect of the quantum observer effect that we hadn't previously considered. In the classic double-slit experiment, the key factor of interest is *what is knowable* about the behavior of a photon. In practice, this means that if it's possible to tell which path a photon takes as it passes through a double-slit apparatus, then the photon will behave like a particle. If it's not possible to tell, then the photon will behave like a wave. Also, the degree to which the photon becomes particle-like or wave-like is proportional to how much information is gained.

In this study, rather than using a double-slit interferometer, we used a transparent diffraction grating. When you pass a laser beam through this grating, you see a couple of discrete spots of light, as compared to the alternating light and dark bands of light produced by a double-slit system. With a diffraction grating optical system, to measure photon interference you can simply measure how much light appears at each spot.

In our apparatus, we recorded the illumination levels at three spots of light. One spot was formed by the laser beam that passed straight through the diffraction grating. On either side of the central spot were two more spots (called first-order maxima) that exist only because of constructive interference of the wave-like nature of light. If a test participant managed to gain information about each photon as it passed through the diffraction grating, then there wouldn't be any wave-like photons remaining in those spots to interfere with one another. In this way, each of the two first-order spots provided an easy way to measure how much interference was in the optical system.

I will spare you the details, because unless you're enthralled by optical physics and the quantum observer effect, there wouldn't be enough coffee in the world to keep you awake. For those who *are* interested in the minutiae, I invite you to read the published journal article.

Now for the magical element. The study was planned for fifty participants. To find them, we sifted through about 100,000 candidates recruited through social media to select fifty finalists. We focused on two groups of experienced participants: meditators and magicians. Each person identified as having the requisite skills was mailed a custom-designed optical interferometer built for this experiment. Three of the fifty participants failed to provide any data for unanticipated personal reasons, so the study results were based on data from forty-seven participants. The finalists included twenty-four meditators and twenty-three magicians hailing from the United States, the United Kingdom, Ireland, Germany, Austria, Denmark, and Australia.

When performance between meditators and magicians was compared, by one measure the magicians ended up with odds against chance of about 10 quadrillion to 1 when they were observing, and odds of 2 to 1 when they weren't. The same analysis for meditators was odds against chance of 124 to 1 and 4 to 1, respectively.

As this was the first test comparing magicians and meditators, we don't know if we will be able to repeat these remarkable results in a future experiment. But the study outcome does hint that the magicians' *outward focus* of attention and intention may be a key factor.

The superior performance of the magicians also provided an amusing irony: To advance our interpretation of quantum mechanics—the pinnacle of today's hard sciences—we might need to include a factor that is so "soft" that it isn't even considered a part of science—magic. This odd turn of events would probably have pleased Isaac Newton and the other founders of modern science, all of whom were deeply into what is now called magic.[36]

Entangled Photons

The existence of psi tells us that certain aspects of the mind have *nonlocal* properties. That is, the mind is not constrained by the everyday boundaries of space or time. Many experiments have shown that nonlocal mind interacts with *local* matter (like dice, RNGs, or as we'll see later, water and plants). But can nonlocal mind also interact with *nonlocal* matter—that is, with matter or energy that is not constrained by distance in space? And if so, would those interactions go beyond what is currently understood by quantum theory?

To be clear, by *nonlocal matter* I mean physical objects that are not located in a specific location but are spread out through space and time. The term for this that most people know is *quantum entanglement*, which refers to connections between two or more particles, such that whatever happens to one particle instantly affects the others, even (in principle) if they're on opposite sides of the universe. From an everyday perspective, it's as though the particles somehow communicate faster than light, but it's not quite that, because entanglement does not involve any form of signal transmission. Nevertheless, these strange connections that transcend space and time have been repeatedly verified as a fact in physics labs, and those demonstrations won the investigators the 2022 Nobel Prize in physics.

With my colleagues Peter Bancel and neuroscientist Arnaud Delorme, I conducted an experiment to see if the mind could interact with quantum entangled photons.[37] The way to detect such interactions was through a measurement called entanglement strength, which refers to how strongly correlated or "connected" pairs of photons are through space and time. The upper limit of that correlation is called the Tsirelson bound, named after Russian mathematician Boris Tsirelson, who calculated the maximum entanglement strength allowable based on today's understanding of quantum mechanics.

If an experiment showed that nonlocal mind could influence entangled strength *above* the Tsirelson bound, it would indicate that whatever psi is, it is not adequately described by quantum theory.

We used an optical system that generates about one thousand entangled photon pairs per second.[38] Each experimental session included short periods of time when a participant's intention was focused on a graph that reflected entanglement strength in real time, as compared to periods of the same length with no feedback and where intention was withdrawn. Delorme and I conducted three experiments at IONS, and Bancel conducted one at a meditation retreat in France.

Overall, the lab studies found evidence with odds against chance of 50 to 1 that nonlocal mind increased entanglement strength. Most of this result was due to the three studies we conducted at IONS, where odds against chance were 5,000 to 1. Control experiments using the same equipment and protocols, but without observers present, showed results consistent with chance. We also conducted a version of this study online, where through a web browser individuals could interact with the entangled photons using a protocol similar to what we used in the lab. That resulted in modest odds against chance of 20 to 1.

We did not find any evidence that entanglement strength could be mentally "pushed" above the Tsirelson bound. That may have been due to a limitation of the optical equipment we were using, or it might be an inherent limitation in what the physical world allows. Our conclusion was that quantum entanglement appears to be sensitive to conscious awareness. That's of course interesting when it comes to interpreting quantum theory, but it is also important to know when developing quantum information technologies, such as quantum computation and encryption, because if such methods are vulnerable to distant mental influence, then the supposed ultra-security promised by quantum encryption techniques is not quite as safe as some have assumed.

PLASMA—IT'S ALIVE!

In 1880 Sir William Crookes, president of the Society for Psychical Research from 1896 to 1899, presented evidence for a "fourth state of matter."[39] Beyond solid, liquid, and gas, this new state, which he dubbed *radiant matter*, consisted of highly energetic, ionized gas. In 1928 radiant matter was renamed *plasma* by the physicist Irving Langmuir.

Electrical plasma is thought to make up about 99 percent of the visible matter in the universe.[40] It is also associated with anomalous luminous effects reported throughout history, including phenomena called will-o'-the-wisps, ball lightning, and von Reichenbach's "Odic light," as well as lights in the sky, including UFOs and UAPs, and unexpected lights associated with certain locations, including Marfa, Texas; Zeitoun, Egypt; and Hessdalen Valley, Norway.[41] Other reports of luminous phenomena, possibly associated with electrical plasma, are associated with the human body, including reports of glowing ectoplasm, moving points of lights observed during séances, and shimmering apparitions.[42]

Some researchers have noted that because of the complexity of the ionic interactions within electrical plasma, at times plasma seems to show signs of sentience.[43] In fact, in the late nineteenth century, at the Chicago World's Fair, Nikola Tesla first publicly demonstrated plasma streams. Tesla, who had closely followed William Crookes's exploration of radiant matter, stated in an interview:

> Inasmuch as Sir William Crookes, that distinguished scientist and my good friend, has not hesitated to state openly his belief

in telepathy, it is a reasonable flight of fancy for me to say that *my machine—so sensitive—may be affected by the human will.* But that is all it is—merely a pleasant speculation, founded on logical grounds. I have no evidence to support it, but I have a perfect right to state it—understand me—as a possibility—no more. (emphasis added)[44]

In the late 1970s, the Stanford University materials scientist William Tiller was exploring the possibility of mind-matter interactions using a custom-designed plasma device as the physical target. The device developed in Tiller's lab was designed to provide a controlled way to study interactions between electrical plasma and what he referred to as "human energy fields." Tiller's conclusion, based on a series of experiments using his gas discharge device, was that "this energy can be directed by the human mind."[45]

Following up on Tiller's work, in the 1990s I explored the use of electrical plasma as a physical target in a series of mind-matter interaction studies. The plasma device I used was a commercially available eight-inch-diameter glass sphere filled with xenon gas and energized by a central high-voltage electrode. This kind of device is inexpensive and marketed as a night-light, a party decoration, and a science toy. The ball generates an aesthetically pleasing, undulating display of dynamic plasma streams that randomly move around inside the sphere. If the glass surface of the ball is touched by a finger, the electrons in the plasma streams will coalesce and move toward the touched location.

While Tiller's experiments involved placing one's hands a few centimeters from his plasma device, my experiment was designed to test if focused intention directed toward the ball from a distance of six feet away would influence the direction of the plasma streams. Effects of the mind were measured by placing a photodetector about an inch away from the edge of the glass. We measured the voltage returned by the photodetector, then invited participants to mentally urge the plasma streams to move toward the photodetector, thus increasing the amount of light in that direction, or to withdraw their attention. While nudging the plasma toward the photodetector, the participants obtained real-time feedback about their efforts in the form of a continuously updated graph displayed on a computer screen.

The results using that apparatus with a half-dozen participants were so consistently positive that I decided they must be due to some sort of mistake. Not having the time to track down the problem at that time, I set aside the plasma ball and focused on other work. A decade later I found that same plasma ball while conducting an inventory of laboratory items, so on a lark I decided to repeat the experiment, this time using a webcam to record the movements of the plasma streams. The results were again remarkably significant, but once more I assumed that I must have overlooked some mundane explanation, so I returned the plasma ball to inventory.

Another decade passed. Then I learned that another researcher had reported apparently robust mental interaction effects with a plasma ball.[46] That encouraged me to revisit this experiment in the IONS laboratory.[47] In the following studies we pointed a webcam at the ball from about eight inches away.

We conducted three studies, each more strictly controlled than the previous one. For the first experiment, the ball and the webcam were placed inside an opaque cardboard box, about twelve feet from the participant (in this case, me). The webcam images were processed by a computer to quantify the amount of illumination. This measure was presented on the computer's screen during attention-toward periods but not during attention-away periods. Each session consisted of twenty alternating twenty-second periods of focusing toward or away from the plasma ball. I ran ten experimental and ten control sessions, the latter with no one watching the computer and with the computer's sound turned off. The results for the experimental data were associated with odds of 300 to 1, and the control results were at chance. That was promising, so I moved on to the next experiment.

For the second study, we placed the ball and webcam on a small wooden table inside the IONS laboratory's two-thousand-pound, solid-steel, double-walled, electromagnetically shielded chamber. Nothing else was in the chamber during the experiment. We left the door of the shielded chamber open so the participants, who sat in front of a computer about twelve feet away from the ball, could see it through the doorway. Other than the plasma ball and the open doorway, there were no sources of light inside the chamber. The webcam's output was carried by a USB extender cable to the computer that controlled the experiment, and the protocol was the same as in the first experiment. This study included twenty planned experimental and control sessions contributed by ten individuals. The experimental sessions resulted in odds against chance of 10 million to 1, and the control sessions 50 to 1.

Now this was even more interesting, although the fact that the control session was also modestly significant told me that I had to completely secure the plasma ball from any possibility of extraneous influence or light. So for the third experiment, the shielded chamber door was sealed shut, and the only source of illumination inside the chamber was the plasma ball. The webcam's digital images were converted into light pulses, then carried by optical fiber through a tiny porthole in the chamber wall (which was designed for that purpose), then on to a computer outside the chamber.

We also changed the protocol a bit. In this study, the participants' task was to imagine that they were touching the plasma ball either on the top or the right side (according to instructions spoken by the computer). The purpose of this dual task was to see if intention caused different outcomes in the plasma stream. That would more directly test if intention really did influence the plasma. In a "relax" condition, participants were asked to withdraw their attention and intention from the experiment. In each test session there were ten aim right, ten aim top, and ten relax phases, presented in a newly randomized order in each session, for a total of thirty twenty-second periods per session. A total of thirty experimental and thirty control sessions were planned. The results showed that the difference in plasma illumination between the aim right versus aim up intentions was associated with odds against chance of 3.7 million to 1.

How can we understand this? As with any psi effect, a completely satisfactory explanation is not yet available, but a speculation by the physicist Ian Thompson offered a possible clue.[48] He pointed out that the equations of a well-accepted theory in physics (called the Standard Model), which describes the behavior of elementary particles like electrons, protons, and neutrons, uses a mathematical trick called renormalization. This trick makes the theory work, where *work* means that the results of the equations provide a reasonably good match to the observable world.

But there's a drawback. It's possible to renormalize equations in many ways, and in so doing one might end up with an entirely different description of how the physical world works. Thompson suggested, based on this flexibility, that the minds of living systems may be able to slightly alter some of the variables in the Standard Model equations to help optimize their survival. He proposed that the mind does this by affecting a physical property called the "permittivity of the vacuum." This tells us how much an electric field can "flow" through a material and how much gets stored in that material. For example, in a vacuum, electric fields can easily flow, so the permittivity is low. In a material like glass, electric fields can't move very easily, so permittivity is high.

If the mind could influence permittivity, even to a miniscule degree, then that would allow for all sorts of interesting physical changes. Such changes would be especially noticeable in charged particles, precisely like those *found in electrical plasma*. In fact, Thompson specifically proposed, without knowledge of this experiment, that the mind might be able to cause discernible changes in the light generated by a fluorescent tube, which is a perfect example of a common practical application of electrical plasma.

Interestingly, there's a traditional form of magical practice that involves plasma. It's called *candle magic*. The hottest part of a typical candle flame, near the blue base of the flame, has enough energy to create free electrons and positively charged ions. That portion of the flame is a plasma that, like the plasma ball used in this experiment, conducts electric charges.

Enchantment on Water, on Plants, and in Healing

My wife was a chef in gourmet restaurants for many years, and I heard stories from her and other chefs about the role of the cook's intentions in how diners perceive a dish. The lore tells us that in a happy kitchen, the food will be especially delicious and your tummy will be happy. If you see kitchen staff who are sad or angry, it's probably best to skip that meal.

MAGIC WATER

I began this line of research through collaborations with Masaru Emoto, who famously promoted the idea that thinking happy thoughts about a bottle of water would cause frozen water crystals formed out of that water to look beautiful, and thinking bad thoughts would create badly shaped or no crystals at all.[49] I conducted two double-blind studies with Emoto. In our lab in California, we prepared bottles of water that came from the same source but were intentionally treated or not treated. Then we sent those bottles to his lab in Tokyo, with the bottles simply labeled A or B, so neither Emoto nor his technician knew the treatment condition of each bottle.

Emoto kindly invited me to Tokyo to watch how these crystals formed inside his walk-in freezer. But the prospect of flying to Tokyo to spend a week inside a freezer was not all that appealing. So I thanked him and managed to bow out of that invitation.

After his technician made and photographed the crystals, Emoto sent photos of the crystals back to us. We asked hundreds of people via a web-based judging process to rate how beautiful each crystal was. Of course, we didn't indicate the underlying water condition of the crystals. Then we analyzed the ratings to see if the results supported what Emoto was claiming. Our first study used a double-blind design, which we followed up with a triple-blind design. In both cases we found modestly significant evidence that aligned with his claims.[50]

Those studies led to an experiment where we wanted to see if intention could also influence pieces of chocolate, such that when it was consumed it would cause a measurable elevation in mood, as compared to the same chocolate that was not intentionally influenced. The influencers in this case were a Buddhist monk and a Mongolian shaman. The results of that study, under double-blind conditions, showed a significant enhancement in mood.[51] This line of research was becoming more interesting, but science demands independent replications to gain confidence in reported effects. So I was pleased when Professor Yung-Jong Shiah, from the National Kaohsiung Normal University in Taiwan, asked if I would collaborate from afar on a new study of the mood enhancement effect.

Instead of chocolate, Shiah suggested a more popular consumable in Taiwan, namely tea. He recruited 189 members of a Buddhist temple and assigned them randomly to two groups. One group was given bottles of oolong tea blessed by a respected monk from the Bliss and Wisdom Buddhist Foundation in Taiwan, along with two other senior monks from the same foundation. The other group drank the same tea that had not been blessed.

Under double-blind conditions, the group drinking the blessed tea reported a modest but significant improvement in mood. And importantly, among those who drank the treated tea without knowing if it was in fact treated (because of the placebo-controlled design), those who nevertheless *believed* that their tea was treated showed a much greater enhancement in mood as compared to those who drank the exact same tea but did not believe it was treated. Odds against chance for the observed difference were 50,000 to 1.[52]

This indicated a strong interaction between the effects of intention and belief. In the light of understanding magic, this is important because it suggests that the efficacy of magic is modulated by the belief of those subjected to the magic. Thus, in any form of enchantment aimed at influencing others, especially glamouring, it's best to not let the subjects of one's influence know about the magical efforts, because if they actively believed it wouldn't work, then they'd be able to bring to bear their defenses, and the effects of the magic might be diminished or extinguished. If they did not know, then they might or might not be able to mount effective unconscious defenses. And if they did erect a defense, then the enchantment might rebound. This is why directing any sort of intentions toward another person, even positive intentions like healing, without that person's permission should be strictly avoided. Such intentions can be risky, depending on who or what you're up against.

MAGIC PLANTS

Shiah and his colleagues, again including me from afar, followed up the successful tea study to see if water blessed by the Buddhist monks would influence the growth of *Arabidopsis thaliana*, a little plant in the mustard seed family. Using a double-blind design where the technicians who were growing the plants did not know what kind of water—blessed or control—they were using, after an assigned period of time they measured the length of the first stem of each seed, called the hypocotyl. Healthy seed growth results in a short, fat hypocotyl because the seed is able to save its energy to continue to push upward and flourish. In our study, the hypocotyl indicated superior growth when hydrated with the blessed versus control water, with the prodigious odds against chance of 10 trillion to 1.[53]

As I was contemplating these results, I found myself feeling sorry for the plants grown in the control water. After all, they didn't receive the obvious benefits of the blessings. It also made me more sympathetic about Emoto's wish to get people everywhere to bless all the waters of the Earth.

We followed up the *Arabidopsis* study with a more complex design to try to tease apart what was going on. Did the effect work on the seeds, the water, or some combination of the two? And could the study be crafted in a way to ensure that the method of growing the seeds was not producing some sort of unintended or spurious result? To find out, Shiah designed a method to test the effect of blessed versus unblessed seeds, blessed versus unblessed water, and two colors of light used in the plant incubation process (blue plus red, or just blue). As in the earlier study, the hypocotyl and several other elements were measured.[54]

The results showed that the *Arabidopsis* plants that were hydrated with blessed water showed enhanced growth, replicating what the first study found but far more modestly, with odds against chance of 25 to 1. The effect of blue mixed with red light also resulted in enhanced growth as compared to blue light, with odds against chance of a billion to one. That last result was expected, because it is well known that blue-red light makes this kind of plant grow better than blue light does. So that outcome provided confidence that the methods, measurements, and means of analysis had performed as expected. So far, so good.

However, the blessed seeds resulted in an unexpected outcome. They showed *reduced* growth at odds of 2,500 to 1. What caused this odd reversal was the best kind of mystery. Unexpected outcomes, like in the photon polarization and scattering studies discussed earlier, are vitally important because they remind you that Mother Nature still has a few tricks up her sleeve, and she's trying to teach us something new by whacking our expectations over our heads.

Faced with the unexpected seed result, we speculated that intention might affect highly labile physical systems, like water, more than it influences relatively inert substances, like seeds. Another idea related to biochemical factors known to be involved in maintaining seed dormancy. These processes stop a seed from germinating before the seed senses that optimal growth conditions are available. Yes, a seed can sense its environment.[55] In any case, could the application of intention to encourage a seed to accelerate its growth put competing forces into motion that simultaneously promoted and inhibited that growth? And could that conflict have produced the puzzling results we observed?

Maybe. This is the fun of science. We ask the universe a question through our experiment, and sometimes we're presented with puzzling results that might provide important hints about how psi works. But research funds are limited. So for the next study, we set aside the plants and tested a more pragmatic target: stem cells.

MAGIC STEM CELLS

A stem cell is a cellular shape-shifter that migrates to injury sites and transforms into the type of cells required to heal the injury. This study explored if human stem cells derived from dental pulp gathered during tooth extractions, then cultivated in a medium made with blessed water, would grow more and show greater shape-shifting capacity (science geek alert: the technical term is "pluripotency") than cells from the same source but grown in control water.

Stem cells from two donors (called cell lines) were cultured in triplicate in a growth medium made from either blessed or control water, and the total number of cells grown were counted on days 3, 6, and 8. Gene expression factors were also studied to see if the stem cells showed greater pluripotency (the ability to develop into nearly any cell type in the body) with the blessed water. As you might expect by now, the combined result of both cell lines showed improved growth with the blessed water with odds of 1,250 to 1. This was due almost entirely to just one of the cell lines. Why, we don't know; it's another mystery for enterprising students to pursue.[56]

MAGIC ENERGY MEDICINE

Energy medicine is a branch of integrative medicine that studies how "subtle energies" may be used to diagnose and treat "energetic imbalances" in the body. This definition includes a bunch of scare quotes because the word *subtle* in "subtle energies" suggests something that is extremely weak. In fact, it's so weak that no available instruments can directly measure these purported energies. To make things worse, the word *energy* in energy medicine is not what most physicists would regard as energy, and the word *medicine* is not what most physicians or pharmacists would regard as medicine![57]

Then what is it? It's a class of healing modalities known by various names, including Reiki, Johrei, therapeutic touch, qigong, thought field therapy, emotional freedom techniques, psychic healing, shamanic healing, spiritual healing, prayer, and so on. The commonality is that the methods are often described in ways that *sound* related to energy, including use of words like *field*, *frequency*, and *vibrations*. Or they refer to Eastern terms that are roughly synonymous with subtle energies, including qi, ki, and prana.

Terms like *vibration* and *frequency* have precise meanings in engineering and physics, which is confusing because this is not what energy medicine is about. Instead, practitioners of these techniques, and oftentimes patients as well, are usually talking about subjectively *felt* energy. That refers to electrical-like or magnetic-like sensations in or around the body. Such sensations, sometimes accompanied by visualizations, can at times be incredibly clear and strong. But when instruments are designed to detect exquisitely small amounts of conventional energies, like electromagnetism, little or nothing shows up. What can be measured are physiological correlations with *something* that does not appear to be physical, at least not in the usual way we think of physical energies. Perhaps subtle energies are a precursor to physicality, or something that modulates the behavior of the physical world.

Some promote the idea that energy medicine is mediated by electromagnetism or quantum mechanics. The desire for an explanation is understandable, because many scientists and physicians will not accept weird healing effects without an explanation despite a growing clinical literature indicating that these modalities are effective with certain kinds of disorders (especially pain). However, except for quantum mechanics, explanatory attempts based on known fields and forces, even ultra-weak effects, cannot be fully adequate, because nearly all energy medicine methods work not only in proximity to the patient, *but also at a distance*. This nonlocal feature is the most intriguing aspect of these therapies and the one where they are most similar to psi and magic.

One possible way to explain energy medicine is *information*. As an example of the power of information, consider a friend whispering very faintly in your ear, "I love you." The energy expended in transforming air pressure is miniscule, but after those signals are decoded by the ear and brain, the physiological response can be gigantic. Now imagine the same scenario, except that with the same expenditure of energy the whispered phrase is "You are going to prison." That would produce a rather different physiological response.

Informational models of physical reality are at the leading edge of physics today. These theories propose that reality is not made up of matter and energy; rather, the fundamental building blocks of the universe are more like simulations running in a cosmic computer. Based on this idea, *everything* we see—those things we call particles, forces, one another, even basic concepts like space and time—are actually much more like software-based virtual realities than objective hunks of material stuff or just givens (as space and time were considered to be, before Einstein's theories of relativity).

From this perspective, we might expect that what is currently called energy medicine may evolve into two or more subdisciplines, with some focused on conventional energies, like pulsed electromagnetic or bioelectromagnetic fields, and others on nonlocal informational effects. A fledgling body of literature is already forming around nonlocal informational effects, including positive studies reported by Nobel laureate Luc Montagnier. But despite intriguing evidence, informational models of reality still have a way to go to convince the mainstream that there's a there there, because it certainly doesn't *feel* like we're living inside a simulation. But perhaps that's because we're inside it, like a fish in water, so we don't have anything to compare it to.

PUTTING BILL IN A BOTTLE

William Bengston was a retired professor of sociology and a research methodology expert who for many years taught at St. Joseph's University in New York. Over decades, Bill developed and tested a method for healing based on rapidly cycling through mental images of things one desires.[58] I view Bill's technique as a kind of mental centrifuge that creates a highly refined, and largely unconscious, form of desire or will. It is, in other words, essentially an enchantment technique.

After many experiments, primarily conducted on mice given lethal doses of mammary cancer (a nasty practice, but that's how medical research is conducted), Bill found that by practicing his rapid cycling method while holding a cage of injected mice, he would get 100 percent full cures of the mice. Even more surprising, mice injected with the same cancer and treated with the blood of the cured mice became immune to that cancer and also enjoyed full cures. This is astonishing, because without that treatment, it is well established in hundreds of conventional experiments that those mice would reliably die in about twenty-seven days.[59]

The Bengston method is not especially difficult to learn, and Bill held workshops, wrote a book, and created a streaming audio program that teaches the technique.[60] As with any learned skill, some people are better at this type of healing than others, but in principle anyone could learn how to use this method, or for that matter most of the other energy medicine techniques. Incidentally, a practice I occasionally use and have found to be both ridiculously simple and remarkably effective for self-healing is the emotional freedom technique or "EFT tapping" method.[61]

The reason Bill's method is interesting from a magical perspective is that he claimed that his process differs from intentional healing. That is, he didn't intently *try* to heal the patient. Instead, by becoming adept at the rapid imaging cycle method, then adding a slight, effortless wish, the healing goal is apparently super-amplified. In the case of an effortless wish that the mice are healed, they are. This is approximately the same as the enchantment aim of applying *effortless striving*.

Another similarity with magic is that the healing can apparently be transferred and "stored" in various materials, like cotton and water, then applied later without the healer present. Such effects had previously been noted by Bernard Grad, a McGill university biologist.[62] This is virtually the same as the concept underlying the formation of amulets and talismans, which are perfectly ordinary objects until they are imbued with magical intention.

While Bill's healing technique works remarkably well in some cases, this kind of healing doesn't easily scale up. That is, if you needed a live healer to do it, it would be Bill-limited, and not everyone who wants to have a healing session could have one. So we set out to see if we could record Bill's healing "energy" (for want of a better term), then play it back later, in the form of a sound, to achieve a healing effect.

To do this, we had three healers, including Bill, practice his method to "charge" cotton inside the IONS's electromagnetically shielded chamber. We used a custom-designed multichannel recording system to capture a broad range of magnetic and electromagnetic signals while the healing activity took place, and also during control periods without healing so we'd have a comparison.[63]

I took the data we recorded and converted it into stereo audio files, and then we used spectral and temporal analyses to see if there were any differences between the healing and control recordings. We did see some interesting data in some recordings at very low frequencies, mainly below 5 Hz. To test if those recordings captured any of Bill's healing effects, we exposed mammary cancer cells to the recording in vitro and looked for gene expression changes. During the playback of the recording, the cells were placed in an incubator with speakers inside it. For the control test, the cells were placed for the same amount of time in the incubator while the speaker system was on, but without the recording playing. In this way, any potential interference from the speakers or the amplifier would be present in both conditions. Note that most speaker systems, including the ones we used, are not designed to reproduce signals at 5 Hz because such sounds are far below what humans can hear. So both the healing and the control recordings sounded like pure static, or a hissing noise.

Results of the experiment showed biological changes when the healing recording was played. Something about healing intention apparently could be recorded, then played back, and it would still work. Live healing by Bill was stronger than the recorded healing, suggesting that our recording did not capture the full effect of a living person performing the healing. But it recorded *something*.

MAGIC HEALING

In another study, we tested if energy medicine would be effective in treating carpal tunnel (i.e., wrist and hand) pain that hadn't responded to any other treatments.[64] We thought this might be a good health problem to work with because it's frequently reported. It's caused by nerves that are compressed by the ligaments and bones at the wrist. As such, it's difficult to treat and can become debilitating because a hand or wrist experiencing nerve pain is practically unbearable.

We recruited 190 people suffering from carpal tunnel pain to have a free thirty-minute treatment by one of seventeen different energy medicine practitioners. Some practitioners delivered their treatments near the client without touching, while others used a light touch. The main outcome measure was self-reported pain. Other measures included the client's expectations about whether energy medicine treatments would work, their sleep quality, their well-being, and so on. We also took a number of other measures, including two of special interest related to enchantment.

First, we found that the post- versus pre-session pain scores decreased 2 points on a 10-point pain scale, and three weeks later it remained significantly lower than their pre-session level. Two points may not sound like much, but it was surprisingly consistent across the clients, and it was associated with whopping odds against chance of 200,000 to 1. Importantly, this effect was not a placebo effect because it was independent of the clients' initial expectations. Measures on the patients' well-being and sleep quality also significantly improved and remained improved at the three-week follow-up visit.

One of the other measures in this study was about the effects of healing intention on the structure of water, specifically hydrogen-oxygen (H-O) covalent bonds.[65] We asked the energy medicine practitioners to directly "heal" samples of distilled and commercial bottled water, and during healing sessions with clients we also had both the healers and the clients wear necklaces that held a little vial of water. Before and after each healing session, we analyzed these water samples using an instrument that can measure the molecular structure of water. (Science geek alert: It was an Attenuated Total Reflection Fourier Transform Infrared Spectrometer equipped with a liquid nitrogen-cooled detector.) The comparison of interest was the infrared absorption portion of the water spectrum before and after the healing sessions.

We found that the distilled water that was directly treated by the practitioners resulted in a modestly significant change in the H-O "stretching" bond, one of many ways that water bonds can behave. We didn't see any effect with the use of bottled water. We also observed that a distilled water bottle worn by the healers during the healing sessions resulted in a more significant change in the same bond, with odds against chance of 2,500 to 1. We saw no changes in the bottled water, and no changes in either type of water in the vials worn by the clients. This study confirmed previous observations suggesting that water structure reacts to healing intentions.[66] It appeared to involve some form of energetic influence, but exactly what caused that change is not known.

A second factor we investigated in this healing study was claims that during energy healing, aspects of the physical environment change in a predictable way: a kind of physical order or coherence arises. The technical term is negative entropy, or *negentropy*.[67] To detect this change, we measured the outputs of truly random electronic number generators before, during, and after the healing sessions.

The results showed significant deviations in the outputs of the RNGs from chance expectation during healing. The peak effects occurred twenty-four minutes into the half-hour session, with odds against chance of 33,000 to 1.[68] By comparison, data recorded from the same RNGs eight hours after each session showed uniformly chance results. This outcome was consistent with what previous healing studies have found, suggesting that during periods of focused healing, physical coherence—meaning less randomness or noise than expected—emerges in the environment.[69]

The relevance of these studies to enchantment magic is that they demonstrate that focused attention and intention directed toward a wide range of physical systems, from photons and electrons to water, plants, cell cultures, and human health, can produce measurable changes in well-controlled laboratory environments. These experiments do not work every time, the effects tend to be small in magnitude, and we still do not have explanations that would satisfy every scientist. But the preponderance of the evidence, formalized using meta-analyses when there are enough similar studies to examine, shows that the effects are quite real. So enchantment exists.

Retrocausation

The idea of genuine enchantment causes some scientists to emit a combination of guffaws, groans, and, in extreme cases, spontaneous face-palming. Some may resort to muttering equations like incantations, as if attempting to banish such heresies. But we're not finished. We're going to wade into extremely strange territory—so strange that quantum physicists might want to clutch their emotional-support Schrödinger's cats.

There are reasons to suspect that enchantment is not just about influencing the present—it also works backward in time. This might seem to violate the commonsense notion that cause can only precede effect. But if science has learned anything about common sense, it's that our everyday experience is a poor guide to what reality allows. In fact, that the present is influenced by both the past and the future is not just an interesting theoretical possibility but has been convincingly demonstrated in "delayed choice" quantum physics experiments.[70] The upshot here is that enchantment and divination appear to be intimately related, or might even be exactly the same phenomenon, just described from different perspectives in time.

But first questions first. Is there any scientific evidence that the future can influence the present? One especially successful experiment that says yes is dubbed a *presentiment* test. That term is used, rather than the more familiar *precognition*, because information in this kind of test is received as a *feeling* rather than as a knowing or pre-*cognition*.

PRESENTIMENT

A real-life version of a presentiment experience may manifest as follows: You're driving along a road that you've taken hundreds of times. Now you're approaching a four-way intersection where the traffic light just turned green. Normally, you'd just continue at speed and drive through the intersection. But on this occasion, for no apparent reason, you suddenly get a *bad feeling*. Something's off, even though there are no obvious danger signs. You can't shake the bad feeling, so you slow down, confusing the drivers behind you and causing the whole row of cars to come to a stop even though you have a green light. Just as the driver behind you starts to impatiently honk their horn, an eighteen-wheeler that was hidden from view and approaching the intersection from a cross street blasts through its red light. You can see the look of panic on the truck driver's face when he realizes the brakes on his truck have failed, but it was too late to stop. If you hadn't paid attention to your "something's not right" feeling and kept driving through the intersection, the truck would have hit your car broadside, causing a massive accident.

What caused that bad feeling? A mundane explanation is that you unconsciously heard the truck approaching. As already noted, we are consciously aware of only a tiny fraction of what is impinging on our senses, so that explanation is possible. A more radical possibility is that the shock of the future event, when you realized that you just saved your life by slowing down, rippled backward in time and retro-causally influenced you to unconsciously feel that reaction in the present. That idea turns out to be testable in the laboratory.

The design is simple. The experimenter uses electrodes to record your skin conductance, heart rate, blood pressure, pupil dilation, brain activity, or a half-dozen other physiological measures. These variables reflect both conscious and unconscious responses, the bread and butter of the academic discipline known as psychophysiology, which began as a result of a mystical experience by the German philosopher and scientist Gustav Fechner.[71] But that's another story. Thousands of published experiments have used these methods to study what happens to your body *after* you're exposed to different kinds of visual, auditory, or other stimuli. In such an experiment, you might sit in front of a computer screen and hit a button; five seconds later a randomly selected calm or emotional image appears. Your body will respond, the data will be recorded, the investigator will analyze the results, articles will be published in journals, promotions will be gained, and honors will be awarded.

The presentiment experiment is run the same way, but with a slight change. Instead of examining the physiological response *after* a randomly selected stimulus, it is analyzed *before* the stimulus. The hypothesis is simple: Before a calm image or a soft sound, your nervous system will remain calm. But before an emotional image or noxious sound, simulating a truck about to run a red light, your nervous system will start to become activated. This study design also rules out unconscious clues, like the sound of a truck.

The earliest known suggestion for this type of experiment was offered by the brother of the eminent British statistician Irving J. Good, in 1961, as follows: "A man is placed in a dark room, in which a light is flashed at random moments of time. . . . The man's EEG [electroencephalogram] is recorded on one track of a magnetic tape, and the flashes of light on another. The tape is then analyzed statistically to see if the EEG shows any tendency to forecast the flashes of light."[72] Several simple experiments along these lines were conducted in the 1970s, but the results weren't strong enough to get researchers excited, so the idea lay fallow for several decades. In the mid-1990s, I had the idea that this experiment might work better if it simulated the real-life emotional stress of almost getting hit by a truck.

We can't put people in real danger in an experiment, but we can present calm and emotional images. So that's what I did, and the results showed that skin conductance (which reflects activity of the sweat glands) clearly reacted a few seconds before a randomly selected emotional photo but not before a calm photo. By 2012, there were many reported independent replications of this design, and they were reviewed using meta-analysis by neuroscientist Julia Mossbridge and her colleagues.[73] That review was updated in 2018 with new studies by the psychologists Michael Duggan and Patrizio Tressoldi,[74] and for this book I combined all these presentiment studies into a single database.

Some fifty-six presentiment experiments were conducted using many different physiological measurements and stimuli, including calm versus emotional images, no sounds versus loud sounds, and winning versus losing in gambling games. Physiological measures were observed before the stimuli, at times ranging from about nine seconds for heart rate measures, to about three seconds for skin conductance, to about a half-second for brain activity. Odds against chance combined across these studies were *11 decillion* to 1. That's an 11 followed by forty-five zeros.

Figure 3 shows the cumulative statistical result of these experiments in order of publication. It shows—in a way that can excite only a statistician—a cumulative Stouffer Z score (named after the statistician Samuel A. Stouffer, not the frozen food company). As more replications were conducted, confidence progressively grew that these studies were not due to chance. This is what we'd expect if the underlying effect is genuine—it should be reproducible by different investigators most of the time. The journal articles reporting these presentiment experiments discussed many ways of examining these studies to see if they might have been due to poor quality designs, or flawed analyses, or failure to report nonsignificant outcomes, and so on. Those possibilities were carefully considered and found to not be viable explanations for these results.

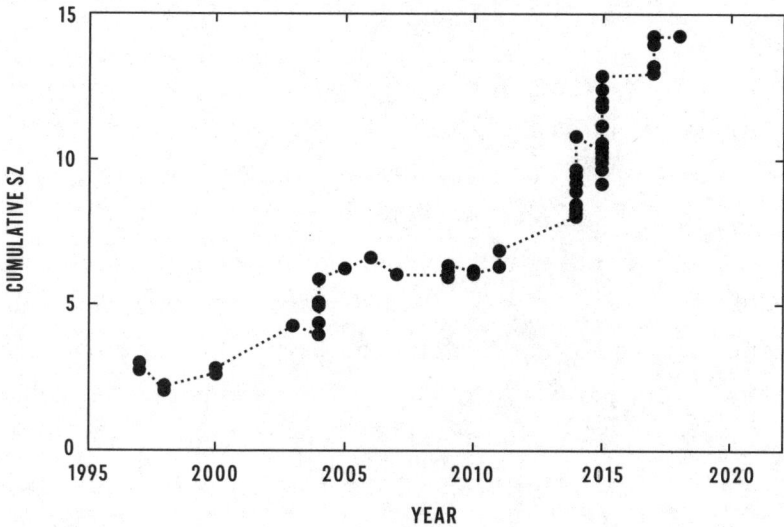

Figure 3. Cumulative Stouffer Z score for fifty-six replications
of the presentiment experiment conducted from 1997 through 2018
by seventeen different investigators. The end point is associated with
odds against chance of 11 decillion to 1.

Z SCORES

A short digression is in order because I will occasionally refer to *z* or
to Z scores. This value is sometimes called a *standard normal deviate,*
not because it maintains a questionable lifestyle, but because it refers
to deviations in a bell-shaped curve. Say you take a bunch of people
and they all take a standardized IQ test, like the Stanford-Binet. Then
you plot how many of these people have each IQ score. You'll eventually end up with a bar plot, or histogram, where the distribution of
scores looks like the shape of a bell; hence the famous bell curve,
which is also known as a normal distribution. The peak in the middle
will be around 100, the center point of the IQ test, and the sides of the
bells will decline as you move away from 100. This is one of the most
common distributions found in the natural world. It's a convenient
way to think about the likelihood of events because you can see at a

glance that measurements far out on the tails of the distribution are relatively rare.

In this way, you can see that a person who has an IQ of, say, 160 on the Stanford-Binet IQ test would be above average in intelligence. But how much above? The Stanford-Binet is designed so the population average is 100 and one standard normal deviate (same as a z score) is 15. An IQ of 160 would therefore be associated with $z = (160-100)/15 = 4$. It's now a simple matter to calculate the probability of getting a z score of 4 or greater. In terms of odds against chance, it's quite rare, about 31,600 to 1. That's impressive, but with a world population of 8 billion, that means about a quarter-million individuals would have that IQ or greater.

PRESENTIMENT IN ACTION

Presentiment in the lab is one thing. Are these effects meaningful in the real world? A 2024 study published in the *Proceedings of the National Academy of Sciences,* one of the highest-impact multidisciplinary science journals, was entitled "Brain Activity of Professional Investors Signals Future Stock Performance."[75]

The study published by Leonard Diederik van Brussel of Erasmus University in the Netherlands and his colleagues used a functional magnetic resonance imaging (fMRI) instrument to visualize the deep brain activity of thirty-six professional investors as they predicted future stock prices. Van Brussel and his team found that the investors could not consciously predict future market performance better than chance. But unconsciously they could. The portion of their brain associated with reward and motivation (called the *nucleus accumbens*) had higher activity for investment predictions that ended up overperforming in the market.

The article reported, "These findings remained robust, even when controlling for stock metrics and investors' predictions. . . . Cross-validated prediction analysis indicated that [the nucleus accumbens's] activity could significantly predict future stock performance. . . . Accumulating evidence does suggest that humans, including professional investors, may share a neural response to stimuli that is related to future market-level performance."

This conclusion was followed by the not-so-subtle hint "suggesting to financial institutions the investment value of collecting such information." In other words, the presentiment effect as observed in the laboratory can be, and most probably already is being, used to make money. That the most successful businesspeople rely on psi is one of those secrets, like magic, that is admitted only quietly among trusted friends after consuming three or more beers.

ASSOCIATIVE REMOTE VIEWING

Later, we'll explore remote viewing (RV), a structured form of clairvoyance (or divination) for perceiving through time and space. One method of remote viewing is called associative remote viewing (ARV), which uses precognition of the future to help make better decisions in the present. I'll provide a brief sketch of the ARV method here as preparation for a similar method that illustrates why enchantment and divination are closely related. For those interested in a comprehensive review of the history and applications of ARV, I can recommend a 2021 book by Debra Katz and Jon Knowles, entitled *Associative Remote Viewing*.[76]

Here's how ARV works:

1. Select two very different objects or images. Say, a photo of a fluffy white bunny and a photo of a rough-hewn black meteorite.

2. You randomly decide to associate the bunny image with a selected stock index that will go up tomorrow, and the meteorite image with that stock index going down tomorrow.

3. Ask a remote viewer to divine an image that you will show to them tomorrow. You don't tell them anything about the bunny or the meteorite, nor about how the images are associated with changes in future stock market prices. The less they know about what you're doing, the better.

4. The remote viewer gives you their impressions. This is recorded in the form of sketches and perhaps a few words.

5. You give those impressions to a panel of judges. For purposes of this explanation, assume that the judges are secured by themselves in a separate room, and they know nothing about the source of the impressions. All they know is that they've been handed some impressionistic sketches and two images, and they're asked to tell you which picture best matches the sketches.

6. In this example, the judges decide that the sketches look more like a bunny. They slip a note under the door with the word *bunny* on it.

7. If they can't decide between the two images, they'll slip a note that says *pass* under the door. This is a signal to the experimenters that they should skip this session because the quality of the remote viewing wasn't good enough.

8. You've already decided that the bunny is associated with the stock going up tomorrow, so you immediately place a buy order on that stock to take advantage of the divined information.

9. Tomorrow comes, you see that the stock price does indeed go up, so you show the remote viewer the picture of the bunny, and the retrocausal loop created by this task is now closed.

10. You make a profit and celebrate by eating a delicious chocolate chip cookie.

Can this method be used to make a profit? Yes, it can.

The Dutch physicist Dick Bierman and the French psychologist Thomas Rabeyron retrieved seventeen reports of the use of ARV to earn money.[77] They found that "most of the series led to profit, and some of them considerable profits." Across these studies, the hit rate in two-target ARV tasks, as in the above example of a bunny versus a meteorite image, was around 63 percent where chance would be 50 percent, and the reported overall profits were about a half-million dollars.

While impressive, because of the sensitivities surrounding ARV (most people using psychic methods to game the stock market are not comfortable readily admitting it) the precise success rate is unknown. However, there are a few well-documented cases where profits were definitely made. For example, Greg Kolodziejzyk, a world record holder in long-distance recumbent cycling and pedal-powered boats, published an article reporting a $146,000 profit using this method.[78]

MANIPULATIVE REMOTE VIEWING

Now for a mind-bending variation of ARV. It's deceptively simple, but its consequences for understanding magic are enormous. It's called manipulative remote viewing (MRV), and as far as I can tell, the idea was first proposed by the psychiatrist Elisabeth Targ, daughter of the co-founder of the US government's classified Star Gate program, the physicist Russell Targ.

MRV proposes that the act of perceiving the future can *cause* that future event to occur. In other words, it explicitly combines precognition with PK, or in the language of magic, it is a combination of enchantment and divination. It suggests that these two magical techniques, which may look and feel quite different from each other, may arise out of the same underlying source. That is, precognition can be thought of as intentionally pulling a desired effect *from the future*, while PK is intentionally pushing the effect *from the present*.

Before explaining the procedure, a bit of background is in order. In 1998 I was in charge of a psi research program at Interval Research Corporation. This was a research lab in Silicon Valley funded by Paul Allen, co-founder of Microsoft. The purpose of the lab, which housed a hundred scientists and engineers poached from such storied R&D facilities as the MIT Media Lab, Apple Computer, and Xerox PARC, was to invent the future of the "wired world" of the Internet. I was conducting psi research there because a small proportion of the lab's program was devoted to "blue sky," projects, of which psi research is the poster child. Everything at Interval was considered a company secret, so for many years what we did on the project, which was code-named the Phenome project, was unpublished. Interval closed in 2000, and Paul Allen passed away in 2018, so any embargo that may have been in place has long since expired.

On the surface, the MRV technique looks similar to ARV, but it includes a novel twist that turns the passive perceptual act of divination into an active act of enchantment. Here's the technique, as described in one of our Phenome reports:

> 1. Before the experiment begins, create twenty-four pools of images, each pool with five images. Within a pool, the images selected should be as different from one another as possible. Label the pools 1 through 24, in random order.

> 2. To begin an MRV session, experimenter 1 programs an RNG to randomly select one of the twenty-four image pools. Let's say it selected pool 6.

> 3. Now experimenter 1 programs the RNG to randomly generate numbers 1 through 5, one new number every six seconds, and to continue this process for ninety minutes. That will produce a sequence of nine hundred random numbers. The last number generated will be used ninety minutes in the future to select one of the five target images out of the selected pool of images.

4. While steps 2 and 3 are happening, experimenter 2 asks a remote viewer to divine a picture that will be shown to them in ninety minutes.

5. The remote viewer does so and hands you their sketches and written words.

6. You give those impressions to a panel of judges secured in a separate room. The judges are also given the five images from pool 6. You ask the judges to rank-order each of the five images according to the best match to the remote viewing impressions, which you'll label image 1, to the worst match, labeled image 5.

7. The judges do their task and hand you their envelopes labeled 1 through 5.

8. At the end of ninety minutes, the RNG will produce a random number from 1 to 5. If that number is a 1, then you show the remote viewer the judges' number 1 best match. If it is a 2, then you show the second best match, and so on.

Now here's the trick: For the remote viewer to end up seeing what they had precognitively perceived, and what the judges selected as the best match and subsequently ranked 1, then in the future the RNG *must* generate a 1 as its last number of the sequence.

Why?

Because if the judges failed to assign the rank 1 to the remote viewer's most accurate impressions of the target, it would create a temporal paradox. So the RNG *is forced* to select 1 as its final number, because otherwise the remote viewer would never get to see what they precognitively "saw."

In science fiction, temporal paradoxes are great fun, but in the real world it's usually not a good idea to fool Mother Nature. The physicist Nick Herbert, author of *Quantum Reality* and other books, once said to me that he knew we hadn't yet created a temporal paradox because the universe was still here. He meant that creating a causal paradox might start to tug on the fabric of reality, and depending on how severe the paradox was, it might even unravel that fabric. That would be bad, because unraveling the fabric of space and time is not something to take lightly.

Fortunately, even with superior knowledge of the future, there are two possible ways of avoiding a causal paradox or a predestined fate: The future *might* be inherently probabilistic rather than absolute or predetermined, and/or precognition *might* also be inherently probabilistic. In either case, accurate divination may or may not turn into enchantment. Perhaps this is the case, as it would help to explain why the universe hasn't yet unraveled. On the other hand, perhaps not, as we'll see.

At Interval we conducted ten MRV trials according to the above protocol. On the very first trial, the participant, a staff member at Interval who hadn't previously tried remote viewing, produced a sketch of his impressions for a waterfall target image that would be selected in the future (Figure 4).

After ninety minutes of randomly generating numbers 1 through 5, the RNG finally finished and generated a 1. So we showed the remote viewer the image of the waterfall, which was by far the best match to his sketch, and then we had to recover from the shock of seeing that this procedure actually worked. It also worked the second time we tried it, and then we really freaked out because we thought we had stumbled upon the psychic Holy Grail. But none of the remaining eight trials produced a first-place match, and we ended up with too many cases where the RNG generated a 2, which the judges had ranked as the second best match. In hindsight, we should have passed on any remote viewing sessions that did not provide clear outcomes, but hindsight is always 20/20. I will leave future replications of this type of experiment to the reader as an exercise. Important safety tip: Please do not unravel the fabric of reality.

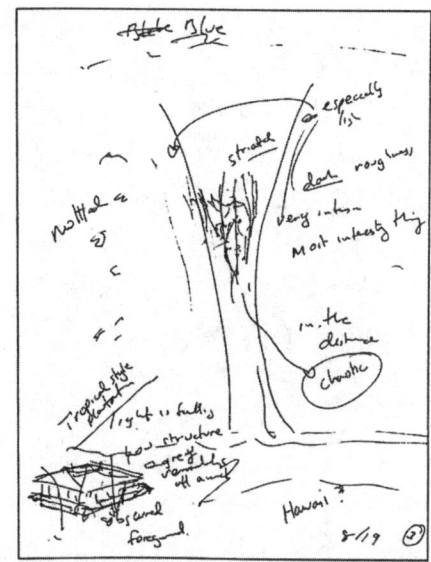

Figure 4. The remote viewing sketch on the right was accompanied by the words "There are rocks . . . definitely a waterfall . . . rapids or a crevasse . . . there is more than just a V-shape . . . separate, striated, serrated components . . . striped and dark . . . not smooth and silvery . . . tall cliffs like Hawaii . . . chaotic, not orderly . . . a redwood tree." The target image, which was randomly selected ninety minutes later, is on the left.

As with ARV, this MRV process can be applied in many ways. For example, instead of forcing an RNG to generate a certain range of possible outcomes, through the same divination-enchanting process you can in principle *force* a selected stock index to go up. In fact, you could in principle force anything to happen, depending on the quality of the remote viewing. If there's ambiguity about the quality of the remote viewing, and the judges find it difficult to clearly rank an image as number 1, then the strength of the causal loop will be weakened and would not be forced to close in only one way.

Here's an example of the kind of high strangeness that can be evoked with high RV accuracy. A colleague (let's call him James) described an instance where the outcome of an MRV procedure would be linked to highly implausible behavior by a person randomly selected out of his personal contact list. The selected person (let's call him Archie) turned out to be an insurance agent whom James rarely spoke to, but by design of the MRV test, Archie would be forced to call James on the phone, late that evening. There was no reason this would ever happen spontaneously, because Archie had *never* called James before, and he certainly wouldn't have done so late at night. Nevertheless, this was the goal of the MRV test to vastly reduce the likelihood of a chance outcome.

The divination portion of the procedure produced a clear answer, so James waited with some friends to see if Archie would call at the prearranged time. To James's and everyone else's astonishment, his phone rang right on schedule. Archie was indeed on the line, but he was very upset because he felt a peculiar *compulsion* that he just *had* to call James at night, *for no reason*. And James could not explain to Archie that he was an unwitting player on the razor's edge of black magic. Viewed from a magical perspective, this was an exercise in remote glamouring. I might add here that James, whom I've known for many years, is a clear-eyed physicist who is not prone to making up or embellishing such events.

LET'S INFLUENCE PEOPLE BACKWARD IN TIME!

As if MRV were not strange enough, this next series of experiments also involved intentionally creating causal loops going backward in time. These studies point toward my best guess about how magic works.

The studies were conducted by Elmar Gruber, an Austrian psychologist who incidentally created one of the most unique private collections of mediumistic art. These are drawings and paintings created by mediums who were "able to temporarily switch off conscious control and leave their bodies disposed to influences that are experienced as coming from outside the boundaries of the person and usually appear personified as spirits."[79]

These experiments were based on a theory of psi phenomena proposed by the psi researcher and psychologist Rex Stanford. His theory proposed that when we need something, we unconsciously scan our environment via psi for a means to fulfill that need.[80] And if some malleable event in the future or the past needs to be nudged to help us achieve that need, then we'll use psychokinesis to move it along.

As an example, let's say it's a hot day, and we are walking along a pleasant street with lots of fine stores. After a while, we find ourselves hot and famished, and we desire a refreshing drink. We can fill that need by looking around the street, spotting a suitable vendor, and then placing ourselves in the desired location by moving our body accordingly. If we forgot to bring money, via psi we can arrange to "find" just enough money lying on the ground a few steps away from where we'd like to buy our desired drink. Someone had "accidentally" and unknowingly dropped the money, and no one else had spotted it. The initial series of events in this scenario is straightforward and part of our everyday experience. The last part is where psi enters. It creates meaningful coincidences—synchronicities—that serve to satisfy our need. What makes this magical is that the creation is not limited in space *or time*.

To test this idea in the laboratory, we would need (1) an organism with a need, not necessarily a human; (2) a source of unpredictable events that can be influenced; and (3) a way to link those events to the desired need. Gruber conducted a number of such experiments involving both gerbils and human participants.[81] The hypothesis was that meaningful coincidences would "magically" appear in the behavior of the gerbils and humans according to the specific intentions of an observer distant in *time*. From a magical perspective, this could be viewed as a form of glamouring, even if it's about glamouring a gerbil. To be clear, glamouring a gerbil, or for that matter any type of small rodent, is not my thing. But don't let my preferences get in the way.

In perhaps the most astonishing of his studies, which Gruber called "biological REG [random event generator]" experiments, participants in the lab were asked to try to remotely influence when people entered a Vienna supermarket *in the past,* and when cars passed through a short tunnel in the center of Vienna during the rush hour, also *in the past.*

For the supermarket experiment, a colleague installed a photoelectric detector at the entrance of a Vienna supermarket; the colleague did not know what it was going to be used for. Every time a person entered the supermarket, the detector would produce a click sound in an intercom, and when the person passed the light beam, it would produce a second click. No one entering or inside the supermarket knew about the purpose of the light beam, and no one could hear the associated clicks, which were recorded on audiotape, because the intercom that sounded the clicks was in an acoustically shielded box.

For the tunnel experiment, the tunnel was small enough that only one car could pass through at a time, and people were not allowed to enter the tunnel. As with the supermarket test, every time a car passed through the tunnel, a detector produced a click that was recorded. The intercom for the photoelectric device was installed in a room in a house located above the tunnel. The person who installed this device did not know the purpose of the experiment; nor was he allowed to be present when the clicks were recorded.

The mind-boggling factor was this: These recordings were made during several weeks in the winter of 1978–79, but they were played back to participants in the laboratory *one to two and a half months later.*

In the lab, the experimenter was in one room with the recording equipment, and the participants were in another room. A third room lay between them to provide acoustic shielding and to prevent the experimenter from accidentally hearing the replayed clicks. To further block the experimenter from possibly hearing the clicks, he listened to a continuous static sound over headphones. None of the participants were aware that the clicks, which they also heard over headphones, were prerecorded. They were led to believe that they had to try to influence the click sounds in real time.

The participants were asked to focus their intention on the click sounds to speed up the click rate, and to imagine during those periods that many people would be entering the supermarket or that many cars would be passing through the tunnel. To help them visualize this task, a humorous movie clip, played faster than normal speed, showed people entering a supermarket or cars coming out of a tunnel. There were ten periods of forty seconds each, during which clicks were played through the headphones, and ten forty-second intervals with no feedback as controls. During those controls, the participants were asked to withdraw their intention from the task and simply relax. After each of the twenty epochs was a twenty-second rest period, followed by a one-second buzzer sound to let the participants know that they should prepare to concentrate again on enhancing the click rate. If no buzzer sounded, then the next epoch would be a control period.

To determine the condition of each epoch, Gruber shuffled a pack of twenty black and white cards twenty times, then placed the pack upside down in front of him. Each successive epoch was determined by picking up the top card, with a white card indicating an experimental period and a black card a control period.

The first three experiments involved a total of twenty-one participants listening to the supermarket clicks. The results showed that more clicks occurred during the experimental epochs than during the control epochs, with modest but significant odds against chance of 20 to 1. The next three experiments, using a similar design, again included twenty-one participants, where this time they were listening to cars going through the tunnel. In this case the overall results had stronger odds against chance of 200 to 1. The combined results of these six experiments were odds of 700 to 1.

What these studies suggest is that the real-time behavior of people entering a supermarket or driving a car through a tunnel, all of whom were completely unaware that their behavior would be used in an experiment a few months later, *was influenced by people in the future.*

Could the clicks have been altered in present time by the test participants, rather than affecting the human behavior that those clicks represented? To explore this possibility, later studies using similar designs made multiple copies of the prerecorded data to see if the data observed in the future changed as compared to the data in the still-unobserved stored copies. The prerecorded data and all the copies of those data were always exactly the same. So the past wasn't changed. Instead, as the events unfolded in their present time, they were apparently influenced from the future.

Neither the participants nor the experimenter in these studies knew how many clicks would be expected by chance, so the analysis simply compared click rates between the influence versus relax epochs. Other than the participants, two other people heard the clicks to ensure that data were being recorded in real time and were correlated with the behavior of the people and cars, but neither of them was aware of the meaning of the clicks because they had no information about the experiment.

OUTRAGEOUS IMPLICATIONS

If Gruber's experiments were the only controlled studies indicating the existence of retrocausal effects, they might be dismissed as outlandish flukes. And they certainly wouldn't be persuasive enough to challenge our everyday intuitions about the nature of causation as a strictly cause-and-effect sequence. But this isn't the end of the story. In a review on the implications of retrocausality, William Braud, a psychologist and pioneer in the study of the effects of focused intention on people isolated by distance or shielding, pointed out that this phenomenon had been successfully experimentally replicated *many times*.[82] The idea that psychokinetic effects might be genuinely nonlocal, meaning they could transcend the everyday constraints of space and time, was proposed by physicist Helmut Schmidt, the pioneer who developed the use of random number generators in psi research.

In 1971 Schmidt considered that because nonlocality had been experimentally confirmed in physics as a perfectly acceptable—if poorly understood—feature of the physical world, then psychokinetic effects might operate just as well backward in time as in present real time. To test this idea, he developed retroPK-RNG experiments that recorded random data that remained unobserved until a future time, when participants were asked to direct their intentions toward those data according to assignments selected in the future (that is, from the point of view of when the data were first recorded). This was the design adopted by Gruber, but in his case the intentions were applied to human behavior rather than to random bits generated by an RNG.

Schmidt published his retroPK-RNG findings in a series of studies in 1976.[83] He reported that time-displaced PK on prerecorded but previously unobserved target events was indeed possible, and that the magnitude of such influences was basically the same as real-time PK-RNG studies. Others were able to successfully replicate this effect.

Schmidt realized that a retroPK study offered the intriguing possibility of conducting a super-secure experiment. Say that RNG data was recorded but not yet observed by anyone. This data could be copied onto several cassette tapes (remember, this was the 1970s) and some of these copies would be held by numerous collaborators, including hard-nosed skeptics. All the collaborators would be told to not listen to or otherwise examine the data in any way until after the experiment was finished. As in all these studies, the intentional conditions would be assigned in the future, *after* the random data were generated.

Schmidt conducted five formal, independently supervised experiments of this kind.[84] I was one of the participants. The overall results produced odds against chance of 10,000 to 1, which provided strong evidence that PK can indeed act backward in time on RNG data, even under exceptionally high security conditions and where skeptical observers were involved.

In 2000 Braud published all known retrocausal studies up to that time, where the target of influence was a living system, ranging from cell cultures to human physiology and behavior. This amounted to nineteen studies conducted by Braud and his colleagues, those run by Gruber, studies by Dutch scientists Frank W. Snel and Peter van der Sijde, and an experiment that I conducted with colleagues in Brazil. The combined results indicated a retrocausal intention effect associated with odds against chance of 3 million to 1. That's pretty good for something that from any conventional perspective would be considered doubly scandalous: mind influencing matter *through time.*

The University of Amsterdam physicist Dick Bierman found twenty-six retroPK-RNG studies published from 1975 to 1993.[85] When combined, the overall results were associated with odds against chance of 18 million to 1. More recently, psychologist Bryan Williams updated that review in 2022 and found a total of forty-two experiments reported from 1975 to 2021.[86] The odds against chance increased to 214 billion to 1.

Not all these experiments had an independently significant outcome, but there was enough consistency in the results to show a remarkably positive effect. William Braud had pointed out that "the emergence of these mental influence effects may depend on the simultaneous presence of a complex and interactive set of physical, physiological, psychological, and even social and cultural factors. If all requisite ingredients of such a complex recipe are not present, or present in insufficient degrees, the effect may not occur."

Magicians have made the same observation. To make "big magic" happen, the beliefs and motivations of the investigators and the participants, plus social factors, the stars overhead, and the phase of the moon, may all need to be optimized. The moon is an especially notable factor in the magical traditions, and interestingly many animal species, including human females, are known to synchronize their reproductive behavior with the phases of the moon.[87] There is even some experimental evidence that precognition performance correlates with reproductive hormonal status in women.[88]

Still, even without optimizing all these factors, the retroPK-RNG experiments demonstrate that retrocausal effects do exist.

Does this mean it is possible to *change the past*? Probably not. Once an event has been observed, it is not likely to "unhappen." What seems more likely is that future intentions can influence events *as they are unfolding* in their present timeframe. According to Braud, "To clarify this interpretation even further, the time-displaced direct mental intervention could be said to 'change' what *would have happened*, but does not change *what did happen*."

In magical practice, the reality of retrocausal influences adds to the enchantment toolkit because a desired goal might be attained by influencing how events unfold in the future *or in the past*. Being able to influence the past instantly doubles the means by which the desired outcome can unfold. It also relieves the magician from having to worry about temporal mechanics. Magic is not constrained by time.

Retrocausality also has big implications for health and healing. The course of a disease or disorder is complex and does not need to follow only one course of action. As we've discussed, spontaneous remissions do happen. If tightly focused and highly motivated healing intentions are directed toward a disease *from the future*, that might influence the present-time course of the disease. If those influences are effective, the results may look like a spontaneous remission. For more information about Braud's experiments and their wild implications, I recommend his 2003 book, *Distant Mental Influence.*[89]

GLAMOURING

I did not say that it was possible; I simply said that it happened.

—SIR WILLIAM CROOKES

Glamouring is a specialized form of enchantment, one that works mind to mind. In psi research this phenomenon is called telepathy, and it has been tested in four primary ways. The first, involving ESP cards, was used mainly during J. B. Rhine's era at Duke University in the first half of the twentieth century. Experiments conducted by Rhine and others from the 1930s through 1970s used many variations of this approach, and the results were clear: Information about the card's identity arrived in the receiver's mind at statistical levels far beyond chance when all other forms of sensory cues were blocked.

We've known for many decades that it is possible to demonstrate the existence of telepathy under laboratory conditions. As reported in an article in *The New York Times* on December 5, 1937:

Prof. Rhine's report on Extrasensory Perception starts wave of experiments. Statisticians approved. They find no fault with conclusions based on card-drawing tests. . . . If the statisticians assure us that Rhine's results are not merely chance coincidences, what have the psychologists to say? As yet *nothing but a questioning of statistical methods.*

Oh, those wacky psychologists. Rhine's co-authored book, *Extrasensory Perception after Sixty Years*, which refers to the period from

1880 to 1940, goes into this line of research in great detail. It also includes a list of all known ESP card replications up to 1940, which among other things makes this book and its analysis of those studies *the first known* meta-analysis. Incidentally, "the first known use" is a repeated refrain in parapsychology. Psi research is so challenging that over the years investigators have been forced to develop new ways of studying and analyzing these phenomena, and those methods were so useful that they were eventually adopted by the scientific mainstream, and then the origins of the techniques were quickly forgotten.

Besides meta-analysis, which is now used in virtually all the life sciences, it includes techniques like the use of double-blind designs to prevent participants or investigators from using their preconceived beliefs to bias the results of an experiment, use of statistics to evaluate results in psychological experiments, the publication of studies regardless of whether they are positive, negative, or null, to prevent selective reporting biases, and even the development of the electroencephalograph (EEG) for studying brain activity.[90]

The second, more modern method for testing telepathy is a ganzfeld experiment, using the German term for "whole field." In this study, a pool of four (usually) different images or video clips is created. One is selected at random and given to a sender secured at a distant location. A receiver relaxes in a comfy reclining chair, and a research assistant tapes halved Ping-Pong balls over their eyes and places headphones playing white noise over their ears. In this unpatterned sensory environment, one feels immersed in a world consisting entirely of pinkish light and staticky noise. After a few minutes, one becomes highly sensitive to mental impressions, like a waking dream.

After the receiver has become used to the ganzfeld state, the sender is asked to mentally send them the randomly selected image or video, and the receiver is asked to speak aloud their impressions. In some experimental setups, anything the receiver says is carried via a one-way audio channel to the sender. This is provided to help the sender adjust their attention, motivation, and mental sending strategy, which refers to what the sender focuses on—colors in the image, or objects, emotions, meaning, etc. After a twenty-minute sending period, a research assistant takes the receiver out of the ganzfeld condition and presents them with four images or video clips. The receiver's job is to select the best match between their mental impressions and one of the targets. By chance, they'd get one out of four guesses correct, for a 25 percent "hit rate." Thousands of test sessions like this have been published since the 1970s. We'll review the results of those studies in the next section.

The third method for testing telepathy is the "telephone telepathy" paradigm. This line of research was started by the British biologist Rupert Sheldrake, who designed the study based on anecdotal reports that when the phone rang (before smartphone ringtones became a thing), some people were remarkably accurate at knowing who was calling, even when the incoming call and the caller's identity were unexpected. Well-controlled experiments, including some that were videotaped to strictly prevent cheating, demonstrated that some people are highly adept at this task, and in general even people with no special abilities can perform beyond chance levels.[91]

The fourth method for testing telepathy involves examining correlations between brain activity in isolated pairs of people. Both EEG and neuroimaging methods like functional magnetic resonance imaging (fMRI) have been used, and overall the results suggest that what has been observed in the three other experimental methods can also be observed in correlated brain activity. We will examine this line of research after looking at the results of forty years of ganzfeld experiments.

Ganzfeld Meta-Analysis

The psychologists Patrizio Tressoldi and Lance Storm published the results of a broad range of frequently repeated psi experiments, including the ganzfeld.[92] Their compilation of studies reported over a half-century, from the 1970s to the 2020s, allowed me to reanalyze these studies and reach a few conclusions.

First, they found 109 publications by forty-two different authors. For the experiments using four possible targets in each trial, the chance expected hit rate was 25 percent. Across those 109 studies, there were a total of 4,754 sessions and 1,495 hits, for a hit rate of 31.4 percent. The statistical likelihood of that hit rate compared to chance is associated with odds against chance of 2.9 sextillion, or approximately a 3 followed by twenty-six zeros. In other words, the combined database of replicated ganzfeld studies is immensely significant.

If we examine a subset of these studies where the participants were not selected for special interest or talent, typically college sophomores participating for credit in their psychology courses, there were sixty-six publications by thirty-four unique authors, and 2,878 sessions with 843 hits. That's a hit rate of 29.3 percent, and odds against chance were 19 million to 1. When we look only at participants who were selected because they were in the creative arts (a known correlate of psi ability) or had previous telepathic experiences, there were forty-three publications by twenty-two authors, and 1,876 sessions with 652 hits. With a hit rate of 34.7 percent, odds against chance were 11 sextillion to 1.

We can also compare peer-reviewed versus non-peer-reviewed studies, whereupon we find odds of a 138 quadrillion to 1 for the former and 273 million for the latter. We can then separate these ganzfeld studies into telepathy, clairvoyance, and precognitive designs. Note that the clairvoyance and precognitive designs required only a receiver, who in real time attempted to perceive one of the four images sitting by itself in a distant room or in a sealed envelope, making it a clairvoyant design, or conducted the same task with the target selected in the future, thus making it a precognitive design.

For the telepathy design, over 3,111 sessions, the hit rate was 32.7 percent, and odds against chance were 77 septillion to 1. For the clairvoyance design, the hit rate over 1,431 sessions was 28.4 percent, and the odds were 757 to 1. For the precognitive design, over 212 trials, the hit rate was 33.0 percent, and the odds were 285 to 1. These odds figures are wildly different but recall that odds are closely linked to the amount of statistical power, which in turn relies on the number of trials. So if you'd like to compare results across studies that have different numbers of trials, you have to use a common effect size, which in this case is most conveniently the hit rate.

From that perspective, we see that the telepathy, clairvoyance, and precognition studies resulted in hit rates of 32.7 percent, 28.4 percent, and 33.0 percent, respectively. These are not so different from one another, especially telepathy and precognition, suggesting that the underlying phenomena may not be different. Such similarities have been observed many times in psi research. The phenomena just seem different depending on the nature of the reported experience.

Figure 5 plots the cumulative average hit rate (and for science geeks, one standard error bar) for all reported ganzfeld studies based on a four-target design, published from 1975 through 2022. At a glance, we can see that this graph provides very high confidence that we are dealing with a real effect. What do skeptics say about this? Either nothing at all, because they believe this result is impossible, or they claim that the effect is due to one or more flaws. So are these studies credible or not?

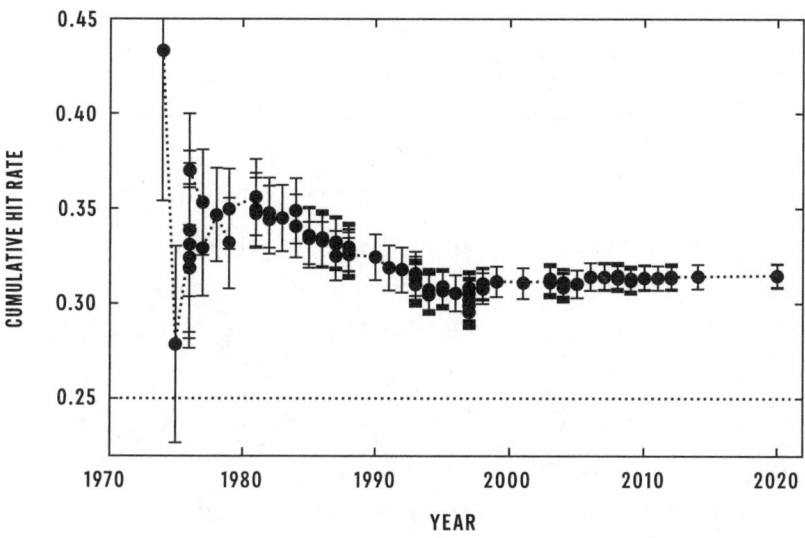

Figure 5. Cumulative hit rate for four-choice
ganzfeld telepathy experiments

ARE THESE STUDIES CREDIBLE?

Robert Rosenthal was a psychology professor at Harvard for many years
and an expert on research methodologies. He was selected as one of
the hundred most eminent psychologists of the twentieth century.[93]
Rosenthal was also an important figure in the debate over the quality
of ganzfeld experiments because he was asked by the US National
Research Council in 1984 to review five areas of research on potential
human capabilities as part of the US Army's interest at that time in a
project called Enhancing Human Performance. One of the research
topics he and his co-author Monica J. Harris studied was the ganzfeld
telepathy experiments. After reviewing all such experiments published
through the 1980s, they concluded that the ganzfeld experiment had
repeatedly demonstrated the existence of telepathy under rigorous
conditions. In a recent essay honoring Rosenthal, Etzel Cardeña, a
professor of psychology at Lund University, wrote the following:

Despite finding that ganzfeld . . . psi research followed the most rigorous protocols of those areas, he and his co-author . . . were "pressured to withdraw our . . . positive evaluation of psi so that . . . reports on other areas would be published." They refused, and he wrote a letter [published] in [the journal] *Psychological Science* mentioning the pressure and his conclusion that "we found the typical methodological quality of the Ganzfeld experiments to be superior to the typical quality of the four other [conventional] areas [of interest to the Army]." The resulting book [*Enhancing Human Performance*] by the National Research Council shamefully does not even include [Rosenthal's and Harris's] names as part of the committee.[94]

I wrote about this sad affair in a previous book,[95] but the backstory is worth repeating because it illustrates why there is continuing doubt about the existence of psi within the academic mainstream. The National Research Council (NRC), an arm of the US National Academies of Science, Engineering, and Medicine, is often asked to investigate leading edge and controversial topics. To do this in a fair way, it maintains a policy of assembling "balanced scientific committees," whose members are required to affirm that they have no conflicts of interest either for or against the topics under study.

On December 3, 1987, the NRC convened a press conference in Washington, D.C., where the chairman of the review committee, John A. Swets, said, "Perhaps our strongest conclusions are in the area of parapsychology." The bottom line was: "The Committee finds no scientific justification from research conducted over a period of 130 years for the existence of parapsychological phenomena." *The New York Times* reported on this portion of the press conference as follows:

Dr. Ray Hyman, a panelist from the University of Oregon in Eugene, said the committee found no evidence of the existence or usefulness of elements of parapsychology, including ESP, telepathy or thought projection, and mind-over-matter psychokinesis. . . . "Even when you look at the best work in parapsychology, it is flawed, even by its own standards," Dr. Hyman said. "We found that many of the studies cited in this field have inadequate controls, lack documentation or make the wrong use of statistics in reaching their conclusions." The panel said there was no scientific justification for the claims of parapsychology and concluded that the Army need not research these phenomena further.

At the time, I was president of the Parapsychological Association, and my colleagues and I knew that that conclusion was utter nonsense. We confirmed our suspicions that the two principal evaluators of psi research for the NRC were Ray Hyman and James Alcock, both skeptical academic psychologists who throughout their careers had accused parapsychology of not being a legitimate science. By contrast, there wasn't a single active psi researcher on the committee, which violated the NRC's policy of assigning members to committees "with regard to appropriate balance."

In addition, while the NRC's report did not mention the conclusions of Robert Rosenthal and Monica Harris, it did quote liberally from two skeptical background papers that supported the committee's false conclusions. To make matters worse, we discovered that the chairman of the NRC committee phoned Rosenthal and asked him point-blank to withdraw his conclusions from the NRC report. Fortunately, Rosenthal refused.

Besides the nasty politics, the NRC report contradicted itself. The committee announced at the press conference that there was no evidence for psi phenomena. And yet the written report admitted that the committee members, including the skeptics, could offer no plausible alternatives to psi for the research it surveyed. Nor did it mention that the army should continue to monitor psi research in the

United States and Russia. It even recommended that the army propose specific experiments to be funded.

When we brought this to the attention of journalists, a reporter for *The Chronicle of Higher Education* asked the NRC committee chairman why he asked Rosenthal to withdraw his favorable conclusions. He replied: "We thought the quality of our analysis was better, and we didn't see much point in putting out mixed signals." He went on to explain, "I didn't feel we were obliged to represent every point of view," which was a strange comment for someone who was required to assemble a committee without conflicts of interest. So what was going on?

The army asked for a public review of psi phenomena, which was spun in a way to sound uniformly negative. That message was then dutifully echoed in all the major news outlets. But while the army was publicly deflecting attention away from psi research, they were secretly funding remote viewing studies as part of a series of highly classified programs now known as Star Gate, one of the code words used in that program.

Why would the army publicly dismiss the very thing it was secretly funding? The answer is in the question itself. That is, the value of a secret project using "exotic" methods, in this case using psi for ESPionage, is inversely proportional to what people think about that topic. If the army had announced in its NRC review that psi was in fact real, then our adversaries would of course have taken closer notice of psi as a threat, and meanwhile the public, many of whom were already wary of the government spying on them, might also become alarmed. Until very recently, we've seen the same playbook used about UFOs and UAPs. In public, the official pronouncement is "There's nothing to see here, just move along." In private, it's often an entirely different story.

QUESTIONABLE RESEARCH PRACTICES REDUX

Remember our discussion about questionable research practices (QRPs), earlier in this chapter? Scientific concerns about QRPs have always been leveled at psi experiments, but then it began to be a concern in psychological experiments, and now the anxiety seems to be spreading. As reported in the journal *Nature* in 2016, "More than 70 percent of researchers have tried and failed to reproduce another scientist's experiments, and more than half have failed to reproduce their own experiments."[96] That finding increased public angst that science may be permeated with fake news and hoaxes. Everything is going to hell because nothing can be repeated, *even in physics.*[97]

Whoa. Take a deep breath and settle down. What is broken is the *myth* that exciting new findings in science should be easy to replicate. *That is hardly ever the case.* Most new experimental findings involve aspects that the investigators are not even aware of, so they're not hiding anything; rather, they just don't know why the experiment worked. In fact, every experiment includes tacit knowledge, that is, activities that the experimenters perform unconsciously, or factors in the environment that are deemed unimportant but nevertheless turn out to be critically important.[98]

For example, the sociologist Harry Collins explored difficulties that physicists had in replicating a laser called the Transversely Excited Atmospheric pressure CO_2 laser, known as the TEA laser.[99] The first lesson Collins learned was that *no one* had succeeded in building this laser by using only the information reported in publications. Second, he found that *no one* had succeeded in building this type of laser where the informant had not already personally built a working TEA laser. Everyone else who had successfully built that laser had attained crucially important tacit knowledge from direct personal contact with somebody else who had actually built one. But even then, not everyone who tried to build a TEA laser was guaranteed to succeed!

Returning to the ganzfeld experiments, what happens if those studies are reevaluated by throwing the kitchen sink of QRPs at them? Do they remain significant? We've already discussed physicist Peter Bancel's approach toward simulating the effects of QRPs in PK-RNG studies. He applied the same technique to ganzfeld experiments. His conclusion, based on an "extreme scenario," was as follows: "It is shown that a broad set of QRPs fails to account for the ganzfeld data, even if these are used in maximal combination and are adopted by researchers at frequencies approaching 100 percent."

In other words, the evidence in favor of telepathy provided by the ganzfeld meta-analysis cannot be explained away by QRPs. This means that the cavalier accusations one sometimes hears, that these experiments can be ignored because of one or more methodological flaws, are flat-out wrong.

Brain-to-Brain Correlations

ESP cards, telephone telepathy, and the ganzfeld technique have been successfully observed in controlled laboratory experiments. The fourth type of telepathy experiment uses the tools of neuroscience to explore the existence of brain-to-brain correlations.

These studies are the essence of simplicity. You recruit a pair of people who report episodes of spontaneous telepathy; let's call them Alice and Bob, a couple who know and like each other, or perhaps identical twins, Dallas and Damien. You wire them up to measure their brain waves, then you securely isolate them from one another by distance, shielding, or both. At a random time, you present a stimulus to Alice or Dallas, like a light flash or a buzzer tone. That stimulus will cause their brains to jump. (The jargon is an *event-related potential* or ERP.) The question is whether Bob's or Damien's brain will experience an ERP at the same time, even if they have no idea when Alice or Dallas were stimulated. If you perform this stimulus-response task many times, and the ERPs align, you will be able to tell that the brains are in sync even when no ordinary signals can pass between them. This is a way to demonstrate an unconscious form of telepathy.

About two dozen of these EEG brain-to-brain correlation experiments have been performed, starting in the 1960s.[100] One of the most prominent yet perplexing studies was published in 1965 in the top-tier journal *Science* by Thomas D. Duane and Thomas Behrendt of the department of ophthalmology at Thomas Jefferson University, in Philadelphia. (I don't know if one's first name had to be Thomas at Thomas Jefferson University, or if it was just assigned to you when you joined the faculty, but it might be worth looking into.)

In any case, neither Thomas was known by anyone in the psi research community. When you look up this study on PubMed, the National Library of Science website, you'll find a one-line abstract: "Alpha rhythms have been elicited in one of a pair of identical twins as a result of evoking these rhythms in a conventional manner solely in the other."[101]

Here's what they did: With the "receiver" and "sender" twins secured in different rooms, the receiver twin's EEG was recorded continuously with their eyes open while the sender twin was periodically asked to open or close his or her eyes. They used this approach because in most people, closing the eyes reliably increases the brain's EEG alpha power, a brain wave frequency at around ten cycles per second. During these closed-eyes periods, when the sender's alpha power increased, Duane and Behrendt examined the receiver twin's EEG to see if their brain also produced more alpha power.

They reported positive evidence in two of the fifteen pairs of twins. They measured this correlation by looking at the raw EEG signals recorded on paper strip charts generated by the EEG equipment. They also conducted the same test with unrelated participants and observed no evidence of a correlation in those pairs.

This study was strange for two reasons. First, getting a telepathy article with positive results published in one of the highest-impact scientific journals in the world was a major anomaly. Nothing like that had ever happened before. And second, the results relied on visual inspection of EEG graphs, not on objective measurements. Because of this second factor, the study was severely criticized by both psi researchers and by scientists from outside the field. What were the editors thinking? It was a mystery.

Four years later a report was quietly filed with the Defense Technical Information Center (DTIC) at Fort Belvoir, Virginia, entitled "Coincidence of EEG Alpha Patterns in Humans," by—you guessed it—Duane and Behrendt. The filing date was long before paperless reports became common, so that report existed only in the form of a paper document buried somewhere in the bowels of the DTIC.

I discovered this document because Tolga Özkurt, a neuroscientist at the Middle East Technical University in Ankara, Turkey, had asked me if I knew about a *second report* by Duane and Behrendt. I had never heard of such a report. But after some searching in dusty corners of the Internet, sure enough I found the report in the DTIC, so I called and asked if I could get a copy. I was told that *no one had ever asked to see this report before.* It was available only in paper form, so it would have to be scanned and digitized. Two months later I received a copy of the report.

In it, Duane and Behrendt described a follow-up experiment that addressed all the criticisms they received about the experiment that they published in *Science.* This time they relied on objective measures, more stringent controls, better isolation between the participants, and so on. They also tested a third "control" person, unrelated to the twins.

The results showed that out of fifteen test sessions, each with identical twins and a control person, eleven sessions produced highly significant results between twins *and* with the control person. This report noted that the study was funded by the Office of Naval Research. Oddly, despite the strikingly positive results, it was never published and languished silently in a file drawer in the DTIC, virtually unknown, for half a century.

AN UNEXPECTED DENOUEMENT

In October 2024, Tolga Özkurt published an article in *Frontiers in Human Neuroscience* that reanalyzed the Duane and Behrendt article published in *Science*.[102] He used an algorithm that converts an image of a printed graph into numerical data to extract the data from the old *Science* article, then used modern EEG analytical tools to see if their conclusions were sound. He found no evidence that the identical twins showed similar brain waves, as originally reported, but he *did* find significant evidence of synchronous brain activity between a twin and an unrelated third person used as a control, just as Duane and Behrendt had found in their unpublished 1969 study. This suggests that there may not be anything super-special about identical twins, and that telepathic connections can occur even between unrelated strangers. We've already seen ample evidence that this is the case from the ganzfeld telepathy experiments. This is another indication that at deep levels of reality, everything, *and everyone*, is interconnected.

OTHER STUDIES

Many other experiments have been conducted between identical twins and strangers.[103] For telepathy studies in particular, both EEG and fMRI designs have been used, and the preponderance of those studies continue to demonstrate that significant connections can arise in brain activity between distant or shielded people.[104]

Such a study was published in 2024 by Richard Silberstein from the Swinburne University of Technology, Australia, and his colleague Felicity Bigelow.[105] They conducted an EEG correlation study in identical twins using a technique that measures brain activity happening simultaneously across different regions of the brain. They found very significant effects in the receiver's brain while the sender was viewing images that were personally meaningful versus neutral images. Odds against chance were 2.5 million to 1.

When we put our magic hat back on, these laboratory studies tell us that mind-to-mind experiences are quite real, which in turn means that glamouring is also quite real. Dozens of conceptually similar experiments show that these connections can also be found between your mind and another person's *body* at a distance. Both conscious-report and unconscious physiological studies have repeatedly demonstrated these connections.[106]

Note that *connection* does not mean control. In lab and life, what it usually means is that you can subtly sense that another person is thinking about you or has an emotional or urgent need for your attention, like a family emergency. These impressions tend to be subtle because practically everything in modern life seems designed to distract our attention. With meditation practice, one can become more sensitive to these feelings. However, becoming hypersensitive without learning how to "turn it off" is not a good idea because you could open yourself to a cacophony of others' thoughts and emotions. One minute, you're minding your business while grocery shopping and the next, you're overwhelmed by a stranger a few aisles away who's having an existential meltdown because they can't find their favorite brand of peanut butter.

COLLECTIVE CONSCIOUSNESS

Magical lore suggests that group rituals may be more powerful than those performed by an individual. What does science say about that?

The Transcendental Meditation organization proposed that groups of meditators practicing their meditative technique can reduce violence and crime in their vicinity. Since 1976 TM has published numerous experiments that apparently demonstrated this outcome in many social indices.[107] The Global Consciousness Project (GCP) is a conceptually similar experiment that since 1998 has been exploring the idea that mind and matter interact in fundamental physical ways, but on a global scale.[108] It is based on decades of studies conducted in the laboratory indicating (as discussed earlier) that when an individual focuses on an RNG with the intention to influence its output, then the RNG's output no longer operates according to chance. The question posed by the GCP was whether *attention alone* could also cause something like coherence, or order, to arise in the physical world, as reflected by the behavior of RNG data.

Numerous "field consciousness" experiments tested this idea starting in the 1990s in small groups engaged in coherent activities, like group meditations and choral performances.[109] Many others have reported successful replications. These studies suggest that something about coherent attention in small to large groups does seem to "cause" RNG outputs to exhibit significant degrees of order in outputs that should have been completely random, assuming there was no mind-matter effect.[110]

To create an automatic version of these one-off field consciousness studies, Roger Nelson at Princeton University spearheaded the creation of a worldwide network of RNGs designed to continuously generate random samples of data every second. The number of RNGs simultaneously active in the network on a given day ranged from three, when the project was launched in 1998, to a peak of about seventy in 2015. Each RNG was hosted by a volunteer in a different city around the world on their own computer. All the RNGs used in the network were required to pass standard randomness and calibration tests to make sure that the data conformed to statistical expectations about truly random events.

Each RNG continuously recorded data every second on its local computer, and then every five minutes it transmitted the data to a web server in Princeton, New Jersey. That resulting database was publicly accessible from the beginning of the experiment, and as of July 2024 it consisted of over 111 gigabytes, representing over 6 trillion individual random bits.

In a formal experiment using this network, when an event of mass interest occurred (or an upcoming mass event was planned in advance), the investigators first defined how long the event was estimated to last, and then after the prediction was formally registered, the random samples corresponding to that time period were evaluated using a pre-planned analysis. After five hundred such events were registered from 1998 to 2015, the formal portion of the experiment was finished, and the accumulated deviation from chance was found to be associated with odds against chance of 3 trillion to 1.[111] This means that the RNG outputs definitely deviated from chance during these five hundred events. The same analysis applied to non-event days did not show these deviations.

Could these results have occurred because (a) millions of people turned on their televisions or computers to watch important events unfold on live media, which (b) caused a surge in demand for electrical power, which (c) caused an increase in ambient electromagnetic fields or power line artifacts, which (d) influenced the RNG electronics? In a word, no. These RNGs were specifically designed to exclude those kinds of influences. Do the results mean that mass coherent attention somehow *forces* the RNGs to work in concert? That is one interpretation, but there is still no firm consensus on exactly *why* RNGs respond to attention and intention. To gain a better understanding of this phenomenon may require entertaining other models of reality (like dual-aspect monism, discussed later).

GCP on New Year's Eve

For fun, I decided to use the entire GCP database to study a predictable event involving the momentary focused attention of billions of people at a specific time and date: New Year's Eve. With twenty-seven years of data and twenty-four-plus time zones, this event offered a straightforward way to see if the physical world is "warped" a little by all that coherent attention just before to just after midnight.

To do this, I retrieved the GCP data for every December 31 through January 1, from 1998 through early 2025, and then I combined all those data from a half-hour before to half-hour after midnight. Then I smoothed the resulting ensemble average by two minutes. The results are shown in Figure 6.

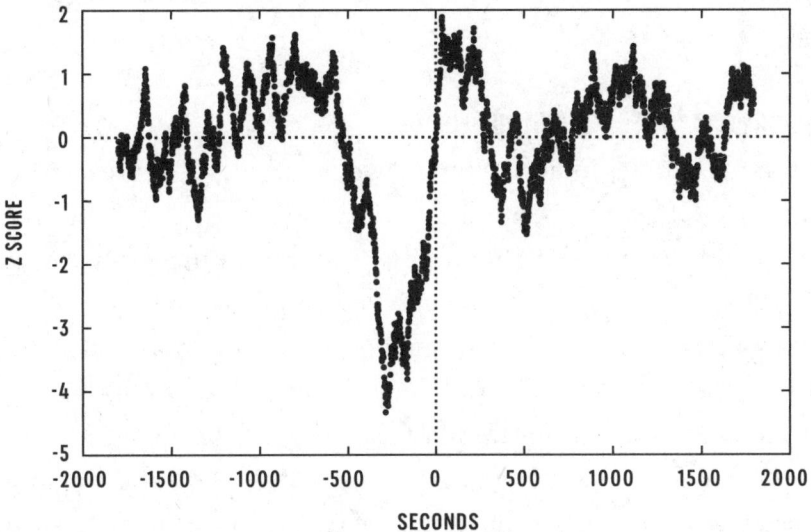

Figure 6. Global Consciousness Project data during
New Year's Eve celebrations

The results suggest that a few minutes before the turn of the year, the rising mass anticipation was associated with a strong negative deviation in the random output of many RNGs distributed around the world, and then a few seconds before midnight that deviation suddenly changed course and became positive. Was this "jolt" in randomness meaningful, or did a deviation of that magnitude occur every so often just by chance? To find out, I ran the same analysis on the transition to midnight for every other day of the year, for example on December 30 to 31, January 1 to 2, and so on. I calculated the joint probability of the magnitude of that drop just before midnight on New Year's Eve, as compared to all the other midnight transitions, combined with the distance in time to midnight, again as compared to all the other midnights. The answer was a probability of $p = 0.01$ for the former and $p = 0.01$ for the latter. The joint probability is thus 0.01×0.01 or odds of 10,000 to 1. That outcome suggests that we'd have to run this same twenty-seven-year experiment ten thousand times, or for 260,000 years, to see this or a better outcome purely by chance.[112]

Sentiment and Presentiment in Twitter

Presentiment studies indicate that individual minds can sense the future. The GCP experiment suggests the presence of a collective mind. Could the collective mind also "feel the future"? That is, if many people are about to experience an unpredictable emotional event, especially an event with strong negative emotion like an act of terrorism, then before that event unfolds do we collectively shift toward a darker mood? And would that shift be detectable in social media data as a decline in *sentiment*? Sentiment here refers to emotions expressed on average by groups of people, from happiness to sadness.

To find out, I retrieved Twitter (or if you prefer, X) sentiment data from Hedonometer.org, a website hosted by the University of Vermont's Complex Systems Center as part of a project in its Computational Story Lab. That project calculated sentiment on a daily basis over five thousand days by automatically retrieving Twitter posts, calculating a happiness score for each word in the posts, and then taking the average. That project didn't attempt to evaluate the content or meaning of each post; it just evaluated the emotions conveyed by the words.

For example, to evaluate English text, each word in a corpus of ten thousand words was rated to provide a "happiness score," ranging from 1 to 9, with 1 most negative and 9 most positive. Thus, the word *love* was assigned an average score of 8.42, and *terrorist* was assigned an average score of 1.3. The Hedonometer.org site provided similarly evaluated sentiment scores for tweets in Arabic, German, Spanish, French, Indonesian, Korean, Portuguese, Russian, and Ukrainian.

I was interested in whether the average sentiment score would begin to decline two weeks before an unexpected highly negative event. I'll skip over the technical details of how I prepared the data because it would bore most readers, but Figure 7 shows the mean and one standard error confidence intervals across ten languages for sentiment scores prior to unexpected and very negative events, shown in the graph as day 0. The downward slope from −14 to −2 days before that event was the measure of interest.

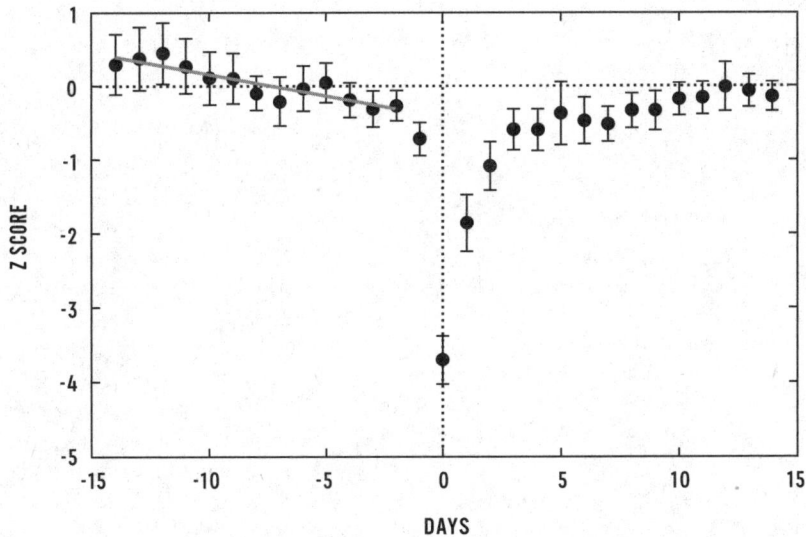

Figure 7. Average normalized sentiment scores leading up to an unexpected strongly negative day fourteen days later

When these slopes were examined across all ten languages, each turned out to be negative, and the combined result was associated with odds against chance of 1,000 to 1.[113] This suggests that trends in collective sentiment scores on social media (at least on Twitter/X) significantly anticipated unpredictable negative events. Given that such events are typically unpredictable acts of terrorism, mass shootings, and the like, it may be possible to perform a prospective analysis that could predict unpredictable events of interest to counterterrorism agencies, law enforcement, and mental health advocates.

CHAPTER 3

SCIENCE OF DIVINATION

Weather forecast for tonight: dark. Continued dark overnight, with widely scattered light by morning.

—GEORGE CARLIN

Divination refers to perception through space and time. In psi research, this ability was traditionally called *clairvoyance* (French for "clear seeing"). That term commonly refers to *real-time* perception through space, while terms like *precognition* and *retrocognition* refer to perception *through time*. Since the 1990s, the term *remote viewing* has also become popular; it refers to the same phenomenon as clairvoyance, but it is also associated with certain training practices. Remote viewing was developed and coined within the US government's classified psi research program to avoid using the sensitive p-words, like *psychic* and *paranormal*.[1] The technique was developed by the talented psychic and artist Ingo Swann. Since then, many variations on a theme have been developed by multiple generations of remote viewing students, and an International Remote Viewing Association was formed in 1999 to promote the study and practical use of this ability.[2]

THE DIVINATION ADVANTAGE

Magical lore says that to effectively perform divination, one needs to achieve the state of consciousness called *gnosis*. Does being in that nonordinary state really enhance divination accuracy?

The psychologists Tressoldi and Storm, whom we've already met, analyzed a closely related question.[3] In a 2021 article, they reviewed eleven meta-analyses involving nearly a thousand experiments conducted over a period of eighty years. These studies investigated perceptual psi performance in the normal waking state of awareness, various nonordinary states like dreaming and hypnosis, and the different ways that the participants responded, like reporting conscious impressions versus the use of unconscious physiological measures.

The bottom line was that the largest psi yield was for free-response remote viewing, in which you are free to be open to any mental impressions you receive about a hidden or distant target. While these experiments produced the strongest effects, being open to any mental impression can be quite a challenge, especially for beginners, because if we get a mental flash of a target as, say, *something yellow*, we might instantly think, it's a banana! The "if you see something, say something" slogan works very well in some situations, but it does not work well when you're remote viewing.

Seeing and saying is a fast, automatic associative process that's hard-wired in our brains. In everyday tasks, this kneejerk response is useful, because if you see a flash of orange and black, you need to react quickly because there might be a tiger about to jump on you. But when you're engaging in remote viewing, if you flash on *yellow equals banana*, it becomes very difficult to stop thinking about a banana. This is why remote viewing training teaches one to open the mind to subtle impressions and to carefully note them, but to then delay analysis of the impressions, especially the urge to *name* them. It takes practice to learn how to do this, but many students will attest that it can be done. It's similar to the practice of mindfulness meditation, in which you can learn to quickly recognize when you're mind-wandering. That too is a hardwired behavior that takes a while to unlearn.

REMOTE VIEWING

Richard Wiseman, a prominent British skeptic, stage magician, and psychologist at the University of Hertfordshire, offered this opinion about remote viewing in a 2008 article in the *Daily Mail*:

> I agree that *by the standards of any other area of science that remote viewing is proven*, but begs the question: Do we need higher standards of evidence when we study the paranormal? I think we do. . . . Because remote viewing is such an outlandish claim that will revolutionise the world, we need overwhelming evidence before we draw any conclusions. Right now we don't have that evidence.[4] (emphasis added)

As I write this some sixteen years after Wiseman's comment, remote viewing still appears to be an especially robust form of divination. But how robust? That's what the psychologists Patrizio Tressoldi and Debra Katz set out to determine. They conducted a meta-analysis of all published remote viewing experiments conducted from 1974 through 2022.[5] They found forty studies reported by twenty-two different first authors, which they categorized according to the type of task.

Precognitive remote viewing experiments asked the participants to gain an impression of a target image that would be selected in the future. Seventeen studies by nine authors produced odds against chance of 162 billion to 1. *Outbound* studies had the remote viewer describe in real time where another person was located. That involved nine authors who reported sixteen studies, and it resulted in odds of 403 quintillion to 1. *Clairvoyant* studies involved images selected at random from a large pool of prepared images, then placed inside an envelope or displayed on a computer screen. The remote viewer, secured in another location, was asked to perceive those images in real time. Some fourteen authors reported twenty-four studies, which re-sulted in odds of over 1 septillion to 1.

So yes, remote viewing, and by association divination magic, can be quite robust. Figure 8 shows the cumulative statistical result for all these studies. The graph's y axis is a cumulative Stouffer Z score, which we've already met. The graph shows that after forty experiments conducted over fifty years, involving thousands of remote viewing sessions, the results accumulated to a Stouffer Z score of about 12, which is associated with odds against chance of 136 novemdecillion to 1, or said another way, 136 followed by thirty-six zeros to 1.

Is that overwhelming enough? It depends on how "outlandish" one regards the claim that psi perception can transcend the ordinary limits of space and time. As we've discussed, if you view reality solely through a simplistic materialistic lens, then remote viewing is indeed ridiculous and impossible. No amount of evidence could convince you otherwise. But when you begin to entertain other worldviews, the very same evidence suddenly becomes obvious.

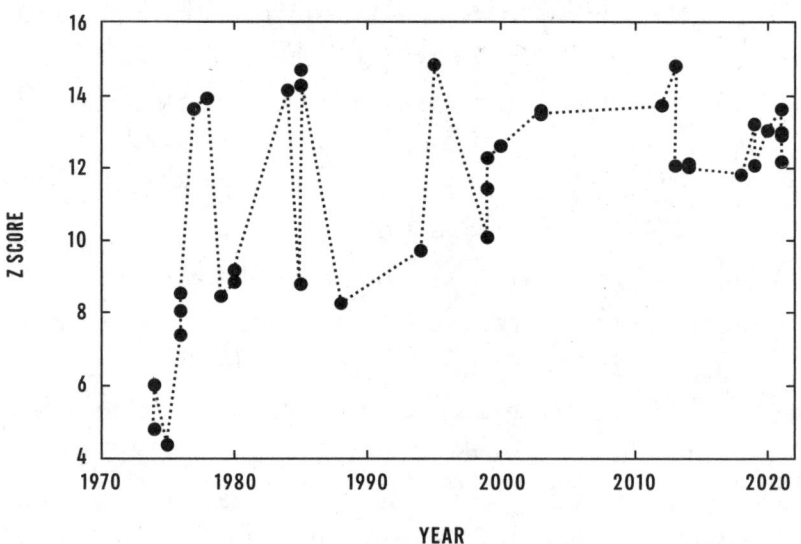

Figure 8. Cumulative Stouffer Z score over fifty years of remote viewing experiments

Kona Blue

If remote viewing is so effective, why was Star Gate, the classified US government ESPionage program, which ran from 1972 to 1995, shut down?[6] Lots of speculations have been offered, but having worked on that program and seeing how effective remote viewing could be when exercised by experts, I was skeptical that government interest went away. There are reasons to suspect it hasn't.

For example, in March 2024 a possible clue was revealed by a report issued by the Department of Defense. It mentioned that a highly classified program, dubbed Kona Blue, had been proposed to the Department of Homeland Security to restart investigations of unidentified anomalous phenomena (UAPs).[7] Kona Blue would have been a continuation of a program managed by the Defense Intelligence Agency from 2009 to 2012. The proposed program would have included "paranormal research (including alleged 'human consciousness anomalies')."[8] That phrase is government-speak for psi. The Kona Blue program was reportedly not funded, but the fact that "human consciousness anomalies" was mentioned suggests that those in the know have remained interested. More recently, disclosures about on-going programs keeping track of UFOs and UAPs, where these phenomena are reportedly involved with consciousness in some way,[9] further indicates that there have been, and probably still are, programs that include remote viewing and other psi phenomena.

CHAPTER 4

SCIENCE OF THEURGY

Everyone who is seriously involved in the pursuit of science becomes convinced that a spirit is manifest in the laws of the Universe—a spirit vastly superior to that of man, and one in the face of which we with our modest powers must feel humble.

—ALBERT EINSTEIN[1]

Theurgy refers to practices aimed at invoking the presence and power of spirits or entities. It can also refer to refining or elevating oneself through spiritual and mystical experiences. The term comes from Greek roots, meaning "divine work" or "work of the gods." Theurgy differs from *thaumaturgy*, which means "wonder working" or "miracle working." Thaumaturgy focuses on performing magic more closely aligned with what I've called enchantment and divination, although in both cases these practices traditionally assume that spirits, entities, angels, or other aspects of the divine exist.

The scientific question about theurgy is whether spirits, or in general "the divine"—meaning related to God or gods, or in general the supernatural realm—*exist*. This question is not possible to answer by scientific means, at least not using current methods. With enchantment and divination practices, we can run controlled experiments to test if they exist, but in the case of spirits or the concept of the divine, we have no way to *directly* engage with such purported entities or realm. We can only explore such ideas *indirectly*, through living humans who claim to see or engage with spirits or other realms, or through the use of electronic equipment where we may infer that any changes observed were due to spirits.

By analogy, in cosmology today the concepts of dark matter and dark energy were proposed to help explain unexpected behaviors of the visible universe. This includes observations like stars at the edges of galaxies that appear to be moving faster than we'd expect based on the amount of matter we can observe, and the unpredicted strength of gravitational lenses, wherein light is bent around massive objects more than can be accounted for in our current theories, by the surprising large-scale structure of the universe, and so on.

In cosmology, the adjective *dark* means we think something must be there to account for these behaviors, but we haven't been able to detect it. Likewise, we might use the term *dark spirits* to refer to experiences claimed to involve spirits or angels, but that word seems unnecessarily sinister, so I'll use a more pleasant term, *ethereal entities*.

ETHEREAL ENTITIES

The closest that science has come to investigating ethereal entities is through the study of phenomena suggestive of the persistence of consciousness after bodily death. This includes cases of reincarnation, near-death experiences (NDEs), out-of-body experiences (OBEs), reports of apparitions, hauntings, and ghosts, electronic voice phenomena (EVPs), instrumental transcommunication (ITC), deathbed visions, after-death communications, poltergeist activity, miraculous healings associated with prayer, mediumship, and terminal lucidity, which refers to instances where patients in comas or with severe dementia suddenly become lucid and freely converse and reminisce with family members, then pass away shortly thereafter.

These phenomena challenge our current understanding of the relationship between brain and consciousness, and the relevant literature reviewing the evidence is immense.[2] That literature is now increasingly expanding into mainstream discussions because of the same paradigm shift that is causing a reconsideration of magic. For example, experiences like NDEs were once condescendingly dismissed by doctors and neuroscientists as illusions of a dying brain. Now these experiences are being discussed in more balanced terms. For example, an article entitled "Lifting the Veil on Near-Death Experiences" appeared in a May 2024 issue of *Scientific American*.[3] In it, neuroscientist Christof Koch acknowledged the transformative and "noetic quality" of an NDE, adding, "They know what they've seen."

Of the ten or so categories of evidence suggestive of survival, most involve spontaneous experiences, like an unexpected sighting of an apparition, having an NDE, or cases of reincarnation, which rely on memories reported by young children. As such, with the exception of mediumship, survival-type experiences cannot be studied in formal laboratory tests. This makes it difficult to provide the rigorously controlled, on-demand, repeatable evidence that science demands. In addition, questions of life and death are among the most intensely motivating topics humans will ever face, so assessments of the available evidence tend to strongly align with one's preferred beliefs about an afterlife.

There are two main critiques about the evidence for survival. The first comes from those who are fully convinced that you are your brain, in which case it is impossible for consciousness, personality, or anything else associated with a living person to survive the death of the brain. The second critique comes from those who accept the existence of psi phenomena but view the evidence for survival as manifestations of psi in the living. This latter view is sometimes called the "super psi" argument, because some types of survival evidence seem to involve "super" forms of psi that are beyond anything typically observed in the laboratory.

My take on super psi is that we really don't understand the limits of psi in the living, in which case virtually any form of evidence for survival *could be* attributed to psi. That is, without a firm understanding of what psi can do when amplified by real-world motivations, as opposed to the relatively weak effects we see in the laboratory, then it is premature to claim that the evidence for survival *cannot* be magnified forms of psi. We just don't know.

Of course, this doesn't prevent some from insisting that there is *proof positive* for survival. That level of certainty is often based on personal experience or strongly held philosophical or religious positions, rather than evaluation of the evidence. This by no means discounts anyone's experiences or ideological convictions, but it does reveal the limits of what can be said from a scientific perspective.

POLTERGEISTS

Poltergeist episodes involve movements of large objects in real-world environments that are not caused by any obvious source. Besides moving objects, poltergeist effects can also involve major electrical disturbances, strange odors or sounds, or other unaccounted-for effects in the environment. Reports of this type of phenomenon can be found throughout history, and they eventually gained the German term for "noisy ghost" (*Polter-geist*). But are these effects due to disembodied spirits? The psychologist William Roll investigated many such cases and published one of the most reliable modern books on this phenomenon.[4] He made a persuasive argument that the source of these effects in genuine cases (they're often faked) is associated with an emotionally disturbed *living* person, typically an adolescent dealing with emotional problems. That is, Roll concluded that what used to be attributed to a noisy ghost was actually due to psi in the living.

I've witnessed two instances of poltergeist-like effects involving electrical systems. In one case, the human source was obvious—a guest visiting our home who, when angry, somehow "caused" all of the electrical appliances to mysteriously and simultaneously stop working. In a second case, which took place in 2019 in a hotel in Paris, the source of the disturbance was unknown, although it may not have been a coincidence that earlier in the day I attended a presentation about a poltergeist case. It involved a prison that was said to house a ghost named Anton. The case was recorded by a physician in 1835 in Weinsberg, Germany, and it was somewhat unusual because Anton was apparently a "traveling ghost." That is, visitors to the prison would return home and experience odd disturbances similar to what was being reported in the prison. The presentation was during the annual conference of the Parapsychological Association and given by Michael Nahm, a biologist and research associate at the Institute for Frontier Areas of Psychology and Mental Health in Freiburg.

Many hours after Nahm's presentation that day, while my wife and I were sleeping in our hotel room, around three A.M. I suddenly woke up because I heard a strange hissing sound, followed by a loud pop. My phone, which was plugged in to charge overnight, had turned itself on. I looked around the room in the dim light from my phone's screen to see what was going on, but nothing looked out of the ordinary, so I started to go back to sleep. About thirty seconds later I heard another hissing sound and pop, this time louder than before. I turned on the light and immediately noticed that the flat-panel TV in the room was bellowing smoke. My wife was up by now, too, and we were both alarmed about a possible fire hazard. Then there was another hissing and an even louder pop, followed by a nasty-looking cloud of acrid smoke gathering around the ceiling.

We looked out the window at a courtyard, where we could see many other rooms in our same hotel. They were all dark, suggesting that whatever was going on was only happening in our room. While we prepared to escape, we peeked out into the hallway and were startled to see that the occupant across the hall was Michael Nahm. He immediately said, half laughing, "It's Anton!" The occupants in the room next to his, and in the room adjacent to ours, were also standing bleary-eyed in the hallway. We were all startled awake by similar electrical disturbances, and these four rooms were the only ones on our floor.

We searched the hallway for an electrical panel, to check if maybe a fuse had blown. We eventually found the panel, but everything seemed in order. We went downstairs to the hotel lobby to alert the night clerk, but he said he hadn't seen anything unusual either. So we returned to our rooms, where things seemed to have settled down. As my wife and I prepared to get back to bed, I switched off the light, but it wouldn't turn off. Instead, the light started to flicker, menacingly, like in a horror movie. This was more than a little unsettling, but having a background in electronics, I was reasonably sure that the disruption was due to an electrical short. I repeatedly flipped the light switch on and off, and after about twenty flips the light finally turned off. I waited a few minutes, everything remained quiet, and we got back to sleep around four A.M. The next morning I mentioned this strange episode to the day clerk, and without any prompting she laughed and said, "Poltergeist!"

The electrical disturbance that blew up our TV set, caused the lights to flicker, and generated an evil-looking cloud of smoke could all have been due to a power surge, a faulty fuse somewhere in the hotel, or any number of other reasons. But the synchronicity of this event happening simultaneously to two parapsychologists, neither of us knowing that we were staying in rooms across the hall from each other, and in the evening after a talk about a traveling poltergeist, was eerie.

While I believe that most of the evidence for survival, including poltergeist episodes, can be attributed to psi in the living, this does not mean that that is the only possible explanation. Occasionally odd events transpire, like our experience with Anton the traveling ghost, that do not have an obvious human source. Of course, if we entertained the possibility that poltergeist-like effects could emerge from unconsciously conjured psi, then Anton may have been a figment of my or Michael Nahm's unconscious. Science fiction fans will appreciate the parallel between this idea and the 1956 film *Forbidden Planet*,[5] which was in turn based on Shakespeare's play *The Tempest*. In the science fiction film, we learn (spoiler alert) that advanced aliens accidentally wiped themselves out by creating machines that manifested their conscious desires, which was great. But unfortunately the machines also manifested their *unconscious* desires, which was not so great.

On the whole, like many people I would prefer that some form of survival after death exists, but with one caveat. As Benjamin Franklin wrote shortly before he died, "In this world nothing can be said to be certain, except death and taxes." My concern is that if there are taxes after death, I'm not sure I would enjoy eternal disembodied life after all.

MEDIUMSHIP

A few classes of survival evidence are amenable to experimental study. They include EVP/ITC, NDE, and OBE, but only a few investigators have conducted these types of studies, so it's not yet possible to conduct meta-analyses to see if the reported effects are repeatable. But there is one class of tightly controlled scientific studies that has been repeated numerous times: mediumship.

Mediums are psychics who report that they can sense and communicate with the deceased. Most mediums are "mental mediums," meaning their communications or visions are subjective. A smaller percentage of mediums are "physical mediums," who hold séances and claim to act as intermediaries between the spirit and physical worlds. Séances are nearly always performed in complete darkness, where the physical medium invites spirits to mysteriously display lights, produce sounds, or move objects. Such séances were in their heyday in the mid-1800s, when they were popular forms of entertainment.

Many physical mediums were eventually unmasked as con artists. Fraudulent physical mediumship flourished because it was an easy way for swindlers to bilk people desperate to believe in survival. The Witchcraft Act of 1735 in the UK was used to prosecute these fraudsters; many years later that act was updated as the Fraudulent Mediums Act of 1951. The many cases of fraud that were uncovered tarnished the reputation not only of mental and physical mediums, but of all kinds of psi research. There are still a few physical mediums today who conduct séances, but precious little research has been conducted to rigorously verify their claims, and the few results that have been reported remain hotly contested. So I have little to report regarding physical mediumship.

This is not the case for mental mediumship. These mediums typically enter a light trance state, or they can go into a full trance and embody a spirit; such mediums are called channelers. Within the magical traditions a version of mediumship is called *necromancy*, from the Greek meaning "divination by the dead." It involves calling upon the spirits of the dead for guidance, insight, favor, healing, or predictions of the future.

In the laboratory, mediumship is tested by asking a medium to contact a specified deceased person and then ask them a set of prearranged questions about, say, the person's physical appearance when they were alive, their hobbies, their home, events that only family members would know, and so on. A well-controlled test typically involves the medium; a sitter, meaning a person who wishes to contact their departed loved one; a "proxy sitter," a third party asked to take on the role of the sitter so as to not give the medium any body language or other clues about the deceased person; and the investigators. Neither the medium nor the proxy sitter is told anything about the deceased person of interest, except perhaps a first name.

The medium then contacts and communicates with the deceased person to gain the requested information, and a recording of the medium's spoken communications is transcribed. Then the medium does this again for a different sitter's requested contact, and a second transcript is prepared. Now the two sitters are each given two transcripts, one corresponding to the medium's communication with their deceased loved one, and the other to the other sitter's loved one. Each sitter is asked which of the two transcripts best matches their loved one. The chance outcome of such a test would be 50 percent. If the result of many such tests was above 50 percent, then that would provide evidence that the medium gained accurate information from a deceased person. And there you go. Laboratory evidence of survival of bodily death.

Well, sort of. This type of test can verify that the medium's *information* was accurate and that it was not gathered using "cold reading" techniques. But it cannot identify where the information came from.

This is a problem because we already know, through the many studies of divination in living people, that we have the capacity to gain information beyond the everyday boundaries of space and time. So we cannot exclude the possibility that mental mediums are especially adept at clairvoyance, thus gaining information that will please their sitters and give them the impression that the medium was in contact with their loved one. Or the medium might be especially skilled at telepathy and gain the information directly from the sitter's mind. That said, clairvoyance and telepathy are generally not the medium's experience; they feel they are in actual contact with the deceased. And maybe they are. The point is that an external observer cannot know this for sure.

What we *can* tell from a neuroscience perspective is that a medium's brain activity is different when thinking about an imaginary person, thinking about a known living person, listening to a recorded biography of a person, or asked to actively interact with a deceased person. Also, brain activity in mediums differs from non-mediums who are asked to identify the cause of a person's death, based solely on a photograph of the person taken when they were healthy. These outcomes still don't tell us where the information comes from, but it does indicate that the act of mediumship is a distinct subjective state that is not the same as ordinary thinking and imagination.[6]

Fourteen laboratory tests of mediums were published from 2001 to 2019.[7] The researcher Matthew Sarraf and his colleagues retrieved these articles and applied all the usual methods for conducting meta-analyses, including assessing the possibility that studies that found no results were conducted but not published. The result in terms of odds against chance was 518 million to 1. That means on average the mediums were able to gain accurate information about deceased people that they did not know. Sarraf also used an alternative statistical method for assessing the outcome of a meta-analysis, called the Bayes factor. This is a way to weigh evidence for a hypothesis as we incorporate the results of each additional experiment. The rule of thumb is that if a Bayes factor is over 100, then that constitutes "decisive evidence" in favor of the hypothesis. In this case, the Bayes factor for the hypothesis that mediums could gain accurate information about a deceased person under strictly controlled conditions was 231. That's doubly decisive. The analysis also found that "certified mediums," those pretested for accuracy, performed better than noncertified mediums.

Does this mean etheric entities definitely exist? Unfortunately, no. These experiments are certainly suggestive of survival, and they are in alignment with the studies on remote viewing and telepathy. But this evidence is provided by living mediums, so we cannot exclude psi in the living as a viable explanation.

CONJURING

In 1973 eight members of the Toronto Society for Psychical Research conducted an experiment to see if they could conjure a spirit.[8] In magical terms, they were making an explicit attempt to evoke a *servitor*, which in other traditions is known as a thoughtform, an elemental, a daemon, a golem, an egregore, or a tulpa. The Toronto group included ordinary people with no special psychic skills but with a deep interest in psychokinesis. They included an engineer, an industrial designer, a scientific research assistant, and four "housewives."

The team made up a story about "Philip," an English aristocrat from the seventeenth century who had a secret love affair that ended in tragedy and suicide. The imagined Philip was given a comprehensive backstory and an image to encourage the story to feel real, as if he were a historically genuine person. The group met weekly, aiming to evoke Philip's "spirit" through their collective focus and visualization, not in the context of a dark séance but rather a serious effort that took place in ordinary light.

It didn't work; there was no evidence of Philip. So they changed their approach and encouraged a much more relaxed and engaging atmosphere. This led to unexplained movements and sounds from a table where they sat, then to the table moving independently and apparently responding to the group's requests. They began to hear knocks and raps in response to their inquiries, as well as answers consistent with how they imagined Philip would respond. If the group changed how they interacted with Philip, the phenomena would also change, suggesting that Philip was a creation of their collective intentions.

The team then created a new character, "Lilith," and with that character they achieved results similar to Philip, which again suggested that the typical range of séance-type phenomena could be recreated by the living through their coherent, collective focus. This experiment confirmed that a motivated group can conjure up apparently independent spirits, where the entities are imagined into existence through coherent, focused intention.

AN ESSAY CONTEST

In 2021 the Bigelow Institute for Consciousness Studies sponsored an essay contest where the topic was "the best available evidence for the survival of human consciousness beyond permanent bodily death." In this context, the criterion for *evidence* was defined as "beyond a reasonable doubt," which could include eyewitness testimony. The idea was that because such evidence was considered suitable in court trials, it would be good enough for this contest. On the one hand, that criterion is useful because except in mediumship, survival phenomena cannot be brought under laboratory control.

On the other hand, "reasonable doubt" as a threshold of credibility is in the eye of the beholder, and eyewitness testimony is notoriously unreliable. Individuals have been convicted of horrendous crimes and put to death based on faulty eyewitness testimony. Some prisoners were incarcerated for years but later found to be innocent due to false or faulty eyewitness testimony. Even if an eyewitness to a crime was under oath and sincerely described their experience, if that information ultimately turned out to be wrong, they would not be charged with perjury because it is well known that memory fades with time and can become distorted.

But setting aside the less than perfect evidence based on eyewitness testimony, some twenty-eight of the 204 entries for the essay context were awarded prizes totaling $1.8 million. How to best interpret the evidence was repeated in many of these essays. Topics covered included all the categories of phenomena associated with survival. The best evidence varied according to the author of each essay, with NDEs, reincarnation, and mediumship often at the top of the list.

Many essays included phenomena that have been reported often enough to gain descriptive labels. For example, the following case was categorized as a "crisis apparition." From Michael Nahm's essay:

> A dog, two adults, and five children were together in a room at 6 pm in May. Suddenly the dog began to bark loudly and jumped towards the corner with the stove. The seven people followed the dog's movements with their eyes. In the corner, they saw an apparition of a child in a shirt that looked like a boy who was a friend of the family and often came to play. The apparition started to float above them, leaving the room through an open window. The dog followed the moving apparition through the room, continuously barking fervently. The episode lasted for about 15 seconds. Later in the evening, the family learned that this boy had died at about the time they saw his apparition.[9]

The essay that to my mind was the most persuasive was not based on anecdotes or even on the highly successful experimental results in mediumship studies. Instead, it was a philosophical argument. The computer scientist and philosopher Bernardo Kastrup proposed a series of arguments based on idealism, the perennial philosophy underlying esotericism and magic. As Kastrup put it:

> I contend that it is, strictly speaking, unnecessary to look to the paranormal for high-confidence validation of postmortem survival. Not that there is anything wrong with doing so, or that paranormal research is unreliable (often enough the contrary is the case); but given present-day cultural sensitivities and prejudices, I believe that an argument for postmortem survival based solely on rigorous reasoning and sufficiently replicated laboratory evidence [in physics]—both of which are not contested by the mainstream—is more likely to resonate.

Moreover, once this argument is presented, evidence of phenomena currently regarded as "paranormal" may be considered with less prejudice, since the argument lays a coherent theoretical foundation to accommodate said evidence.[10]

The laboratory evidence Kastrup refers to is from quantum and relativistic physics. Experiments in those realms indicate that the everyday, commonsense impressions we hold about reality, which includes self-evident properties like space, time, matter, and energy, are illusions. When examined in detail, commonsense is understood to be a simplistic, cartoonish picture of what is "really" going on. Kastrup continues:

Indeed, decades of progressively refined and repeatedly replicated experimental results in foundations of physics have refuted physical realism: Physical entities have no standalone existence and, as such, are merely a superficial appearance of a deeper, fundamental but nonphysical layer of reality. This alone refutes mainstream physicalism and its implications regarding postmortem survival.

If spacetime and matter are off the table as fundamental aspects of reality—for now they are understood to be merely cognitive representations in human consciousness—the notion that the loss of spatial integrity of the material body at the time of death implies the end of consciousness loses whatever couching in logic it might otherwise have. The most we can say is that death is an event in consciousness: in the consciousness of the dying and of those observing the dying process and its aftermath. Any extrapolation beyond this is logically unfounded, regardless of how tempting it might be from a culture-bound perspective.[11]

I think that nicely sums up the philosophical argument in favor of magic. If consciousness is all there is, and it's more fundamental than the physical world, then magic is happening all the time whether we realize it or not, and it becomes increasingly likely that there are indeed ethereal entities of one form or another.

PART III

UNDERSTANDING MAGIC

Okay, so psi and magic exist.

Then why is there so much resistance to these phenomena in the academic world? Why aren't they part of the scientific mainstream?

Good questions.

We'll examine what the skeptics have said about magic, then we'll discuss theories of magic from the perspectives of both the magician and the scientist.

And then we'll see how it all fits together.

CHAPTER 5

TAKING MAGIC SERIOUSLY

If you wish to be considered a scientific-minded person, you probably know that you really shouldn't believe in the occurrence of events commonly referred to as "supernatural." If there was something to that sort of thing, surely the greats of science such as Newton, Bacon, Boyle, the Curies and Einstein would have told us.

—ANDREAS SOMMER, FORBIDDENHISTORIES.COM

Yes, surely they would. And they did. And still do. Many scientists to-day believe in so-called paranormal and supernatural topics. They've just learned to not talk about them in public.

THE TABOO

Taboos are social agreements, and as such they move at the plod-dingly slow speed of society and are highly effective in controlling public discourse. The taboo against psi and magic has been especially tenacious because we've been endlessly told by skeptics and other malcontents that only crackpots hold those beliefs. Some religious leaders also sustain the stigma because they loudly insist that these topics are demonic. Academics studiously avoid psi and magic except when whispered about behind closed doors, or discussed in historical terms, or portrayed as what people foolishly believe as "weird shit."[1] The taboo is reinforced from all sides, yet everyone remains fascinated by psi and magic because most people—including the majority of academic scientists at top-tier universities—have personally had one or more psychic or magical experiences.[2] Despite this, as historian Andreas Sommer notes:

> Anybody who has carefully studied . . . the vast psychical research literature produced since the 1880s (and the critical responses to it) should agree it can no longer be doubted the data suggests that something strange is going on. . . . In short, we are dealing with pretty revolutionary stuff, clearly demonstrating that the still prevailing worldview of nineteenth century physics is in urgent need of a facelift, to put it mildly.
>
> But ask a random scientist if he or she has ever . . . studied any of the psychical research data published over the past 150 years. Chances are that your question will either be met with a shrug or a reference to Wikipedia entries debunking all these studies as obvious pseudoscience.[3]

Those entries are written by skeptics who presumably believe they are saving science from charlatans who are trying to scam us with pseudoscientific gobbledygook. But the reality is that skeptics uncritically toss everything they don't like into the same unacceptable basket, then they actively lobby to prevent legitimate research from taking place.[4] The sociologists of science Harry Collins and Robert Evans, who studied these organizations, felt that scientists should call them out. They wrote:

> After all, among other things, scientists are there to help us know whether there are paranormal effects . . . but their input should be based on their best scientific efforts; ex-cathedra

statements, or dirty tricks, are of no special value, nor should scientists pass their responsibility to outside groups.[5]

Unfortunately, as Yoda might have said, "powerful, the taboo is." So powerful that it turns out that Karl Popper, one of the most prominent philosophers of science of all time, was "convinced of the existence of 'paranormal' phenomena, but absolutely rejected the idea of studying them scientifically—without bothering to offer a rational explanation why."[6]

There are endless contemporary examples of willful ignorance that sustain the taboo. I'll describe a few examples followed by a few counterexamples.

The Strange Case of Freeman Dyson

In *Scientific American*, the journalist John Horgan wrote a blog with the title "Freeman Dyson, Global Warming, ESP and the Fun of Being 'Bunkrapt.'" That last term meant "rapt" or "fascinated" with obvious bunk like religious beliefs and superstitions. Freeman Dyson was one of the most prominent physicists of the twentieth century, spending much of his career at the acclaimed Institute for Advanced Study in Princeton, New Jersey. The bunk in question is that Dyson admitted in an interview that he believed in ESP (extrasensory perception). This bothered Horgan, who asked, "Should a scientist who believes in extrasensory perception—the ability to read minds, intuit the future and so on—be taken seriously?" Apparently not, because it encouraged Horgan to add insult to injury by writing:

> Dyson disclosed this belief in his essay "One in a Million" in the
> March 25, 2004, *New York Review of Books,* which discussed a
> book about ESP. His family, Dyson revealed, included two
> "fervent believers in paranormal phenomena," a grandmother
> who was a "notorious and successful faith healer" and a cousin
> who edited the *Journal of the Society for Psychical Research.*

Oh, the horror, the horror. The peer-reviewed journal mentioned in that passage has been published continuously since 1882. The society that publishes it, the Society for Psychical Research, was founded by the most prominent British scientists and intellectuals of the day, including several Nobel laureates, and it continues to report peer-reviewed historical, scholarly, and empirical evidence. But besides glossing over that important piece of history, Horgan failed to report what Dyson actually said about his grandmother's and cousin's interests. Dyson said, "They may have been deluded, but neither of them was a fool. Their beliefs were based on personal experience and careful scrutiny of evidence. Nothing that they believed was incompatible with science."[7]

But Horgan wasn't deterred. In another piece for his blog, he asked, "Brilliant scientists are open-minded about paranormal stuff, so why not you?"[8] His choice of brilliant scientists included the computer pioneer Alan Turing, the Nobel laureate physicist Wolfgang Pauli, the Nobel laureate physicist Brian Josephson, and once again, Freeman Dyson. Horgan quoted Alan Turing, who said that paranormal phenomena such as telepathy and telekinesis

> seem to deny all our usual scientific ideas. How we should like to discredit them! Unfortunately the statistical evidence, at least for telepathy, is overwhelming. It is very difficult to rearrange one's ideas so as to fit these new facts in. Once one has accepted them it does not seem a very big step to believe in ghosts and bogies. The idea that our bodies move simply according to the known laws of physics, together with some others not yet discovered but somewhat similar, would be one of the first to go.[9]

In response, Horgan asked, "Should the fact that Turing et al. took psi seriously mean that the rest of us should, too? Not necessarily. Brilliant scientists believe in lots of things for which there is no evidence." Sure, but Turing didn't say he believed in something with no evidence. He specifically said that *the evidence* for telepathy was overwhelming. And the evidence for telepathy is far better today than it was in Turing's day. Horgan also overlooked a few other brilliant people who believed in psi. In fact, he failed to mention more than two hundred famous scientists, authors, poets, artists, and inventors, including thirty-three Nobel laureates.[10]

The Curious Case of John Wheeler

Martin Gardner was a mathematics and science popularizer who wrote extensively about skepticism and pseudoscience. In a 1979 article in *The New York Review of Books*, entitled "Quantum Theory and Quack Theory,"[11] Gardner wrote:

> Earlier this year, at the annual meeting of the American
> Association for the Advancement of Science, Dr. J. A. Wheeler
> startled his audience by asking the AAAS to reconsider its
> decision . . . to dignify parapsychology by giving its researchers
> an affiliate status in the association.

Gardner continued by lauding Wheeler's background and many contributions to physics, including the idea that

> We no longer can think of a universe sitting "out there" as if
> separated from us by a thick plate of glass. To measure a
> particle we must shatter the glass and alter what we measure.
> The physicist is no mere observer. He is an active participator.
> "In some strange way," Wheeler has said, "the universe is a
> participatory universe."

Wheeler's ideas were widely cited by psi researchers because his concept of a "participatory universe" supports the reality of mind-matter interaction. But given the taboo, Wheeler was desperate to disassociate his ideas from psi research. So when he was invited to speak at an AAAS conference, he used that venue to clarify that in his view measurements in quantum mechanics had nothing to do with consciousness.

Then Wheeler discovered that his talk was part of a panel discussion that included two physicists who were conducting remote viewing research at SRI International (and would later be known as the founders of the US government's classified psychic espionage program). The panel also included a parapsychologist, Charles Honorton, who was studying dream telepathy at the Maimonides Medical Center in Brooklyn, New York.

To express his dismay, Wheeler ended his talk with "And let no one . . . postulate any 'quantum interconnectedness' between separate consciousnesses. Both are baseless. Both are mysticism. Both are moonshine." Wheeler added an appendix to his written paper that, wrote Gardner, "[has] shaken the world of parapsychology more than any remarks made by a distinguished scientist in the past half-century." Wheeler's appendix was a letter written to the AAAS council, entitled "Drive the pseudos out of the workshop of science." It opened with this barrage:

> The author would be less than frank if he did not confess he wanted to withdraw from this symposium when—too late—he learned that so-called extrasensory perception . . . would be taken up in one of the papers. How can anyone be happy at an accompaniment of pretentious pseudo-science who wants to discuss real issues about real observations in real science? . . . With the decade of permissiveness now well past, [I] suggest that the Council and the Board of Directors will serve science well to vote "parapsychology" out of the AAAS.

The council ignored Wheeler's rant, and no action was taken for the simple reason that he had *refused to look* at the empirical evidence supporting the existence of psi. Wheeler was undoubtedly agitated by skeptics like Gardner to be afraid, very afraid, of the stigma of the woo-woo taboo.

The Odd Case of Sean Carroll

The last example is similar to the Wheeler episode. In a blog, the physicist Sean Carroll, the Homewood Professor of Natural Philosophy at Johns Hopkins University, author, and prominent science popularizer, opined on his belief that psi is impossible:

> There are many things we don't understand about biology and neuroscience, not to mention the ultimate laws of physics. But there are many things that we *do* understand, and only the most basic features of quantum field theory suffice to *definitively rule out the idea* that we can influence objects from a distance through the workings of pure thought.
>
> There is no room for extra kinds of mysterious particles clinging, aura-like, to the matter in a spoon. . . . We know exactly how much energy is available in a spoon; we know the masses of the atoms, and the kinetic energy of thermal motions within the metal. Taken together, we can say *without any fear of making a mistake* that any new particles that might exist within a spoon would have been detected in experiments long ago.[12]

Having no fear might be great as a sports slogan, but as Carl Sagan warned at a 1987 meeting of the skeptical society known as the Committee for the Scientific Investigation of Claims of the Paranormal (CSICOP), "You can get into a habit of thought in which you enjoy making fun of all those other people who don't see things as clearly as you do. We have to guard carefully against it."[13] I guess Carroll didn't get Sagan's message, because he added fuel to the fire:

> You don't need to set up elaborate double-blind protocols to pass judgment on the abilities of purported psychics. Our

knowledge of the laws of physics rules them out. Speculations to the contrary are not the provenance of bold visionaries, they are *the dreams of crackpots*.

Given the above, I would put the probability that some sort of parapsychological phenomenon will turn out to be real at something (substantially) less than a billion to one. . . . The total budget for high-energy physics worldwide is probably a few billion dollars per year. So I would be very happy to support research into parapsychology at the level of a few dollars per year. Heck, I'd even be willing to go as high as *twenty* dollars per year, just to be safe. Never let it be said that I am anything other than open-minded.

I will let the skeptical philosopher Bertrand Russell respond to that smirk: "The trouble with the world is that the stupid are cocksure and the intelligent are full of doubt."[14]

THE EVOLUTION OF SKEPTICISM

At times it seems no one can hear a calm discussion about the evidence for psi phenomena because debunkers have been so effective at sustaining a cacophony of confusion. For example, one of the most common critiques about psi used to be "There isn't a shred of scientific evidence." That argument was shown to be false through the use of meta-analysis, a well-accepted method now used in many scientific disciplines to assess whether independent experiments show the same results, and to estimate the magnitude of the effects under study.[15]

Then the critique morphed into "Well, maybe there's some evidence, but it's flawed." That's an anemic argument because there's no such thing as a perfect experiment in any discipline, and in any case, as we've seen, the effect of *potential* flaws—in the form of "questionable research practices"—has been studied in detail, and even throwing the kitchen sink of possible flaws at the evidence doesn't eliminate the highly significant results we've discussed. So the flaw argument doesn't hold either.

Next, informed skeptics began to admit that there is valid evidence for psi,[16] but because no one knows exactly what psi is, then it can't be called psi. This odd nonargument follows a twisted logic called the experimenters' regress.[17] Say you're studying a mysterious experience we'll call telepathy. You conduct an experiment that provides evidence supporting the idea of telepathy. But without already knowing exactly what telepathy *is*, and how it's supposed to manifest in an experiment, then it's not so easy to tell if the evidence is supportive of telepathy or not. This circular complaint has the advantage (from the skeptic's perspective) of never having to admit that telepathy is established— at least until the absurdity of this argument is made clear.

The next crop of critiques focused on the extraordinary proposal that science itself must be broken, because use of proper methods has produced evidence that cannot be denied but also cannot be accepted. That unresolvable paradox was sidestepped by the astonishing assertion that psi is flatly impossible, so there's no need to pay attention to the evidence.

I'm not kidding. That is the leading skeptical critique.[18]

But now even that argument is dissolving. The "impossible" objection is often used as a cudgel by those who haven't noticed that we're no longer in the nineteenth century. In fact, during the first few years of the twentieth century, three principles were identified that captured our best understanding of the physical world at the time: *reality*, *locality*, and *causality*.

Reality was based on two related ideas: first, that physical objects have definite properties, regardless of whether anyone is observing them, and second, that different observers observing the same object will see the same thing. As Einstein put it, it is reasonable to assume that the moon is still there even if no one is looking at it. *Locality* is the idea that the only way objects can be influenced is through direct contact, and that those influences cannot travel faster than the speed of light. This means any sort of influence at a distance is prohibited. Again, as Einstein put it, locality is required because otherwise there would be *nonlocal* "spooky action at a distance." *Causality* assumes that the arrow of time points in only one direction, and thus that the cause→effect sequence is strictly and absolutely fixed.

By the second decade of the twenty-first century, all three of those self-evident laws were repealed. We now know through experiments published in top-tier science journals that (a) different observers measuring the same object can experience different realities; (b) in spite of Einstein's opinion that "spooky action at a distance" doesn't exist, experimental demonstrations of nonlocality won the Nobel Prize in physics in 2022; and (c) retrocausal influences can and do occur in quantum mechanics.[19]

So with reality, locality, and causality no longer legitimate objections to the existence of psi and magic, skeptics raised the bar again and said sure, but those laws are observed at the quantum scale. And humans are so large compared to the quantum world that for all practical purposes our brains act according to nineteenth-century physics.

That would hold true if only living creatures didn't operate according to quantum principles. Until recently, many physicists dismissed that possibility because they believed that quantum effects could not be sustained in the warm, wet environment of living systems. But like the nineteenth-century view of what is allowed in physics, that belief is quickly disappearing. For example, a mid-2024 search on the topic of "quantum biology" on ScienceDirect.com, a large online scientific bibliography, retrieved 87,700 articles, reviews, encyclopedia entries, and book chapters, most published since 2015.

We are learning that quantum effects are not just *found* in living systems but seem to be *required* for living systems to operate the way they do.[20] Quantum properties are associated with the rate of catalytic effects (substances that increase the rate of chemical reactions), protein folding (the process by which a sequence of amino acids acquires a three-dimensional shape), photosynthesis in plants, birds' ability to literally see the magnetic fields of the Earth, and so on.[21] In addition, there is growing evidence for quantum processes operating in the brain.[22] As this line of research becomes more persuasive and accepted, the missing quantum-psi link will become increasingly accepted, as proposed back in the 1970s by physicists interested in psi.[23]

This does not mean that quantum mechanics in its present form adequately *explains* psi or magic. That would be like staring at my finger rather than where I'm pointing. Quantum mechanics today tells us that physical reality is *compatible* with the core features of psi and magic. History tells us with high confidence that physics will advance beyond today's best theories, and that those advances will continue until one day it will become glaringly obvious that psi and magic do not merely exist, but *must* exist. When this is likely to happen is not yet clear, but with the help of artificial intelligence we may see a breakthrough by midcentury or sooner. What used to take decades of painstaking work by thousands of scientists may, by then, take place in weeks or even days.

ANTIDOTES TO THE TABOO

> Pay no attention to what the critics say; no statue has ever been erected to a critic.
>
> —FINNISH COMPOSER JEAN SIBELIUS

Criticism plays an important role in winnowing the wheat from the chaff, and major advancements in knowledge are always met first with disbelief. This is par for the course. Fortunately, it is possible to be rigorously skeptical and profoundly open-minded at the same time. Here are a few examples.

Magical Candy

James Fallon was a professor of psychiatry, anatomy, and neurobiology at the University of California, Irvine (UCI). He held a Sloan Fellowship, a Senior Fulbright Fellowship, and a National Institutes of Health Research Career Award; he was chair of the UCI Faculty and Academic Senate, chair of the UCI College of Medicine and Medical Center Faculty, an expert for the Pentagon in the field of cognition and warfare; vice-chair of the American Land Forces Institute; and he served on the Vatican Arts and Technology Council. I recite these bona fides to demonstrate that Fallon was a solidly mainstream academic and, as such, was well aware of the woo-woo taboo.

Fallon was asked to review an article describing the experiment I did that tested whether pieces of chocolate "blessed" by intention would cause a mood elevation in people who ate it without knowing if the chocolate was blessed or not. As discussed in Chapter 2, the results of that study showed that people eating the blessed chocolate had a significantly positive change in mood as compared to those who ate the unblessed "control chocolate." The article was ultimately published based partially on Fallon's recommendation.[24] I knew Jim Fallon because at that time we were both members of a discussion group that had been meeting monthly for over a decade. But I had no idea that he was invited to be a referee for that paper; nor did I really know what he thought about it until he mentioned it in a foreword for a book. He wrote:

> I was asked to review a research manuscript in 2007 on the effects of "intentional foods" on mood. This was the first, and only, time until that year that I reviewed a research paper on psi. The manuscript arrived from the editor-in-chief's office, and I settled down to read it, fully prepared to toss grenades . . . and blast away at this monstrosity. . . .

I was so bucked up I had to do the first reading standing up. After the initial read, I sat down and thought about the paper for several hours. Something bothered me beyond what I had expected. So a second more thorough and responsible perusal was in order. Then, after a night of sleeping on it . . . a third quiet careful reading followed the next day. And I took notes, and read the referenced articles. And checked a statistics manual. And so on. Finally, after a fifth read I had to take a knee.

What became annoyingly clear . . . is that the authors had followed, and gone beyond, what I was used to reading. And not only mainstream neuroscience articles ultimately published in rigorous journals, but also articles published in the top four science/medical journals. In spite of the rigor of the manuscript, I gave it only a tepid "accept" to the editor, not because I believed in the reported effect—after all, it couldn't be true—but because structurally, the methods were sound, and the statistics, derived double blind, were solid.[25]

Other scientists, when faced with incredible results, dream up imaginary flaws to reduce their discomfort, but Fallon worked through his incredulity, which allowed him to reach a positive conclusion. He added:

What stunned me and made me shift uncomfortably in my chair was that these psi researchers were doing it better than most of my mainstream colleagues in their publications and grants. Virtually every scientist I have ever met has a recurring story—that they or someone close to them have experienced the seemingly impossible. . . . Many will tell you that (1) we actually know little of the fundamental structure of reality, (2) we know very little of the basis of broadly accepted experiences, and (3) that even though we think that something like psi may actually exist, *we would never admit it outside of a happy hour where no other scientists are present.*

No Really, They Flew

In a scholarly book reviewing the history of Catholic saints who were said to have levitated or bilocated (that is, witnesses reported seeing them in two or more locations at the same time, separated by far distances), the author, Carlos Eire, a prominent historian of religion, acknowledged the taboo as follows:

> To write a history of the impossible is risky for any scholar nowadays, especially if one suggests, even tentatively, that the assumed impossibility of certain events deserves closer scrutiny. . . . Counterintuitive as this might seem—given that the impossibility of certain events is deemed unquestionable in our dominant culture and that dogmatic materialists tend to think of themselves as the only truly objective skeptics—this sort of nonconformist skepticism is necessary if one is to claim any kind of genuine objectivity.[26]

After reviewing dozens of historical cases in detail, Eire concluded:

> Levitation and bilocation accounts are as hard to dismiss as to prove true. . . . Moreover, these accounts do more than raise significant questions. They also reveal the *power of belief* to shape mentalities and the *power of social facts* to shape thought and behavior or to determine the limits we place on what might be possible. (emphasis added)

Eire then commented on the reluctance of scholars to even hint that they are interested in these phenomena by reproducing an observation by the historian of religion Jeffrey Kripal:

> I cannot tell you how many times I have heard an otherwise admired colleague say something like, "Well, it does not really

matter if Joseph of Cupertino flew up into the tree after a scream, or if Teresa of Avila floated off the floor as her sisters piled on top of her to avoid a social embarrassment. What matters is how the popular belief in such presumed levitations was disciplined, controlled, and maintained by the church and later constructed as sanctity and as a saint."

This is how truly mind-boggling historical events, reported by hundreds of credible witnesses, are discussed by anthropologists, scholars of religion, and psychologists. It's okay to discuss magical beliefs in distant, rational terms of what those silly medieval people believed. It is not acceptable to suggest that those events might have been real. Eire continued with Kripal's comment:

A super-pious Italian man ecstatically flies into a tree and has to be retrieved with a ladder, or a raptured Spanish nun cannot keep herself on the floor in front of some visiting noblewomen, and these physical events do not matter to you? Uh, excuse me, if either of those things actually happened (and our historical records suggest strongly that they did), such anomalous events change pretty much everything we thought we knew about human consciousness and its relationship to physics, gravity, and material reality. Either [one of these events] would fundamentally change our entire order of knowledge. And you don't care? Don't you find that disinterest just a little bit perverse?[27]

More than a little perverse. Some of the smartest people go into apoplectic denials when faced with well-documented historical cases and contemporary laboratory evidence that contradicts their beliefs. That this happens is not surprising because all of us tend to identify with our ideas and beliefs. If someone challenges those beliefs, it feels like a physical attack. Our defenses go into high gear, so we lash out first and ask questions later.

It Cannot Be, So It Isn't

Two articles on psi phenomena were recently published in *American Psychologist*, the flagship journal of the American Psychological Association. The author was Lund University psychologist Etzel Cardeña, and the first article appeared in 2018. That paper is one of the most-read articles among the millions tracked by a company that does that sort of thing. Here's the entire abstract of the article:

Throughout history, people have reported events that seem to violate the common sense view of space and time. Some psychologists have been at the forefront of investigating these phenomena with sophisticated research protocols and theory, while others have devoted much of their careers to criticizing the field. Both stances can be explained by psychologists' expertise on relevant processes such as perception, memory, belief, and conscious and nonconscious processes. This article clarifies the domain of psi, summarizes recent theories from physics and psychology that present psi phenomena as at least plausible, and then provides an overview of recent/updated meta-analyses.

The evidence provides cumulative support for the reality of psi, which cannot be readily explained away by the quality of the studies, fraud, selective reporting, experimental or analytical incompetence, or other frequent criticisms. The evidence for psi is comparable to that for established phenomena in psychology and other disciplines, although there is no consensual understanding of them. The article concludes with recommendations for further progress in the field including the use of project and data repositories, conducting multidisciplinary studies with enough power, developing further nonconscious measures of psi and falsifiable theories, analyzing the characteristics of successful sessions and participants, improving the ecological validity of studies, testing how to increase effect sizes, recruiting more researchers at least open to the possibility of psi, and situating psi phenomena within larger domains such as the study of consciousness.[28]

Now here's the abstract of a response to that article, written by two retired professors of psychology, Arthur Reber and James Alcock, and published in the same journal one year later:

Recently, *American Psychologist* published a review of the evidence for parapsychology that supported the general claims of psi (the umbrella term often used for anomalous or paranormal phenomena). We present an opposing perspective and a broad-based critique of the entire parapsychology enterprise. *Our position is straightforward. Claims made by parapsychologists cannot be true. The effects reported can have no ontological status; the data have no existential value.* We examine a variety of reasons for this conclusion based on well understood scientific principles. In the classic English adynaton, "pigs cannot fly." Hence, data that suggest that they can are necessarily flawed and result from weak methodology or improper data analyses or are Type I errors. So it must be with psi effects. What we find particularly intriguing is that, *despite the existential impossibility of psi phenomena* and the nearly 150 years of efforts during which there has been, literally, no progress, there are still scientists who continue to embrace the pursuit. (emphasis added)[29]

I was pleased to see the first article published in such an august, top-tier academic journal. My reaction to the second paper was astonishment that any editor of a scientific journal would have considered publishing it. After all, the authors didn't even bother to debate the evidence. They just ignored it and declared that the results of over a thousand published experiments in peer-reviewed journals were impossible. That's the equivalent of an adolescent schoolyard taunt. It's not a valid scientific argument.

Magic Is WEIRD

Most Americans believe in one or more aspects of the paranormal. One of the highest categories of belief is psi phenomena.[30] These beliefs have been stable for many decades and are reflected by psi themes in innumerable TV shows and feature films.[31] The academic world pays very close attention to popular culture. Does it also pay attention to the possibility that psi and magic might actually exist?

In a word, no.

At least not among WEIRD populations, an acronym used in sociology that means Western Educated Industrialized Rich and Democratic. Among WEIRD cultures, which attract most of the attention of psychologists and sociologists, paranormal beliefs are referred to with the highly sophisticated technical term "pseudo-profound bullshit."[32] That slur virtually guarantees that academics, regardless of what they may personally believe, can never safely or publicly endorse the reality of anything regarded as paranormal if they'd like to retain their jobs.

Academic avoidance of such malodorous topics can be demonstrated by noting that there are only two accredited universities in the entire world, among fifteen thousand institutions of higher learning, that have the word *parapsychology* in the name of one of its departments or is explicitly named as a topic one can concentrate on. One is in India (Andhra University), which is very much not WEIRD. The other is in California, which arguably is indeed WEIRD. Another forty or so universities have at least one faculty member known for having serious interests in psi research.[33] What this sorry statistic means is that despite perpetual fascination by billions of people, psi *as real* is willfully ignored by over 99 percent of the academic and scientific world.[34]

When it comes to the study of magic, or at least magical lore, the situation is somewhat different. As of 2024, the University of South Carolina in the United States and Exeter University in the United Kingdom offered advanced (and accredited) degrees in magical studies.[35] The department of religious studies at the University of California at Santa Barbara and the department of religion at Rice University offered courses with a focus on Gnosticism, Hermeticism, and other esoteric traditions, as did departments at Arizona State University, the Divinity Schools at Yale and Harvard, the University of Amsterdam, the University of Sydney, the University of Gothenburg, the University of Warsaw, the University of Helsinki, and on and on. These programs, as well as many others, reflect growing academic and popular interest in esotericism, which includes the study of magical practices.[36]

It's fine to study esoteric ideas from a historical perspective. But even a cursory survey finds hundreds of journal articles on mistaken *beliefs* in the paranormal. Analysis of those articles indicate that psychologists, anthropologists, and religious scholars focus on why modern peoples believe in preposterous things like magic and psi.

The problem is the term *paranormal*. That word is far too vague because some experiences labeled paranormal are perfectly amenable to controlled scientific investigation. That includes nearly all types of psi experiences, and because of the psi-magic overlap, it also includes all sorts of magical experiences.[37] In addition, because beliefs are closely correlated with personal experiences,[38] widespread belief in psi and magic may be due not to cognitive deficits or wishful thinking but rather to firsthand experience. After all, cultures other than WEIRD have very different levels of acceptance of psi and magic, and in those cultures beliefs in these topics are considered ho-hum normal, not pathological.

Some may object that relying on personal experiences as a form of evidence is invalid because we are all subject to frailties of memory and perception. That's true, and yet our personal experiences will always be the strongest reason we have to believe in anything. Everything else we believe is based on trusting those we perceive to be authorities.

Another objection is that most people are not trained to assess the actual likelihood of coincidences or other factors that might appear to be psychic.[39] That's also true, but those biases are taken into account in laboratory studies that are designed to investigate psi, and when such frailties and biases are excluded, positive evidence remains.

At one time it was considered an "ontological confusion" to believe that properties of the physical world would be affected simply by looking at them. That phrase, by the way, is a fancy term that allows a professor to call a naïve student's scatterbrained beliefs bullshit, but without being so vulgar. Part of the present ontological confusion is related to the idea that if you don't look at the moon, it's no longer there. That's why playing peek-a-boo with babies and dogs is fun. They're easily confused about the true nature of reality. And as it turns out, most adults share those same confusions.

The thing is, after quantum mechanics, we know that the world "out there" *does not exist* completely independently of observation.[40] To be more precise, the elementary properties of an object, like its mass, spin, momentum, and so on, are not strictly defined before an object is observed. That sounds crazy, but at the scale of the micro-world, experiments definitively show that it's true. In any case, it means that this particular ontological confusion—that the world exists independent of our observations—turns out to be false. It was the professors who were confused, not the babies and dogs.

In fact, all sorts of ontological beliefs once taken for granted are now being reexamined by leading scientists who are questioning the assumption that brain activity *causes* consciousness. Instead, as we'll discuss in more detail later, we are now awash in other philosophical ideas, like *panpsychism* (everything including subatomic matter has bits of consciousness in it), *dual-aspect monism* (mind and matter both emerge from something even more fundamental), and *idealism* (all is mind).[41]

Likewise, UFOs and ETs, once reliable inhabitants of the paranormal, have become reframed as UAPs due to credible reports that governments around the world have known for decades that there are strange things flying in our skies and our oceans.[42] In many other historical examples, repeatedly reported phenomena that were once considered anomalous or paranormal because they violated expectations about what was possible were eventually accepted as genuine, like meteorites and ball lightning.

Incidentally, some may imagine that psi researchers are "believers," and as such they're insufficiently skeptical to conduct trustworthy science. But studies of the cognitive styles of those who are actively engaged in psi research have shown that psi researchers are actually much more similar to inveterate skeptics than to lay believers.[43] This is worth highlighting because it counters another false meme about psi research—that only believers get positive evidence. Not so. The primary difference between skeptics who proudly wear a flaming S on their shirts and psi researchers is that the latter actually do research, whereas the former just complain about it.

DISENCHANTMENT: MAGIC SUPPRESSED

I shall not commit the fashionable stupidity of regarding everything I cannot explain as a fraud.

—CARL JUNG

Where did the woo-woo taboo come from in the first place?

When the historical period known as the Enlightenment was beginning to form in the sixteenth century, Martin Luther and John Calvin sparked the Protestant Reformation in response to the corruptions of the Catholic Church. One of the core principles of Protestantism included the rejection of supernatural rituals, the veneration of saints, and miraculous powers.

Strike one against magic.

Around the same time, the founders of modern science, including Francis Bacon, believed that commonly reported experiences like ghosts and mind-matter interactions were facts of the natural world, not the supernatural. And Galileo argued in his 1623 essay *The Assayer* that to advance science, one must rely only on "principal" factors, by which he meant objective, measurable facts. "Secondary" subjective factors, including conscious experience, should be set aside as unreliable.

Galileo linked science with the objective world to avoid conflicting with key elements of the Catholic Church's doctrine, as specified in its *Index Librorum Prohibitorum,* or Index of Forbidden Books. That list was created during the church's Council of Trent by Pope Paul IV in 1559, when Galileo was five years old. Some fifty-four years later, when he wrote *The Assayer,* the church's stranglehold over "acceptable" knowledge was still absolute, and it continued to constrain the development of science. The Council of Trent had declared that the church would control the "power of spirit," which in modern terms can be understood as anything to do with the mind. In that light, Galileo's definition of science was strategic to avoid the wrath of the Inquisition, but it still cost him dearly: He was held in house arrest for the rest of his life. It set the entire academic enterprise on a course that would eventually exclude consciousness from scientific inquiry.

Strike two.

As tales of apparitions, witchcraft, and magic were ejected from serious consideration, academics began to dismiss magic not merely as drivel but as dangerous nonsense.[44] Years later, as the fledgling discipline of psychology began to form in the nineteenth century, the influence of Galileo's mandate was still so strong that any consideration of supernatural, exceptional, or anomalous experiences was viewed as damaging to the credibility of that budding field.

Strike three.

A fourth factor that arguably accelerated the rise of science and began to seriously challenge the authority of religion was the Black Plague, which ravaged Europe in the mid-fourteenth century.[45] An estimated 75 to 200 million people died from the plague, ranking it among the worst catastrophes in history. The devastation forced a reconsideration of medical practices and prioritized the development of medical science. It also raised doubts about religious authority because the church failed to protect the devout, whether poor, wealthy, noble, or royal.

Strike four. Magic, begone foul spirit!

Historians of science refer to this confluence of suppression as the *disenchantment* of modernity. That term was popularized by the German sociologist Max Weber, who argued that one of the defining features of the modern world (which at the time primarily referred to Europe), and the feature that clearly distinguished modernity from previous historical eras, was the rejection of universal belief in supernatural concepts. That led to many benefits. As psychologist Roderick Main writes in *Breaking the Spell of Disenchantment,*

> The process of purging magic from our images of God and nature can be argued to have created space for the development of more theoretical, intellectual, rational modes of thought. Over time this has led to the emergence of science with its provision of empirical explanations, effective predictions, and the ability to manipulate and control the environment. This in turn has resulted in extraordinary

advances in technology, agriculture, construction, manufacturing, transport, and communication, with vastly improved economic conditions for many, unprecedented availability of education and health care, and an overall enrichment of lifestyles.[46]

On the downside, the shift from an ancient to a modern worldview had an unintended consequence. As the modern world aggressively moved into an objective, mechanical, industrial, and scientific future, it moved away from the subjective side of reality, which included mind and magic. In the process, a nihilistic worldview emerged.

The term *nihilism* comes from the Latin word *nihil*, which means "nothing." It's the idea that life is ultimately random and meaningless. It rejects the idea that there is any purpose to anything. Instead, nihilism as a philosophy promotes the importance of maintaining freedom from any preconceived ideas about life or destiny. It is commonly associated with the German philosopher Friedrich Nietzsche, who famously wrote that "God is dead." Nietzsche meant that not in a religious sense but as a way to express what was happening to society as religious authority declined and secular ideas advanced.

As nihilism took hold, modernity did not simply reject the importance of meaning, purpose, magic, mystery, and spirituality. It actively denigrated these factors. This was a problem because, to borrow a phrase from Matthew 4:4, we do not live by bread alone. Humans are hardwired with a strong psychological need to feel a purpose for living. But the modern worldview stripped that away, leading to the discouraging phrase that captures the most that any modern person can aspire to: "He who dies with the most toys, wins." We see the effects of such emptiness in unfathomable selfishness and greed, the cavalier disregard of the environment, and rising suicide rates among the young.

Eventually, a three-part narrative emerged to reject claims about psi and magic: Dismiss anecdotal evidence as unreliable, loudly assert that experimental evidence that seems to support psi or magic is solely due to flaws or fraud, and then write off these phenomena as impossible because they supposedly violate physical laws. These are the only acceptable narratives currently allowed in articles about psi on Wikipedia. It's not easy to overcome centuries of suppression and taboo.

And it's not as though academics are oblivious to this problem. For example, a July 2024 article in *Nature,* one of the most prominent scientific journals in the world, was entitled "Neuroscientists Must Not Be Afraid to Study Religion." It expressed the problem as follows:

> Scientists interested in the brain have tended to avoid studying religion or spirituality *for fear of being seen as unscientific. That needs to change.* Despite the manifest importance of faith as an influencer of human behaviour, neuroscientists have tended to steer clear of studying how people's beliefs affect their brains and vice versa. This includes investigation of the effects of beliefs in supernatural agents or miracles, practices around worship or prayer and participation in rituals.
>
> Such avoidance probably stems in part from centuries of powerful religious institutions resisting scrutiny and interrogation. But researchers and funders are also *fearful* that any investigation of religiosity or spirituality could be seen either as promoting a particular religion, *or as flat-out unscientific.* (emphasis added)[47]

In other words, the witch-hunting Inquisition of the Middle Ages was so effective that centuries later it still strikes fear in the hearts of academics. And regarding the skeptical assertion about fraud, the fact is that there's only one well-documented case of *experimenter* fraud, and one suspected case, in the entire 150-year history of parapsychology. It is noteworthy that a leading critic of parapsychology for many decades, the psychologist Ray Hyman from the University of Oregon, called out baseless allegations of fraud about psi studies that had appeared in *Skeptical Inquirer* magazine as "a dogmatism that is immune to falsification."[48]

Another consequence of the taboo is that the histories of psi and magic are still distorted beyond recognition or are just blithely ignored. As Andreas Sommer put it:

> It is not widely known that . . . psychiatrist Hans Berger's development of the electroencephalogram (EEG) was driven by what he believed was a dramatic "crisis telepathy" experience involving his sister; mathematician Kurt Gödel became convinced of the reality of telepathy after conducting experiments with his wife; physicist Wolfgang Pauli saw a link between quantum mechanics and "poltergeist"-style mind-matter interactions; and physicist Albert Einstein expressed his conviction that telepathy "deserves the most earnest consideration, not only of the laity, but also of the psychologists by profession."[49]

In a letter to the psychologist James McKeen Cattell—known for establishing one of the first experimental psychology laboratories in the United States, at Columbia University—William James confessed, "I used to think the story of the peripatetic astronomers who wouldn't look through Galileo's telescope at Jupiter's moons (preferring aloofness coupled with authoritativeness) was a fable, but the complexion of the time gives it proof."[50]

What is fascinating about the disenchantment is that the same academic and religious skeptics who were dismissing magic as contemptible were just as disdainful about the growing reliance on the experimental sciences! As Sommer points out:

> Those who began to laugh magic and spirits out of intellectual discourse also often mocked the new scientific experimentalism

of the Royal Society as a trivial, eccentric fad, unworthy of men of culture and common sense. . . . Leading Enlightenment intellectuals did not so much debunk marvels as ignore them.

Why then, given this powerful taboo, do supernatural, magical, and religious beliefs persist into the early twenty-first century? The easy answer is that we believe in magic because life is uncertain and death is certain. That generates existential angst in any thoughtful person, which in turn forces us to adopt comforting beliefs wherever we can find them. So it is undoubtedly true that some aspects of belief in magic can be attributed to wishful thinking. Some beliefs will be mistaken or perpetuated by con artists. Some will be due to mental illness. And it is also easy to become colossally stupid by listening to endlessly repeated lies and the highly efficient brainwashing technique behind the power of propaganda. Incidentally, the modern meaning of the word *propaganda* can be traced to Pope Gregory XV, who in 1622 established propaganda as an official activity of the Catholic Church by forming the Sacred Congregation for the Propagation of the Faith.

There's another reason that belief in psi and magic has persisted despite centuries of pressure to eradicate it: Personal experiences continue to confirm their existence. That's where "reenchantment" begins.

REENCHANTMENT: MAGIC RESURRECTED

Reenchantment is not a rejection of science or its materialistic worldview. It's a more nuanced understanding of human existence, one that admits the importance of both material and mental aspects of reality. Despite a shrinking cadre of hardcore skeptics who wring their hands over others' tawdry beliefs, the fact is that modernity is becoming reenchanted.

One way to see this is through the explosion of scholarly articles on consciousness. Not long ago such articles appeared only in philosophy journals with arguments that were largely unintelligible to ordinary humans. Now, besides a rash of new journals devoted to consciousness studies, in 2024 an unusually long journal article was published by Robert Kuhn, a neurophysiologist and host of a public television program called *Closer to Truth*. His "landscape of consciousness" article was 140 pages in length, listed nearly a thousand references, and reviewed some 225 theories about consciousness. One of the categories was "anomalous and altered states," which included psi.[51]

There are also articles appearing in unexpected places that mention psi without apologizing. To give just one example, in 2023 a high-impact journal called *Technological Forecasting and Social Change* published an article entitled "Game Changers in Science and Technology." It was authored by thirty-four representatives from top-tier industrial and academic centers around the world.

The purpose of the article was to list game-changing leaps in science and technology, sorted on their expected potential to change our everyday lives, from tomorrow, to the next ten years, to thirty years and beyond.[52] Short-term future topics were predictable: gene editing, artificial intelligence, synthetic biology, and so on. For the next ten years, the authors discussed new classes of highly effective medications, "neuromorphic processors" that can effectively simulate the brain, quantum computing, nanobots, and so on. For the next thirty years, the article delves into "topics that are characterized by largely uncharted territories today but [would have] an enormous game-changing impact, even a shattering of current scientific world view." The first four sections resemble plausible science fiction scenarios. And then there's section 4.4: "Understanding If Parapsychological Effects Do Exist."

I can't overstate how important this is: a major article in a high-impact journal, forecasting future trends in science and technology, by mainstream authors, that includes psi as a target of interest in a mere three decades. That article, plus dozens of popular, scientific, and scholarly conferences on consciousness around the world, plus a growing number of centers for consciousness studies at universities and private institutions, all demonstrate how reenchantment is in the process of unfolding.

At the heart of the reenchantment is a recognition that physics can no longer ignore the role of consciousness in the physical world. Quantum physics has been a major contributor to this shift in perspective because it describes, and experimental facts confirm, that the physical world is deeply interconnected through space and time, and that "reality"—the idea that the world is completely independent of observers—seems to be intimately linked to consciousness in ways that nineteenth-century scientists couldn't have imagined. Not all physicists subscribe to this idea, but at the edge of the known, there's hardly anything that everyone agrees to. The point is that it's a concept that's now discussed seriously within physics, and contrary to the opinions of some skeptics, it's definitely not New Age flapdoodle.

Indigenous and esoteric wisdom are also being reassessed as part of the reenchantment. Many indigenous traditions are based on animism, the view that everything in the natural world is alive, and as such all creatures have a responsibility to honor and care for the planet. Taking that wisdom to heart within science may lead to new ways of observing Nature, and it may be more important than simply gaining knowledge. A case can be made that until recently the disenchanted "take no prisoners" approach to exploiting natural resources has been slowly and efficiently killing the entire planet and in the process dooming us to extinction. Continuing along that path while hoping for a different outcome is the definition of insanity, so reassessment of other worldviews is not just a nice idea, it has become an imperative.

TWO MORE CLOUDS

In 1895 the physicist and mathematician William Thomson, also known as Lord Kelvin, was president of the Royal Society, founded in 1660 as the Royal Society of London for Improving Natural Knowledge. In commenting on the possibility of flying in something other than a balloon, Lord Kelvin famously said, "Heavier-than-air flying machines are impossible." In 1902 he doubled down with "Neither the balloon, nor the aeroplane, nor the gliding machine will be a practical success."[53] In 1903 the Wright brothers flew their heavier-than-air airplane. As the saying goes, "It is difficult to make predictions, especially about the future."

In 1900 the very same Lord Kelvin gave a lecture to the Royal Society. He stated that physics was so successful that it was essentially complete, except for "two clouds."[54] The two clouds would come to be known as the "luminiferous ether" and the "ultraviolet catastrophe." The luminiferous ether was a theoretical medium proposed to explain the propagation of light through space. Scientists at the time believed that light required a medium to travel through. But no such medium could be detected. The ultraviolet catastrophe was the violation of the Rayleigh-Jeans law, which predicted that an object that was sufficiently heated would emit an infinite amount of energy at ultraviolet and shorter wavelengths. It's a good thing that "law" was wrong, because anything that emits infinite amounts of energy would melt the universe.

Both of Lord Kelvin's clouds referred to anomalies that did not fit the predominant view of what is now called classical physics. But both clouds were assumed to be problems that would eventually be mopped up by a few minor tweaks added onto existing theories.

Eight months after Lord Kelvin's statements, the German physicist Max Planck presented a crazy new idea at a meeting of the German Physical Society, held in Berlin. Planck's idea resolved the looming cloud of the ultraviolet catastrophe and in the process it founded quantum theory. Five years later Albert Einstein explained the luminiferous ether with his theory of special relativity.

These unexpected turns of events, out of many in the history of science, remind us why anomalies, those strange things that go bump in the lab, are worthy of very close attention. Sometimes those odd observations are found to be mistakes or can be explained by slightly revising existing ideas. But if they are puzzles that persist for decades or centuries, when explanations are finally discovered they can lead to startlingly new concepts that affect the course of civilization. Over the course of the twentieth century, Lord Kelvin's two clouds transformed the Western world from the industrial age into the atomic and information ages.

Today we are faced with two different but equally persistent clouds, known as qualia and quanta. *Qualia* refers to first-person subjective experience, and *quanta* refers to quantum objects' mysterious sensitivity to being observed. Interestingly, both clouds raise major questions about the role that consciousness plays in the physical world. As such, both clouds present immense challenges to the prevailing scientific worldview. That's because until very recently many scientists, especially physicists, have taken it for granted that consciousness plays no role in physics at all. That assumption was a powerful and persistent consequence of the disenchantment.

The two clouds associated with qualia and quanta also persist because there are still a few philosophers and neuroscientists who insist that qualia is not a problem because consciousness doesn't exist. They claim that the subjective mental world is an illusory side effect of brain activity.[55] That's another holdover of the disenchantment. Still others propose that any sufficiently complex physical system, presumably even a bunch of tin cans connected by pieces of string, could in principle develop conscious awareness. So consciousness is nothing special.[56] And some physicists believe that the quantum observer effect is not mysterious at all, because what looks like an observer is really just quanta interacting with other quanta.[57]

My sense about this ongoing debate is that quanta and qualia are red flags that are frantically waving. They're trying to tell us that existing theories are wrong, and that radical change is necessary. Instead of viewing these two clouds as wispy puffs that will eventually evaporate, I see them as presaging a paradigmatic thunderstorm. That's because the two clouds aren't the only challenges. There are many more on the horizon. They include the phenomena of genius, savants, near-death experiences, mediumship, cases of reincarnation, psi phenomena, and yes, magic.[58] These phenomena are stretching the "you are your brain" explanation to the breaking point.

CHAPTER 6

THEORIES OF MAGIC

Anyone who says I'm a mystic is an idiot.

—CARL JUNG

Esoteric traditions and religious texts have much to say about magic, but those explanations are typically expressed in supernatural, spiritual, or prescientific concepts. Modern magicians tend to focus on the pragmatics of what works, and some point to elements of quantum theory as supportive of magical ideas. Scientists have proposed five classes of theories to explain psi phenomena, which can just as easily be used to explain magic.

MAGICAL THEORIES ABOUT MAGIC

Gerhard Mayer is a psychologist at the Institute for Frontier Areas of Psychology and Mental Health, a major psi research organization in Freiburg, Germany. In studying the theories and practices of modern magicians, Mayer found that when it comes to enchantment, experienced magicians believe there are four key elements that lead to success: *motivation, connection, belief,* and *effortless striving.*[1] I would add three more: focused *intention, clarity,* and achieving the state of *gnosis.* Let's examine each of these in more detail.

- **Motivation:** You must have an intense emotional need for the outcome of the magical act. It is useful to make a distinction between *want* and *need*.[2] At times, we all would like to have a shiny new object or a fun experience, but such *wants* are not essential for basic survival. By contrast, we *need* food and shelter, and that's the type of powerful motivation that drives magical success. With practice, you can cultivate this type of strong motivation even without the immediate urgency of food and shelter.

- **Connection:** Maintaining an empathic relationship, or the ability to intimately identify with the goal, improves magical success. If that goal seems too abstract or difficult to imagine, clarify it to create greater harmony with the desired outcome.

- **Belief:** You should have no doubt about the effectiveness of a magical act. Before and after performing magic, you can be as skeptical as you like. But during the practice itself, belief must be absolute.

- **Effortless striving:** Extreme motivation must be applied, but without any effort. This paradoxical state is similar to states of deep meditation, where high mental focus and dissociation from the ego go hand in hand. As Gerhard Mayer writes, "In Chinese Daoism, this concept is called Wu Wei. This attitude means not to be attached to the action and also not to the result, but on the other hand also not to lose sight of it."[3] As it says in the ancient Chinese classic *The Secret of the Golden Flower*, "The essence of the great Way is to act purposefully without striving."[4]

- **Intention:** Any magical act involves a goal or desire. It might be to influence something in the physical world, as in enchantment, or to gain knowledge, as in divination.

Whatever the goal may be, it requires tightly focused attention narrowed with a specific intention. How long you should hold that focus is not as important as its clarity and intensity. The primary challenge in holding attention, even for short periods, is mind-wandering or external distractions.

- **Clarity:** What happens as a result of a magical act depends on the clarity of the intention. Performing an enchantment to win a lottery is a clear goal, but a better purpose would be to specify why you want to win. What would you do with that money? This is important to clarify because winning any reasonably large lottery is unlikely, even with a magical boost. But if the reason underlying your desire is that you need a more reliable car to get to work, then that's a much better goal because there are many more ways that could potentially happen than winning a lottery. Gaining clarity helps optimize the likelihood that your desire can manifest, or manifest within a time span that would be useful.

- **Gnosis:** Magic, like psi, is primarily effective in a nonordinary state of awareness. This includes meditation, chanting, rituals, trance, dreaming, dancing, drumming, extreme physical activity, psychedelic states, and so on. For a fledgling magician, achieving these states at will may take disciplined practice for months or years. At advanced stages, after you learn to recognize the difference between ordinary and nonordinary states, especially states *that work for you*, then it can become relatively easy for you to drop into or out of an optimal state.

On the flip side, magical efficacy is reduced by five elements: *mistakes, mind-wandering, attachment, fear,* and *self-deception*:

- **Mistakes:** If you had a plan for the magical act, whatever that may be, or if you wished to follow a certain ritual and it didn't go well, that could introduce doubt about its success, which would in turn reduce the efficacy of the act.
- **Mind-wandering:** Mind-wandering is a lack of focused concentration, and magic is ultimately a mental act. If the mind wanders or is too easily distracted, that can reduce the likelihood of success.
- **Attachment:** Overly strong desire blocks success. If effortless striving becomes effortful, pushy, or struggling, that will limit the outcome.
- **Fear:** Anxiety about the result of the magical act, or concerns about possible side effects, encourages distraction. Such concerns, including doubt, can be contemplated before and after the magical act, but not during it.
- **Self-deception:** If the goal of a magical operation violates your true nature, or it's in conflict with what you truly believe to be right and proper, that will reduce, eliminate, or even reverse the intended magical outcome.

Magical Formulas

Mayer noted that Frater U.D., the magical moniker of the German magician Ralph Tegtmeier, proposed a simple formula to further define a magical act: magical act = will + imagination + gnosis.[5] A more complex formula was proposed by the chaos magician Peter J. Carroll in *Liber Kaos*.[6] Carroll proposed two equations of magic, derived from experience, which he described as a way to calculate the likelihood of a successful enchantment or divination:

$$P_m = P + (1-P) \times M^{1/P}$$
$$M = G \times L \times (1-A) \times (1-R)$$

The P in the first equation is the probability of achieving a desired outcome purely by chance, and the M is what Carroll calls the *magic factor*. The second equation, which defines M, has in turn four factors: G is *gnosis*, L is the *magical link*, A is *conscious awareness*, and R is *subconscious resistance*. The magical link L refers to the clarity of one's association with the target of the magical act. That is, the magician must be able to imagine or feel a connection to the target, otherwise the likelihood of success decreases. The variables *conscious awareness* (A) and *subconscious resistance* (R) both act to reduce the effectiveness of magic.

Carroll explains, "Much of the paraphernalia and theory of magic, including [my own] theory, exist partly to convince the magician that he or she is a magician, and magic is possible in a cultural climate that is heavily antagonistic to such notions." In other words, maintaining strong belief and motivation, however that is achieved, is essential for enhancing magical efficacy because they directly influence all the other factors.

Each factor in Carroll's equations ranges on a scale from 0 to 1, including the magic factor. Based on these equations, we see that factors G, L, A, and R must all be close to 1, or the magical act is unlikely to be effective. For example, if all factors are 0.5, then the overall magic factor M will be 0.0625. Plugging that into the probability equation P_m, you will find that the overall probability of success will be extremely low, because whatever the probability of the desired outcome was (factor P), it will be multiplied by a very small number.

If it were possible to raise the magic factor M to 1, then P_m would also equal 1. In that case, according to Carroll's set of equations, magic can achieve literally anything imaginable. Of course, it is not so easy to produce a 1 on any of these factors, to say nothing of all of them. But occasionally, when everything is perfectly aligned, then in principle, according to Carroll, some very strange things could happen.

Traditional Laws of Magic

The traditional laws of magic were based on esoteric beliefs about the nature of reality. Some of those beliefs were based on experience and others on assumptions about the nature of the supernatural.[7] I'll describe four of the most important laws.

One of the core principles is the Law of Knowledge, also called the Law of Names. As the magician Isaac Bonewits put it, "If you know all there is to know about something, then you have absolute and total control over it."[8] This law is tantalizingly similar to the quantum observer effect, because both concepts rely on the amount of knowledge one can gain. In other words, from both a magical and a modern physics perspective, knowledge is power to shape reality.

The Law of Similarity, or "like produces like," means that one can influence an object or event by using something that resembles it. This is the basis of practices like voodoo and to some extent homeopathy. In a cartoon sense, if you want to make a broom fly, you could put bird feathers on it and wave it around. A variation of this law is also found in mainstream medicine. For example, a large dose of digitalis, a compound derived from the foxglove plant, can kill you. But in small doses, it is an effective treatment for congestive heart failure and atrial arrhythmias. The same principle underlies the use of vaccines. A dose of the vaccine Ervebo, which is derived from the Ebola virus, will protect you from getting Ebola.

The Law of Contagion means that objects that have been in contact with each other continue to influence each other after separation. The similarity to quantum entanglement is clear, and demonstration of that effect won the 2022 Nobel Prize in physics. This effect is also found to inflate the price of buildings with historical markers of notable men and women who lived there.[9] That's considered a form of "magical thinking," a phrase that in academia carries a negative connotation, but behaviors based on the Law of

Contagion are nevertheless found universally in both children and adults.[10]

The Law of Correspondence, or "as above, so below," is the idea underlying astrology, that the location of the planets correspond to human personalities and affairs. It may also be related to recent findings that the structure of the universe and the structure of neurons in the human brain share remarkable similarities.[11]

WORLDVIEWS

All of physics is either impossible or trivial. It is impossible until you understand it and then it becomes trivial.

—ERNEST RUTHERFORD

Before we look at scientific theories about magic, to better appreciate the direction that science is headed, and why it's increasingly compatible with an understanding of magic, it's useful to discuss the assumptions underlying the scientific worldview. This is not as onerous as it may sound, so bear with me.

Materialism, the idea that everything is made of matter and energy, has been the guiding assumption in science for the last few centuries. It's been immensely successful in explaining many aspects of the physical world. But it cannot provide an explanation of conscious experience because it focuses exclusively on what might be called "physics from the outside"—that is, things that everyone can observe given the right tools, like microscopes or telescopes. What materialism doesn't address is "physics from the inside," meaning what it is like *to be you*, your personal awareness and *experience*.

Like all scientific disciplines, the neurosciences developed under the assumption that materialism was the best way to think about the nature of reality. This led to the dogma that tells you that you are literally your brain, that we're all ultimately just a pack of neurons, or moist robots, or machines made of meat.[12] The proof of the pudding offered to support this dogma is based on the *neural correlates* of consciousness, or the observable relationships between brain activity and both conscious and unconscious mental behavior. Neural correlates are so robust that they've become the basis of brain-computer interface developments like Neuralink, variations of which are sometimes called "synthetic" or "artificial telepathy."[13]

The sticking point is the word *correlation*.

As every statistician will remind you, correlation does not imply causation. Some flowers turn their face toward the sun as the sun moves across the sky during the day, so the flower-sun correlation is clear. But that doesn't mean that the flower *causes* the sun to move in the sky. Given that the sun is really big, and the flower is really small, and the Earth is rotating in space, it is likely that the sun causes the flower to move. Notice I didn't say the sun *definitely causes* the flower to move. I said it was likely. Establishing proof of causation is not always as easy as it may seem. In this example, the reason some flowers point toward the sun seems reasonably certain, but in less obvious or more complex circumstances, it is not so clear.

Several billion dollars have been spent on research programs aimed at tracing all the electrochemical signals and mapping all the neural networks in the brain. The idea was that once we were able to create a model of a fully digitized brain, down to the molecular level, then we'd understand everything there was to know about the brain, including our own consciousness. Those projects have produced some pretty pictures of the brain, but someone must have forgotten to tell the funders that an *external* map of the brain—what we can objectively observe with our instruments—tells us nothing about what it is like to have subjective experiences *from the inside*. As the philosopher Jerry Fodor put it in 1992, and his comment still rings true today, "Nobody has the slightest idea how anything *material* [like the brain] could be conscious. Nobody even knows what it would be like to have the slightest idea about how anything material could be conscious."[14]

Once that limitation is appreciated, we are motivated to consider other assumptions, like *dualism*, the philosophy that mind and matter are different "substances," one internal and the other external. We know that mind and matter interact because if you chug a case of wine, or you drink five energy drinks in a row, there's no question that both your mental and physical states will change in predictable ways. But how can two profoundly different aspects of reality—mind and matter—interact? If they do interact, then they couldn't be all that different in the first place. So dualism, while appealing at first glance, has a problem.

An alternative is *panpsychism*, which proposes that consciousness is just part of the fabric of reality, present at all levels of existence, including atoms, electrons, and subatomic particles. This idea leads to a universe permeated with consciousness. One of the conceptual problems with panpsychism is the combination problem, or how endless numbers of elementary "particles" of consciousness can combine to form "larger," uniform types of consciousness. That is, we experience a single awareness, not billions of pieces of tiny awarenesses. Panpsychism also raises the possibility that inanimate objects like rocks, as well as simple living systems like insects, worms, and plants, are conscious.

While *panpsychism* was once dismissed as a throwback to the ancient idea of *animism* (everything is alive), there is a growing consensus among biologists and philosophers that all living systems are indeed conscious, including octopuses, crustaceans, fish, insects, and even plants.[15] Now we can't even be vegetarians or vegans without feeling guilty. The only things remaining to eat are air and sunlight, which is what "breatharians" claim to consume.

Let's take a short diversion to briefly review claims that it's possible to live for extended periods of time without food or water. Note that this is not about fasting for a while—this is about consuming *nothing* for months or years without dying.

The idea that one can live perfectly well without food and water, also called *inedia*, might seem so ridiculous that we could just reject it out of hand. But serious studies of this phenomenon give reason to pause. Some contemporary cases of inedia were found to be due to delusion or outright fraud. But not all of them. A skeptical examination of thirty-eight modern claimants found that eleven cases were considered sufficiently anomalous to justify further investigation. Nine of those cases involved continual monitoring that confirmed no food or fluid had been consumed over a range of 14 to 68 days, and in two cases food but not water was deprived for 365 and 411 days. Fraud was ultimately established in ten of the thirty-eight cases, where the methods of deception were described as "creative,"[16] like hiding a candy bar in your shorts. But that left twenty-eight puzzling cases.

There are also intriguing historical cases, like that of Alexandrina Maria da Costa (1904–55).[17] This Portuguese woman was said to have survived for *thirteen years* nourished only by a Eucharist Communion wafer, received once a day. To test her claims, from June 10 to July 20, 1943, she was monitored around the clock in a hospital room without access to food or drink, subsisting entirely on a daily Communion wafer for a total of thirty-eight days. By the end of that period, the two skeptical physicians who had closely supervised the investigation attested that her claims were true.[18]

Returning to philosophy, as panpsychism begins to look more plausible, what's next? "Shy" photons? "Thoughtful" electrons? Such ideas were once considered unspeakable by scientists, but they are becoming acceptable and materialism as the only imaginable scientific worldview is fading fast. If panpsychism seems a bridge too far, a more digestible alternative may be *dual-aspect monism*.

Dual-Aspect Monism

Dual-aspect monism proposes that mind and matter are *epistemic* aspects of an underlying holistic realm, out of which mind and matter arise.[19] The word *epistemic*, from the Greek term *epistamai*, refers to what can be known.

A philosophy similar to dual-aspect monism is called *neutral monism*. It too assumes that mind and matter are part of a more fundamental "psychophysical" realm, but unlike dual-aspect monism, it assumes that mind and matter are *ontic*, referring to what actually exists, from the Greek word *on*, meaning "being."

The epistemic versus ontic distinction is important because anyone can propose the true nature of reality (the ontic side). But given that our perceptions are only a tiny slice of reality, the best we can actually do is gain bits of knowledge (the epistemic side) about reality through our experience.

For example, every second about 10 billion bits of "raw" information go into your eye and land on the retina.[20] Of them, about 6 million bits per second pass through the optic nerve, and about 10,000 bits per second end up in the brain's visual cortex. From that, we are consciously aware of about 100 bits per second. This means that what we consciously see is about one hundred-millionth of the information entering our eyes, and so what we perceive is an enormously simplified brain-mediated construction, like a cartoon. This is why eyewitness testimony may be useful in court cases, but only when there's no other available evidence.

The other senses also heavily compress raw sensory input into a tiny conscious trickle. This means that our best understanding of "reality" is a crude model at best, like a paper map of a large geological area. It's easy to forget that the map is not the territory, just as our most precise scientific models, including quantum theory, are at best epistemic and not ontic.

Returning to dual-aspect monism, the psychiatrist Carl Jung called the primordial, fully interconnected holistic realm the *unus mundus*, or "one world."[21] This concept, of an underlying unity from which aspects like mind and matter emerge, is found throughout the world's esoteric traditions and in descriptions of mystical experiences. It also permeates philosophy, science, mathematics, and cosmology.[22]

The *unus mundus* is said to split into aspects of the world that we can experience because of meaning. That in turn posits a special kind of relationship between mind and matter. The word *meaning* here refers to a felt sense of special significance related to a symbol or a word. In the present context, meaning may be thought of as a mediator, or connector, between subjective mental experiences and the objective physical world. That is, meaning is a mind-matter *relationship*. Under certain circumstances, when this relationship is especially vibrant or imbued with unusually intense need, the correlation between mind and matter becomes tightly bound, like two sides of the same coin. This is straight-up philosophy, but it's starting to sound a lot like magic.

For example, consider the correlation between sales of ice cream and instances of near-drowning in public pools. Over time, these two variables will be seen to closely correlate because both events tend to occur more in the summer than in the winter. But increased sales of ice cream do not *cause* more near-drownings; nor do more near-drownings *cause* increased sales of ice cream. The correlation is purely a relationship that arises out of something common to both factors (the summer heat).

To appreciate why dual-aspect monism is an appealing philosophy for understanding magic, consider synchronicities.[23] These are *meaningful* correlations between the mental and material worlds. A mundane explanation for synchronicities is that with 8 billion people in the world having perhaps a thousand unique experiences per day, some of the resulting 8 trillion experiences will include remarkable coincidences purely by chance. From the perspective of an individual who experiences one of those coincidences, it might seem exceedingly unlikely to be due just to chance, so whatever that coincidence was, it *must* be meaningful. However, when dealing with such a large sample size, even a one-in-a-billion outcome would be consistent with pure chance. Someone will always win a lottery by dumb luck. Still, sometimes coincidental events are so awe-inspiring, and seem so unlikely to occur by chance, that tales will be collected and inter-preted as evidence of some influence from beyond, often cast in terms of spiritual or divine guidance.[24]

To test if pure chance is the only possible explanation for syn-chronicities, since the 1930s researchers have conducted mind-matter experiments in the laboratory where chance outcomes are known in advance. Experiments using tossed dice, true random number genera-tors, and dozens of other physical targets, as discussed in Chapter 2, all indicate that mind can indeed influence matter beyond chance.[25] This means that some synchronicities are real in the sense that mind, matter, and meaning can coalesce into remarkable "planned coinci-dences."

The strength of dual-aspect monism, endorsed by renowned physi-cists like Wolfgang Pauli, Arthur Eddington, John Wheeler, David Bohm, and many others, is that it offers a satisfying framework for understanding psi and magic. Consider an experiment seeking to demonstrate, say, a telepathic connection between an isolated pair of people. If the person assigned as the telepathic receiver successfully describes a randomly selected image that a distant person is attempt-ing to mentally send, then that outcome is considered a meaningful "hit" rather than mere coincidence because the experimental proto-col *assigned meaning* to that particular outcome and context. In this way, an experimental protocol can be understood as transforming an otherwise pure chance event into a meaningful event. Based on many observations of correlations between what a sender sends and a re-ceiver receives, we can gain increasingly higher degrees of confidence in the existence of telepathy.

In this way, the substantial body of evidence that supports the exis-tence of psi, whether observed in the lab or experienced spontane-ously, may be understood as synchronicities, and laboratory studies as a form of "evoked" or designed synchronicities. Psi experiments are persuasive to those who appreciate research methodologies and statistical methods, but to fully grasp their importance, there are also real-world synchronicities that are so outrageously unlikely that they feel a lot like magic. I have experienced several such synchronicities.

Synchronicities

I described one of these events in a previous book, but it's worth retelling because it's a good illustration of the power of intention to create synchronicities. After this episode occurred, I knew it was so strange that my memory of it might become distorted with time. So I wrote it down while the experience was still fresh to get the facts right.

It began in 2000, when I was setting up a new psi research organization with several colleagues. We called it the Boundary Institute. After looking for a suitable office, we eventually settled on a space in a quiet office park in Los Altos, California, a suburb of Silicon Valley. About a month after moving in, I noticed a sign on an office around the corner from our location with the name tag PSIQUEST, INC. We all thought that was a funny coincidence, because obviously our understanding of psi and whatever that company's use of that term was could not be the same thing. We were confident about this because serious psi research is a tiny discipline, with no more than fifty people actively working on it full time, and just a handful of organizations dedicated to psi research worldwide. We personally knew nearly everyone in the field. So we thought.

The second synchronicity was that a few weeks later, I walked toward our office from a direction I hadn't taken before. As I approached the entrance, I passed the office adjacent to ours and saw a little sign. It read PSIQUEST RESEARCH LABS. Now, this was more interesting, because whatever that PsiQuest company was doing, it had a research lab. But again, we thought it was undoubtedly something like "personnel services lab." Why a personnel services company would need a laboratory was beyond us, but we all had a big laugh about it.

Still, with my curiosity now piqued, I knocked on the door of the PSIQUEST RESEARCH LABS to introduce myself. No answer. For the next week I checked every day, sometimes several times a day. Finally, someone was there. A man opened the door, looked at me, blinked a few times, and his jaw dropped. He had such a shocked expression on his face that I didn't know what to think. I cautiously said, "Hello, I wanted to introduce myself. I'm your neighbor next door. My name is . . ." But before I could finish, he managed to croak: "Dean Radin?"

I hesitated. "Yes," I replied cautiously, wondering how he knew who I was. He said nothing and just continued to stare at me. After an uncomfortable pause, I said, "I'm your neighbor next door. I just wanted to introduce myself and see what kind of work you do here."

After a long moment the man replied, "I'm doing what you're doing." Confused, I asked, "What do you think I'm doing?" He replied, "Psi research . . . parapsychology."

Now it was my turn to stare, dumbfounded. Unbeknownst to me or to any of my colleagues, here was an unknown lab engaged in psi research, *located next door to our new office.*

The third synchronicity was that the president of PsiQuest, Jon K., was not only thoroughly familiar with psi research but was at that very moment engaging *in a magical practice* to manifest me. Jon was practicing a variation of Yoga Nidra, a Tibetan dream yoga technique that involves alternating three-hour periods of sleeping and waking, repeated over the course of twenty-four hours. During the waking periods, he was intensely wishing for a sign that his business was on the right track. One of those signs was for me to contact him, somehow, so I could join his board of directors. But he had no idea where I was or how to contact me. In fact, hardly anyone at the time knew that I was living in Silicon Valley, even fewer knew that I had co-founded a new institute, and fewer still knew where it was located.

This is why when I opened the door to Jon's lab, he was speechless.

He couldn't tell if he was awake or still dreaming. From his perspective, my appearance on his doorstep was literally an act of manifestation magic. When he was able to tell me what was going on, I too felt seriously disoriented. We both had to sit down, our heads spinning.

The fourth synchronicity is that the month before all this unfolded, I was focused on visualizing what our new offices and laboratory space should look like. I was drawing sketches of my ideal lab configuration on a whiteboard in my office and imagining a certain kind of reclining leather chair, an electromagnetically shielded room, and other types of equipment that would be useful to have in the lab. I knew all this would be expensive, and our budget was limited, so I figured we wouldn't be able to afford much of it in the short term. But that didn't stop me from visualizing what I needed.

Returning to the story, after recovering from the shock of our meeting, Jon invited me to tour the rest of his facility. As we moved from one room to the next, I could hardly believe my eyes. Jon had the reclining leather chair, the shielded chamber, and all of the other pieces of laboratory equipment I had been actively imagining. And all of it was located *on the other side of the wall* from my desk, no more than six feet from where I had been sketching what our lab should look like. I had literally drawn what I desired into being.

This episode was a sort of dual enchantment. Imagining how it came about is instructive because it illustrates two ways of thinking about how magic works. One way would have required a fantastic level of coordination and control among lots of people and parts moving in space and time. We can think of this mechanism as magic "pushing" the present state forward *in real time,* so it lands on the desired future state. A second way is that magic pulls the present into the desired future state, *from the future.*

My guess is that the more likely mechanism was the second—a retrocausal goal-oriented process that pulled me and Jon into a mutually desired future, rather than both of us "pushing" our desires in the present. This turns out to be a leading explanation for psi effects as well. We'll discuss this in more detail later in this chapter.

Here is a more recent example of a synchronicity. In early 2023, I was awarded a grant to experimentally investigate the quantum observer effect. I described this as the SIGIL experiment in Chapter 2. Finding talented participants for this type of mind-matter interaction study is not easy, and it can also be expensive if they are required to travel to the lab. So I designed a study where we would conduct a worldwide search for suitable candidates, then mail each person an optical interference system they could use to perform the experiment in the comfort of their home, and at their own pace. I wrote a grant proposal to cover the costs, and I was pleased to receive the award from the Bial Foundation, an organization in Portugal that generously offers competitive grants every two years.

My grant proposal assumed that one of our staff members at IONS would provide the necessary work and equipment at no cost. That exceptionally gracious offer allowed the grant to be funded, because otherwise the proposed budget wouldn't have been sufficient to cover all the costs.

But just as the grant was awarded, my colleague unfortunately had to withdraw from the project. I was in a minor panic because there wasn't enough in the budget to hire someone to make the required optical devices. I was faced with one of two choices: Either return the grant funds or find an additional $25,000 to allow me to design and build the optical systems myself. I did not relish the thought of returning the grant, so I set my intention to resolve this problem in a more favorable way. I *needed* a solution, and soon.

A week later I received an email out of the blue from a new organization in the UK called the Research Network for the Study of Esoteric Practices, which included traditional magical techniques.[26] I hadn't heard of this organization before, nor did I know anyone involved in it. But the founders kindly invited me to be on their advisory board. One of their initiatives was to sponsor a scientific test of a magical practice. I asked how much the grant would be. The answer was €25,000. I applied for and was grateful to receive the grant. That's one of the reasons I revised my original experimental design to compare performance in meditators versus magicians. As it turned out, that too was a fortuitous outcome, as we saw in the discussion of the SIGIL experiment results.

FROM MAGIC TO SCIENCE

A 2024 article in *Scientific American* by science writer Anil Ananthaswamy discussed "one of the most confounding concepts to emerge from the cauldron of early twentieth-century physics." It's the notion that "outcomes in quantum mechanics depend on observations."[27] Why does observing, say, photons in an optical interferometer, as discussed in Chapter 2, cause the photons to change their behavior?

Ananthaswamy went on to say, "Scientists have largely avoided thinking about the observer until recently." Well, not all scientists. Psi researchers have been discussing this puzzle since the 1950s, and those discussions gave rise to a theory about psi that is directly relevant to enchantment magic. It's known as the Observational Theory (OT), and it proposes that a motivated observer can intentionally influence probabilistic events at the quantum scale.[28]

What's amazing about the OT is that it predicted that mind-matter interaction effects would not be limited to unfolding in present time but would also be effective *backward in time*. The reason is that the effect depends on *when* the observation takes place. That is, if the observation takes place after measurements are recorded but not yet observed, and observation influences those measurements, then that requires the influence to go backward in time, a *retrocausal* influence. This had never been observed or even imagined before in psi research. But the theoretical prediction was tested, and to everyone's shock, it worked, as discussed in Chapter 2.

Ananthaswamy's article in *Scientific American* didn't mention those studies because most scientists and journalists aren't familiar with psi research. But the author did note that "if measurement outcomes are relative to observers, that calls into question the entire scientific enterprise, which depends on the objectivity of experimental findings." Indeed it would. That would be quite a radical outcome, and that is precisely what psi research has been telling us for half a century, and what magical practices have been telling us for millennia: Mental influence goes forward and backward in time. That's how goal-directed effects, or teleological "pulls" from the future, happen.

There is more evidence that physics is catching up with psi research. For example, a book about the strange properties of quantum mechanics, again by Anil Ananthaswamy, was reviewed in *Nature*. The review noted that:

> In some versions, nature seems magically to discern our intentions before we enact them—or perhaps *retroactively* to alter the past. In others, the outcome seems dependent on what we know, not what we do. In yet others, we can deduce something about a system without looking at it. All in all, the double-slit experiment seems, to borrow from Feynman again, "screwy."
>
> Odder, the pattern vanishes if we use a detector to measure what slit the particle goes through: It's truly particle-like, with no more waviness. Oddest of all, that remains true if we delay the measurement until after the particle has traversed the slits (but before it hits the screen). And if we make the measurement but then delete the result without looking at it, *interference returns*. (emphasis added)[29]

That last line is the key, because it implies that *observation requires consciousness*. That is, apparently a conscious being has to gain knowledge about what happened. This raises all sorts of interesting questions, like is a human the only thing that can make an observation? If a dog or cat observed the data first, would that partially "collapse" the waves into particles? Would a second observer make it collapse even more? Once again, psi research is ahead of the mainstream because experiments exploring these questions were conducted in the 1970s and '80s in a series of clever PK-RNG experiments by the physicist and psi researcher Helmut Schmidt. His results suggested that if a first observer fully "collapsed" a collection of data, a second observer could no longer affect those data.[30]

Many explanations have been offered to explain the observer effect, usually in conventional terms that don't require consciousness. But as science writer Philip Ball explained, so far none of those explanations are widely accepted: "With apologies to researchers convinced that they have the answer . . . *there is no consensus.*"[31]

Perhaps this is because physicists have overlooked the mystical origins of quantum theory. The historian Juan Miguel Marin reviewed this largely forgotten story. As he put it:

> Not only was consciousness introduced hypothetically at the
> birth of quantum physics, but the term "mystical" was also used
> by its founders to argue in favour and against such an
> introduction. In private conversations, at least as early as the
> 1927 Solvay Congress, the founders discussed ideas about
> quantum theory, mysticism and consciousness.[32]

Those founders included a parade of the most foremost physicists of the twentieth century, such figures as Bohr, Eddington, Jordan, Planck, Pauli, Heisenberg, Schrödinger, Jeans, London, Wigner, Wheeler, and von Neumann.[33] Wolfgang Pauli speculated that consciousness would be the next field to be incorporated into a truly unified quantum field theory, which would incorporate aspects of the psyche. He added, "I do not believe in the possible future of mysticism in the old form. However, I do believe that the natural sciences will out of themselves bring forth a counter pole in their adherents, which connects with the old mystic elements."[34]

Erwin Schrödinger expressed his conviction about the quantum observer effect as follows: "The observer is never entirely replaced by instruments; for if he were, he could obviously obtain no knowledge whatsoever. . . . Many helpful devices can facilitate this work . . . but they must be read! The observer's senses have to step in eventually. The most careful record, when not inspected, tells us nothing."[35]

Incidentally, Schrödinger's famous wave equation was structurally similar to but not exactly the same as equations commonly used to describe water and sound waves. As Philip Ball asked:

> Why wasn't [his wave equation] identical? Schrödinger didn't explain his reason, and it now seems clear that he didn't exactly have one. He simply wrote down what he thought a wave equation for a particle such as an electron ought to look like. That he seems to have made such a good guess is even now rather *extraordinary and mysterious*. . . . Schrödinger's wave equation, which is now a part of the core conceptual machinery of quantum mechanics, was built partly by *intuition and imagination*. (emphasis added)[36]

Today, with a growing appreciation of the role of the observer in understanding physical reality, the mystical origins of quantum theory can no longer be easily shelved as hippy-dippy nonsense. Instead, whether conventional physicists like it or not, magic may have been hiding in the very foundations of the most accurate physical theory to date. As John Wheeler once quipped, "Not machinery but magic may be the better description of the [quantum mechanical] treasure that is waiting."[37] Wheeler wasn't talking about the kind of magic we're discussing.

Or was he?

Consider Philip Ball's comment regarding the delayed choice quantum eraser experiment proposed by Wheeler. That experiment confirmed that quantum effects are not just mysteriously reactive to observation, but that this sensitivity transcends ordinary space and time:

> That's to say, we won't try to detect the photon's path until after it has passed through the slits [in a double-slit optical system]. It's not sufficient simply to set up a detector far behind the slits, for nature seems somehow to know in advance whether it's there or not. No—we won't actually put it there until we know for sure that the photon has passed through the slits. *Surely nature doesn't have some magical window into our intentions?*[38]

Or perhaps it does. Like many scientists concerned about their perceived credibility, John Wheeler tried valiantly to avoid being associated with mystical ideas, but as Ball noted, Wheeler

> offered an extraordinary view of cosmic evolution that depends on such consciousness-induced collapse of the wavefunction. If "noticing"—that is, observation—doesn't just report on but *actually produces* phenomena, crystallizing "what happened" out of "what might have happened," could the presence of beings capable of "noticing" transform a multitude of possible pasts into one concrete history? . . . More generally, by "noticing" how things are today, we might be selecting which of many quantum paths they took in the past—and in this sense we become participants in the evolution of the universe since its very beginning.[39]

In his book *Quantum Revelation*, Paul Levy dove deep into Wheeler's writings to show that he often used the term *magic* to express his amazement at the implications of quantum theory:

> [Wheeler] makes the point that the magic inherent in the universe by itself isn't sufficient, but rather, what is needed is "magic plus the prepared mind." It's as if the magic inherent in

our universe wanted to reveal itself through the vehicle of hard science, and abracadabra the result is quantum physics. Wheeler, wondering about the universe in his inimitable style, asks, "Is it all just a Magic Show?"[40]

The cognitive scientist Don Hoffman drew similarities between his "interface theory of perception" and Wheeler's notion of a participatory universe. Hoffman wrote, quoting Wheeler:

> "What we call 'reality' consists of an elaborate papier-mâché construction of imagination and theory filled in between a few iron posts of observation." We don't, according to Wheeler, passively observe a preexisting objective reality, we *actively participate in constructing reality by our acts of observation.* "Quantum mechanics evidences that there is no such thing as a mere observer . . . of reality. The observing equipment, the registering device, 'participates in the defining of reality.' In this sense the universe does not sit 'out there' [independent of us]."[41]

The physicist John Bell, famous for developing a rigorous way to experimentally test if quantum entanglement was physically real or just a mathematical abstraction, wrote: "Suppose that when formulation beyond 'for all practical purposes' is attempted, we find an unmovable finger obstinately pointing outside the subject, *to the mind of the observer,* to the Hindu scripts, to God, or even only gravitation. Would that not be very, very interesting?"[42]

Yes. It would.

SCIENTIFIC THEORIES ABOUT MAGIC

Five classes of scientific theories have been proposed to explain psi and, by association, magic. They are quantum-based theories, hyperdimensional theories, field theories, retrocausal theories, and what I'll call integrative theories.

First, quantum-based theories propose that consciousness plays a key role in quantum mechanics and by extension in the physical world at large. These theories suggest that consciousness can probabilistically influence physical systems through the quantum observer effect, which we discussed earlier as the key tenet of the Observational Theory. These theories also propose that the mind-brain relationship is a quantum phenomenon operating at the level of neuronal synapses, or other aspects of brain function at the microscopic scale, which is where quantum properties are most influential.[43] The theories support the idea that consciousness is inherently nonlocal and as such it's capable of perceiving and affecting reality at a distance.

A related theory relies on quantum-like principles applied to systems of any size or complexity, not just to particles at the microphysical scale. Called the Model of Pragmatic Information (MPI), it was inspired by how meaningful coincidences, or synchronicities, appear to be mediated by *meaning* (as in the philosophy of dual-aspect monism). The MPI makes two key proposals: First, "psi phenomena are nonlocal entanglement correlations . . . induced by the pragmatic information [that is, *meaning*] which creates the system." And second, "any attempt to use a nonlocal correlation as a signal transfer makes the nonlocal correlation vanish or change the effect in an unpredictable way."[44]

Second, hyperdimensional theories propose that consciousness exists in higher dimensions above the three dimensions of space and one of time. In particle physics, taking a multidimensional mathematical approach led to developments called string theory, brane theory, and more recently, M-theory. These models attempt to describe all known forces observed in the physical world, including gravity.[45] But in the present context, these hyperdimensional theories propose a reality that is composed not just of physical dimensions but of both physical *and mental dimensions*.[46]

Third, field theories, like Rupert Sheldrake's theory of morphic fields, propose that consciousness operates through or is influenced by nonphysical or quasi-mental fields, somewhat similar to but distinct from physical fields like electromagnetism.[47]

Fourth, retrocausal theories replace forward-only causality with relationships that connect past, present, and future.[48] The claim is that all known quantum phenomena, and importantly all psi phenomena, can be accommodated in a simpler and less mysterious way than the more challenging concepts of quantum theory. Similar ideas have been proposed based on considerations of entropy and time-symmetry. The physicist Daniel Sheehan notes:

> For three centuries, the fundamental equations of physics have predicted both "positive-time" and "negative-time" solutions and, by proper extension, both causation and retrocausation. Despite this, the scientific community has rejected the negative time retrocausal solutions as unphysical. However, as experiment and theory probe more deeply into the physical world, it becomes increasingly evident that these negative-time solutions may, in fact, play a largely hidden but perhaps equal role in establishing reality.[49]

Fifth, integrative theories seek to combine the various ways that psi and magic can manifest into a single, high-level model. These models differ from the others because they do not dwell on identifying an underlying physical mechanism, like retrocausation or quantum-inspired connections. But they do provide an especially useful way to think about how magic works.

Integrative approaches are not new. After years of conducting psi tests in his lab at Duke University, J. B. Rhine wrote, "Psi seems to function as a normal, healthy ability, responsive to motivational drives, and as part of the general unconscious system of the individual. . . . The various types and forms of psi seemed to hang together too well to be fundamentally independent. General properties, also, seemed to apply to all four types: telepathy, clairvoyance, precognition, and psychokinesis."[50]

The first fleshed-out version of this idea, proposed by the psychologist Rex Stanford in the 1970s, was called psi-mediated instrumental response, or PMIR.[51] A later variation was dubbed psychopraxis theory by the psychologists Michael Thalbourne and Lance Storm.[52] A third version, by psychologist James Carpenter, was called First Sight theory,[53] and a fourth was called decision augmentation by physicist Edwin May and his colleagues.[54]

These integrative theories suggest that psi operates unconsciously to manifest an individual's desires by continually scanning the past, present, and future. The first three flavors of these theories also assume that psi can influence the environment via PK. In so doing, a meaningful synchronicity is evoked that satisfies your desire. It assumes that perception and influence act "outside" of time, as artistically portrayed in the 2023 Oscar-winning movie *Everything Everywhere All at Once.*

In this way, psi unconsciously influences your decision to go here versus there, to do this activity versus that, to pause or accelerate your plans, to remember or forget something, to make a useful mistake (like dialing a "wrong" number at just the "right" time), or to influence others or events in a similar fashion. The result, provided that the underlying desire and motivation are sufficiently strong, and that the desired goal is realistically achievable, is that everything will come together in just the right place and time to satisfy the desired goal. It will end up looking like a happy coincidence, or a synchronicity.

One way this theory has been tested was to recruit people (usually college students) to engage in a boring task without their realizing that the study was actually a psi experiment. That is, the psi target system might be a random number generator running in another room. The behavior of that RNG would determine if the student would have to continue to do the boring task or be allowed to leave and do something more interesting or pleasant.

A number of studies based on this idea were conducted, and while the results were not consistently positive, overall they did show intriguing support for this unconscious integrative theory. Of course, as in any lab study, what one is allowed to do in an experiment is constrained for ethical reasons. But if one imagines this scenario in a real-life, super-strong motivational context, like a magical act, then the results might be much more consistent and impressive.

Still, a reasonable question one might ask is, if psi is so powerful that it can scan across space and time, then why doesn't magic work all the time? Perhaps the clearest answer to that question is a lack of sufficient motivation or need. Another answer is that our desire may be unreasonable, or not possible to achieve in a short period of time. We can bend reality only so far and so fast before the fabric of reality begins to crack, or before the intentions of other people get in the way and push back with the magical equivalent of "oh no you don't." Another possibility is that we may think we know what we desire, but that's only true some of the time. As the psychologist David Luke has put it:

> If anyone can be psychic at any time you might well ask what stops us from actually being omniscient and omnipotent all the time? Why, we want to know, aren't we gods? The answer might well be us ourselves, as both parapsychological theorists, such as Rex Stanford, and occultists, such as Austin Osman Spare, have indicated—that our own unconscious desires often conflict with each other, thereby preventing pure desires and needs from manifesting.
>
> It may come as no surprise that a vast reservoir of psychic information can be found lurking in the body or hiding in the unconscious mind. For this reason the study of altered states has a lot to offer in the pursuit of both psi and magic, because, broadly speaking, altered states tend to make the unconscious conscious.[55]

In any case, the integrative psi theories developed by scientists to help explain the outcomes of psi experiments, and similar theories independently developed by magicians, suggest that this idea is headed in the right direction. As Luke noted in a later article:

> The philosophy of chaos magick officially began with the publication of [a book] by Ramsey Dukes in 1974 . . . the same year that [Rex] Stanford published his first PMIR papers. Following on from the lead of Dukes, *chaos magick* grew to fully incorporate Spare's . . . doctrine of magickal manifestation and perception, which, it will be shown, *has a direct correspondence* to both expressive psi (psychokinesis) and receptive psi (ESP) as they are conceived within the PMIR model proposed by Stanford. (emphasis added)[56]

The underlying theme of these integrative psi/magic theories could be expressed as "I want X to occur," and by then applying optimal forms of intention, motivation, or belief, X will indeed occur. It may not happen the way that you thought it would, but it will nevertheless happen, and often in the easiest or simplest way.

PART IV

PRACTICAL MAGIC

There are thousands of books on the practice of enchantment and divination magic. This part discusses some of the more popular methods.

The best way to learn any skill, including magic, is to practice, preferably under the tutelage of a teacher who knows what they're doing and has a stellar reputation.

My personal website (DeanRadin.com) has a section listing technical tools useful for practicing psi and magic, as well as organizations that teach these skills.

CHAPTER 7

DOING MAGIC

Just as in sex, no one is good the first time they do magick, and it takes a degree of practice before you can even begin to do it properly.

—ALAN CHAPMAN[1]

The practice of magic consists of two factors: doing and being. The *doing* part is fairly easy. It involves following a few principles and actions. The *being* part is more difficult. It's about achieving the state of consciousness called *gnosis*. We'll first discuss doing, then spend some time on being, which may take months or years of practice before a reliable degree of skill can be achieved.

It would be wonderful to be able to say that with enough practice anyone can learn to perform Merlin-class magic. Unfortunately, that's not the case. Anyone can learn to play golf, but only a few will play in the Masters Tournament, and even fewer will win. The same is true with magical talent, but you won't know whether you have talent until you try, and even minor proficiency in magic is better than no magic at all. Also, there are innumerable forms of magical practices, and perhaps your talent lies in one style but not in others.

Roald Dahl's *The Wonderful Story of Henry Sugar* describes the level of practice necessary to achieve some degree of mastery in the magical arts.[2] The story is about Henry, a spoiled, self-centered aristocrat who performs no useful work and idles away his time playing cards, dreaming of hitting it big. Henry learns of a man who claims to be able to see without his eyes, and he imagines that if that was for real, and he could learn the trick, then he'd be able to win endless amounts of money in a casino.

Henry eventually learns that the skill is indeed for real, but it requires training the mind. The guru who knows the method explains, "You must learn to concentrate in such a way that you can visualize at will one item, one item only, and absolutely nothing else," for at least three and a half minutes. Henry imagines that surely that's not so difficult, but the guru adds that it would take an ordinary person about *fifteen years* to achieve that level of concentrated attention because within seconds the mind starts to wander.

But Henry is highly motivated, and after months and then years of daily practice, he eventually finds that he can indeed see without his eyes. He can see the front side of a playing card just by glancing at the back. He tries out his skill in the casino and easily wins.

But Henry soon tires of being able to win endlessly because it's no longer a challenge. The moral of the story is that being wealthy for the sake of being wealthy soon becomes meaningless. But he decides to keep on winning so he can dedicate all his money to building orphanages around the world. The conscientious training of his mind transformed him from a selfish ne'er-do-well into a compassionate philanthropist.

Training the mind to perform powerful magic requires a similar level of practice, and it may well have a similar transformative effect. So be advised that while an initial attraction to magic may be to gain money, fame, and sex, the ultimate prize may be a dramatic change in your personal values that is far more meaningful and beneficial to all.

ELEMENTS OF PRACTICAL MAGIC

Eight factors of practical magic are repeatedly mentioned by magicians. I regard three as essential: *belief*, *practice*, and *gnosis*. The other five factors involve concentrated *attention, intention, imagination, clarity,* and *motivation.* Belief is essential because it modulates the effectiveness of the other factors. Practice is essential for reasons already discussed. And gnosis is indispensable because that's where the engine of magic resides.

Of these factors, belief, attention, intention, and gnosis have been studied in some detail in psi experiments, as described in earlier chapters. All four of these factors have been found to be effective modulators of psi performance in dozens to hundreds of repeated experiments. The other four have not been as thoroughly investigated in the laboratory, but based on anecdotal accounts and my own experiences, I am persuaded that practice, imagination, clarity, and motivation are also key elements.

There are two other things to keep in mind when doing magic. First, magic works, sometimes with staggering speed. But that's the exception rather than the rule. If your enchantment involves finding a dollar bill on the ground in a busy mall or parking lot, that might be achievable in less than an hour. But if your goal is to mysteriously find an extremely expensive gold-plated sports car in your garage, for no discernible reason, that could take a while. As the magician Donald Michael Kraig says in *Modern Magick,* "The key difference between the 'magic' in fairy tales and in movies and 'magick' as practiced by tens of thousands of people around the world today and in the past is that most real magick does not occur instantaneously."[3]

Second, I will not delve into the practice of evoking spirits. That path is fraught with pitfalls. Do-it-yourself books are available on this topic, but my advice is that if you wish to go down that rabbit hole, be sure to find a well-regarded and highly experienced guide. At minimum, the danger is psychological trauma, but it may be more than that.[4] The risk is that if you encounter things you're not prepared to deal with, it can be so destabilizing that you'll go crazy. As the magician Alan Chapman wrote:

When I first began dabbling, I thought a lot of what I read about the pitfalls of magick was a touch melodramatic. But that was ok, because I was a dabbler. When I became "serious" about magick, I went out and found other "serious" magicians. I then watched a few of them go barking mad.[5]

In sum, theurgy—the realm that deals with spirits and entities—is a serious business that requires serious expertise. So before dabbling in that realm, you might want to recall the play *No Exit*, by the existentialist philosopher Jean-Paul Sartre. Near the end of that play, which takes place in a single room that's a metaphor for hell, one of the characters, Garcin, understands that "Hell is other people." With that in mind, imagine the unholy hell you may accidentally unleash by opening doors to innumerable hordes of imaginary or actual non-human entities. Don't say Sartre didn't warn you.

MAGICAL ETHICS

This section is short because the ethics of magic are simple: Follow the golden rule.

Versions of the golden rule can be found in virtually all religious and moral traditions: *Treat others with the same consideration and kindness that you desire for yourself.* In the Jewish tradition, this is expressed within the Talmud, Shabbat 31a, as "What is hateful to you, do not do to your neighbor. This is the whole Torah; the rest is the explanation; go and learn." In Buddhism, Udana-Varga 5:18: "Hurt not others in ways that you yourself would find hurtful." And so on.

Second, if you have any doubt, don't do it.

Third, if you are a masochist, I can't help you.

Fourth, if you have no capacity for empathy, then may your god of choice have mercy on your soul, because karma's a bitch.

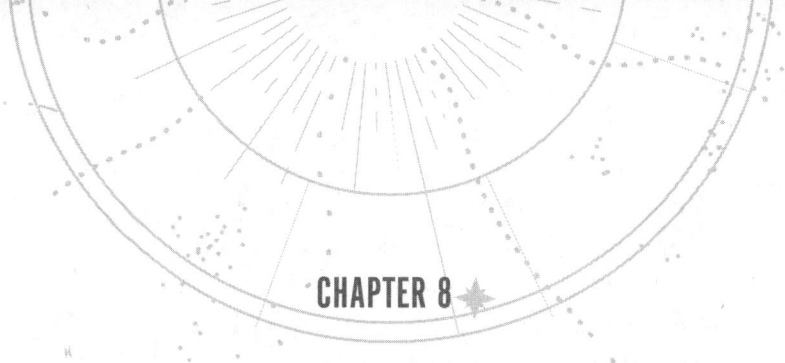

CHAPTER 8

ENCHANTMENT

One man's "magic" is another man's engineering. "Supernatural" is a null word.

—ROBERT A. HEINLEIN

Enchantment is about manipulating the physical world with your desires. Magical lore and some experimental evidence suggest that you may be more effective at such manipulations on or within a day or two of the full moon.[1] But people are different, so maybe that is true for you, and maybe not. Maybe your magical efficiency improves more after eating wheat crackers and cheddar cheese between the hours of eleven A.M. and one P.M. on alternate Saturdays. You'll never know if you don't keep track. That's why recording the results of each magical act is important.

The practice of enchantment, across many magical traditions, follows the same seven steps.

> 1. **Believe** that the process will work. If you cannot avoid some doubt, then suspend your disbelief. We have no problem when Marvel characters like Wolverine or Deadpool demonstrate their superhuman strength and regenerative powers. So suspend your disbelief and unleash the same type of awe and delight you reserve for your favorite superheroes.

2. **Clarify** your intention. Be crystal clear on exactly what it is that you want, including possible unintended consequences. In principle, anything you desire is possible to receive, but the likelihood of success is related to the probability that your desire could happen by dumb luck. It would be easier to magically win a three-pick lottery than to magically be appointed the president of a major bank if you have no experience in banking, are not particularly interested in banking, have a known gambling problem, and just declared bankruptcy.

3. **Create a symbol** that stands for your wish. Later in this chapter we'll discuss the various forms this symbol can take, including a sigil, a word, an image, a knot, or a talisman or amulet.

4. **Charge** the symbol in a state of peak motivation and attention while you are in a state of gnosis. This can be a highly energetic or supremely calm state of awareness, whichever works for you. The former includes drumming, ecstatic or swirling dancing like the Sufi whirling dervishes, extreme physical exertion, or sexual excitation. The latter includes meditation, dreaming, or in general entering a state that a yogi would call samadhi. (Later I'll give some hints on how to achieve this state.) Charging a symbol is a way to force your desire deep into your subconscious, which is closer—figuratively—to the magical engine of reality.

I prefer calm charging because I'd rather not have to get up from the couch or change my clothes to do magic. This is not to deny that magic is a serious business, but it doesn't need to be deadly serious. The cosmos has a sense of humor, so there's no contradiction in acknowledging the playful nature of reality by putting a slice of baloney in your shoes so you'll feel funny (nod to comedian Steve Martin), while simultaneously being a responsible magus.

5. **Release** the intention. Some magicians suggest that once a symbol is suitably charged, you should burn it (if on paper), bury it (if an object), hide it, or otherwise put it out of sight so you don't obsess over the outcome. While the mechanism of magic is not constrained by ordinary space and time, it usually takes some everyday clock time for magic to manifest.

6. Maintain a state of **effortless striving**. This means pushing your desire with the greatest intensity and motivation you can possibly muster, but without any effort at all. This paradoxical state is a subtlety that takes a while to learn, but it is possible.

7. **Record** what happens and celebrate your successes. Share the successes with supportive friends and family, but don't tell strangers or anyone who will just shake their head and mumble about tinfoil hats. Maintaining belief is essential even *after* you achieve the goal because magical time is not linear, and future doubts may retroactively influence the success of past efforts. That might sound crazy, except that there's good evidence that backward-time influences do exist.

The rest of this chapter describes a half-dozen enchantment practices. But there's nothing special about them. That is, many methods have been developed because people have different backgrounds, predilections, interests, and skills, but the key point is that they all share the same essence. The magician Alan Chapman condensed the process of enchantment into five steps, to which I've added a few comments.[2]

1. **Decide** what you want to happen. Clarity is important.

2. **Ensure** that what you want has a means of manifestation. The simpler, the better.

3. **Choose** a magical experience. It could be a traditional method or something new that you devise.

4. **Believe** that the magical act is effective.

5. **Perform** the act.

WORD MAGIC: THE POWER OF IDENTITY

Word magic uses the creative power of language to manifest intentions and shape destiny. Historians of magic have said that "the power of words was thought to be practically unlimited."[3] It's one of the most ancient methods of spellcraft, and it's found at the core of chanting, mantras, incantations, and sigil construction. It is based on the magical Law of Correspondence, or the Law of Names, whereby obtaining the name of something, its symbol, or knowledge about it, brings power over it.

The Brothers Grimm tale of Rumpelstiltskin captures the essence of word magic.[4] Similar tales can be found in many cultures. For example, in Scotland there's the tale of Whuppity Stoorie, while in Old English folklore the character is known as Tom Tit Tot. Comparable stories can be found in Spain, France, Germany, Italy, and Russia.

The fairy tale tells of a poor miller who, in an attempt to impress the king, falsely claims that his daughter can spin straw into gold. The king tests his claim by locking the miller's daughter in a room filled with straw, demanding that she spin it into gold by the next morning, or she will be executed.

Desperate, the miller's daughter is visited by a strange little imp who offers to spin the straw into gold in exchange for something of value. She agrees, and in return, she gives him her necklace. The next day the king is pleased but becomes greedy, so he locks her in a larger room with even more straw. Again, the imp appears and spins the straw into gold, this time in exchange for her ring.

Now the king locks her in an even larger room filled with heaps of straw, promising to marry her if she succeeds. This time the imp demands her firstborn child as payment. Desperate to escape this impossible situation, she agrees. So the imp spins the straw into gold.

The king marries the miller's daughter, and they have a child. The rascally imp returns to claim his payment, but the daughter, who is now the queen, pleads with him to let her keep her child. The imp, confident in his secrets, gives her three days to guess his name. If successful, she may keep her child. If not, all is lost.

The queen sends messengers throughout the land to discover the imp's name. On the third and last day, a messenger reports that he overheard the imp dancing and singing in the forest and saying his name, Rumpelstiltskin. When he returns to collect his prize, the queen triumphantly announces his name, and the impish rogue flies into a rage and disappears, defeated.

This story is a parable about the power of words. Across many cultures and magical traditions, knowing someone's name, or the word for something, is said to give power over that person or thing. This is because within the Law of Correspondence, a name is identical to the thing it represents, so knowing the name makes that thing vulnerable.

We are all aware of the power of words by watching how some people become so incensed by words that they are motivated to ban books. Laws are passed making it a crime to have certain books in the library. Books are ritually burned by those who fear their words.

The Power of Names

I learned the power of names in an accidental way that I don't think I would have believed if I hadn't experienced it firsthand. I am allergic to grass and tree pollen, and most of the places where I've lived are just saturated with seasonal pollen. So during the spring growing season, I consume antihistamines like candy.

The Institute of Noetic Sciences, where I've worked since 2001, was for many years located on two hundred acres on top of a beautiful mountain in Sonoma County, California. The golden hills of California are also home to every sort of pollen imaginable, so for about four months of every year, I stayed indoors as much as I could.

One day a naturalist visited our campus and offered to give the staff a tour of the ample flora in the picturesque countryside. I wasn't thrilled about walking through fields of pollen, but the naturalist said that if I knew the names of the grasses and plants, they would become my friends and would not attack my immune system. To say I was skeptical would be an understatement, but many of the staff were going on the walk, so I bowed to social pressure. I decided to give each plant a name to help "know" it, Rumpelstiltskin-like, with the hopes of encouraging them to be my friends.

I was introduced to wild oats. I called them Walter. Foxtail barley became Fred. Purple needlegrass, Paul. Manzanita, Marvin, and so on. Why I chose male names, I have no idea. After the walk, I realized to my amazement that I wasn't experiencing any allergic reactions. None. My new friends Walter, Fred, Paul, and Marvin didn't attack me because now these buds were my buddies. Days later I noticed that even if I didn't know the proper name of a plant, if I gave it a friendly name, like Bob or Martha, I experienced a much milder allergic response than I did beforehand. Was this a form of word magic? At the time I had no idea what to call it, but in hindsight it was consistent with the magic associated with names and knowledge.

SIGIL MAGIC: SYMBOLIC INTENTIONS

Sigil magic is a modern magical practice whereby you craft a symbol that stands for an intention that then manifests in the physical world. Developed in the early part of the twentieth century by the British artist and occultist Austin Osman Spare, sigil magic has become one of the more popular magical techniques because it's simple and quick. It's based on the idea that symbols do not merely represent an intention; in a deeper magical sense, a symbol *is identical to* an intention. This repeated theme is found in all enchantment techniques.

There are many websites and smartphone apps that will make a sigil for you, but I recommend the pen or pencil and paper approach, because taking time to personally create the symbol helps to focus your mind better than touching a computer screen or a keyboard. For those younger than twenty who may not be familiar with the terms *pen* and *pencil*, these are small magical wands that allow you to draw symbols on flat pieces of white flexible parchment, and they don't require batteries.

The traditional process of creating a sigil involves several key steps:

1. **Define your intention:** Think carefully about what you want to achieve or manifest. Be specific, clear, and concise. When you are first experimenting, the simpler, the better. An example of an intention: *I am pleasantly surprised to find an unexpected gift.*

2. **Write your intention:** Write your intention in a single sentence. Confirm that the goal is crystal clear to reduce the likelihood of unintended consequences. Write in a positive, present tense. Example of a written goal: *I find a ten-dollar bill.*

3. **Remove vowels and repeating letters:** Reduce the sentence by removing vowels and double letters. Example: *I find a ten-dollar bill becomes fndtndrb.*

4. **Combine the remaining letters:** Merge the remaining letters into a single symbol, creating a unique and personalized sigil. See Figure 9 for an example.

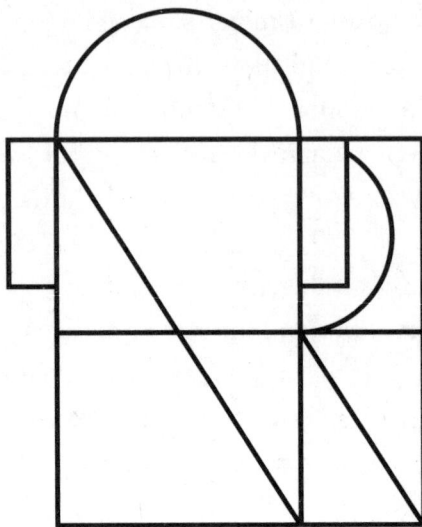

Figure 9. Stylized sigil for the intention *I find a ten-dollar bill*

It doesn't need to be fancy, unless you like fancy. You just need to know that this symbol is more than a representation of your intention; in the magical sense, it *is the same* as your intention. You've taken a subjective wish and manifested it in symbolic form into the physical world. You have taken a step toward making your desire come true.

5. **Charge it:** Concentrate your intention into the sigil, visualizing your desired outcome. This can be done in an energetic or calm state of gnosis.

6. **Release it:** Release the sigil's intention into the universe, allowing it to work its magic through your unconscious. There are two modes of thought about this. Some recommend destroying the sigil so you don't end up obsessing over it. Others say put it somewhere in plain view, so you'll be periodically reminded of your desire. Again, your choice. Experiment to learn what works for you.

Does this work? Readers have told me that shortly after creating a sigil, they were startled to find a ten- or twenty-dollar bill lying on the ground later that same day. In one case, it freaked out the person so much that they stopped playing with magic. As the magician David Thompson says, "The psycho-magical consequences are sometimes quite incalculable. As is well known, the real problem with magic is not so much the question of *whether* it works, but rather the fact that it *does*."[5] Be careful what you wish for.

KNOT MAGIC: BINDING INTENTIONS

Knot magic involves tying knots in string, leather, yarn, or other strips of material, to represent the binding of thoughts and desires. The act of creating the knot is a tangible representation of the intention, like sigil magic, but the additional act of pulling the knot closed and tightening it helps to focus one's desire kinesthetically.

Applications of knot magic include both enchantment and divination. For example, you can make a binding knot to use for protection from psychic attack (also known as a banishing ritual). To do this, you mentally place the unwanted "energy" or situation into the knot and squeeze it tight to capture it. You may loosen a knot to represent undoing an obstacle. You can also tie a knot to secure a desired outcome, or you can unravel a knot to reveal a hidden truth or gain insight about a confusing situation.

- The specific type of cord or string doesn't matter. Select whatever is most appealing or meaningful to you. You might want to associate certain colors with different outcomes, like red or green for manifestation and blue or black for binding.
- As with any magical practice, clearly define your goal and visualize the outcome as you tighten or loosen the knot.

The type of knot doesn't matter unless you believe it matters.

- Repeat this activity several times, reinforcing your intention with each knot.
- When the spell is complete, either destroy or bury the knot if the intention is to bind something or remove an obstacle. Or you may keep the cord for a future spell if the intention was to gain insight.

Knot magic is a simple but effective way to practice spellcraft. Many find the kinesthetic act of creating or loosening a knot to be a powerful way to reinforce their desired intention. When I use knot magic, I like to repeatedly make knots in a piece of yarn and craft it into the shape of a little man. I don't know why. I just do.

CANDLE MAGIC: GO INTO THE LIGHT

Candle magic uses the symbolic power of light and fire to manifest one's desires. This practice is the essence of simplicity. As with all methods of enchantment, first clarify your intention and state it in present-tense, positive terms. Example: *I am healthy, wealthy, and wise.* Avoid stating desires negatively or vaguely, as in *Maybe someday I'll feel slightly better and not be completely bankrupt.*

Light the candle and focus on your intention until the candle burns out. The natural movements and fluctuations of the flame will remind you that mind-wandering is inevitable, so just keep returning your focus to your intention. Imagine that the flame itself is amplifying and radiating your intentions out into the universe.

To begin, you'll want to use one of those small birthday cake candles that lasts a few minutes and not a foot-long storm candle, otherwise you'll end up staring at a candle for twelve hours. If you like, you can use several candles with different colors, each representing a different facet of your intention. As with knot magic, you can select the color of the candle to correspond to your intention, typically red or orange for health and strength, green for wealth, white for spiritual guidance, and so on. You may wish to light an incense stick as well.

Avoid burning down the house. Stay focused, but not so intently that you deplete your energy and fall asleep with a burning candle in front of you, unless it's secured in a safe place. Respect the flame. Let the candle burn out naturally, representing the release of your intentions. The final wisp of smoke from the wick can be imagined to diffuse the intention to go where it needs to go.

In Chapter 2, I mentioned that part of a candle flame is made of plasma, and an experiment using a plasma ball showed that it seems to be unusually responsive to intentions. This may be why some have proposed the use of candles as a way to practice and strengthen magical intentions. You could alternately focus on making the flame lengthen and grow brighter, or shrink almost to the point where the flame goes out.

TALISMANS, CHARMS, AND AMULETS: MAGICAL OBJECTS

A talisman, charm, or amulet is an object, like a ring, a rock, a gemstone, a crystal, a rabbit's foot, a bracelet, a necklace, or even a piece of parchment. The object is imbued with intentions to attract, repel, or neutralize magical influences. It is typically worn as jewelry, hidden in a pocket, or placed under a pillow. The object may also be a liquid in which one's intention is imbued, a potion that one applies as a salve, or a beverage that one drinks. Intentional brews overlap to a large extent with the origins of herbalism as a mode of medicine, which in turn evolved into the pharmaceutical business. To do this topic justice would require a book-length treatment, so I'll save liquid magic for a future work.

Talismans, charms, and amulets are unique labels that carry different connotations. A talisman is typically intended to attract or manifest a specific desire, like love or money. A magic wand or a knife is a type of talisman. These objects are designed to be tools to help focus one's magical intentions. An amulet is more commonly used for protection, traditionally against the "evil eye." A charm might be a symbol for good luck, like a four-leaf clover, a horseshoe, or a medallion honoring a religious saint. These objects remain just as popular today as they were millennia ago and can be found in virtually every culture.

Creating a magical object follows the same steps as any enchantment practice. Be clear what you want the object to help you achieve. Imbue your focused intention into the object. Imagine that the object absorbs your intention and now embodies and radiates it. To "activate" the object, you may wish to perform an additional ritual to support your intention. That could include an incantation, anointing it with oil, or passing the object through smoke or fire. Magical lore also recommends that the object be periodically cleansed of any unwanted or negative energies, and recharged typically by exposing it to sunlight or moonlight, or by smudging it with sage or other herbs.

Does any of this actually work? Can intentions really be imbued into a physical object, which then accomplishes something that would otherwise not have happened? As we saw in Chapter 2, there is evidence that the answer is yes. Those experiments focused not on the usual magical desires for power, money, and sex but on outcomes more easily measured in the lab or clinical settings, like changes in water structure, an enhanced growth of plants, improved moods, and intentional healing.

GLAMOURING MAGIC: TEMPTATION AND ILLUSION

Glamouring is the ancient practice of manipulating how others see us. In today's world, glamouring has become the multibillion-dollar beauty, makeup, and perfume industries. Glamouring in fiction is sometimes portrayed as shape-shifting.

The practice of glamouring involves visualization and intentional projection of how one wishes to be perceived. To be most effective, glamouring is often used along with adornments, appropriate fashion and colors, grooming, or friendly body language, and by charisma. The intentional goal added to this mix, perhaps boosted with an appropriate talisman, is to create an alluring, friendly, or confident aura. Techniques for enhancing the intentional aspects of glamouring are the same as those used in word, sigil, or knot magic.

Glamouring is perhaps most commonly experienced in its pure magical sense as the "feeling of being stared at." That is, if you intently stare at another person without their knowledge, in a minute or less they may turn and look directly at you. If your intention is friendly, they may respond kindly. If you glare or seem menacing in any way, they are likely to respond negatively. Scientific experiments have tested this ability in experiments with both conscious and unconscious measures, and in both cases there is evidence that this phenomenon exists.

ENCHANTMENT QUIZ

Here's a short quiz to see what method of enchantment may be best for you. Record how many A's, B's, C's, and D's you select.

1. What do you resonate with more?
   a. Whispering winds, a gentle breeze (Air)
   b. A crackling fire, a transformative flame (Fire)
   c. Grounding, the embrace of the Earth (Earth)
   d. Flow of water, ebbing tides (Water)

2. What is the source of your strength?
   a. Intellectual, ideas and thoughts
   b. Passions and emotions
   c. The physical, tangible world
   d. Feelings and intuition

3. What is your intentional goal?

    a. Clarity to divine truths

    b. Transformation to ignite change

    c. Protection and grounding

    d. Healing, physical or emotional

4. What is your preferred method of magical expression?

    a. Pen and paper, symbols, words, and sigils

    b. Candles, flames, herbs

    c. Stones, crystals

    d. Water, oils, and potions

5. What time of day do you feel most energized?

    a. Dawn

    b. Noon

    c. Twilight

    d. Night

RESULTS

Mostly A's: Writing Magic or Sigils

Mostly B's: Candle Magic

Mostly C's: Knot Magic

Mostly D's: Water Magic or Potions

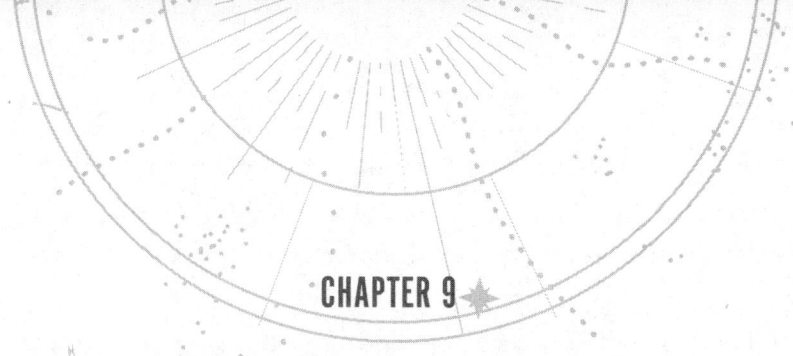

CHAPTER 9

DIVINATION AND THEURGY

Science is magic that works.

—KURT VONNEGUT

The histories of divination and theurgy, and dozens of associated techniques and practices, are described in many fine books.[1] There's no need to repeat those methods here, because they often involve technical aspects or symbolic dictionaries, and each technique can easily fill an entire library. So instead, I'll use this short chapter to provide background for the evidence that was presented in Chapter 2.

DIVINATION

Divination involves methods for perceiving through space and time. As a magical practice, it's typically used to forecast the future or to assist in making decisions. There are four main classes: those that rely on randomness, on unconscious physical movements, on calculations, and on interpretation of symbols and visions.

Class 1 includes the use of playing cards, tarot cards, runes, and the *I Ching*. These practices involve tossing dice, coins, sticks, stones, or shuffling cards, then interpreting the results according to a set of rules or by referring to a dictionary of symbolic meanings. On the surface, these methods rely on randomness, but from the magical perspective, what appears to be random is assumed to be synchronically or meaningfully arranged to reflect the questioner's intentions. This class of divination techniques is therefore not significantly different from a psychokinetic effect.

Class 2 includes the use of pendulums, dowsing rods, muscle testing, and Ouija boards. These methods take advantage of unconscious physiological effects or movements (the technical jargon is *ideomotor* movements) as a way of reflecting mental activity below the level of awareness, which is where gnosis usually resides.

Class 3 includes calculated techniques like numerology and astrology. Interpretation of the resulting information can be performed algorithmically, which is why many computer programs are available to automatically perform these divinations. Expert practitioners may use the calculated outcomes to help spark insights, so what might appear to be a purely technical procedure is more like a starting point for contemplation rather than the end point.

Class 4 involves interpretation of impressions and visions. Methods include dream interpretation; *scrying*, or gazing into a mirror, a crystal ball, or a pool of water; *augury*, or interpreting omens based on the behavior of birds, entrails of sacrificed animals, patterns in smoke or water, or tea leaves; *palm reading* and its close cousins, *face* or *iris reading*. All these methods rely on *clairvoyance* or its modern euphemism, *remote viewing*.

THEURGY

Theurgy involves ways of interacting with purported spirits, nonhuman entities, deceased humans, extraterrestrials, fairies, and so on. There are three main categories. The first is *invocation*, which involves calling in or inviting a spiritual entity, force, or quality into oneself, so as to align or become one with a higher power, deity, spirit, or universal energy. Through this practice, one might experience a profound sense of connection, transformation, or empowerment. Or go quite mad. Think about the movie *The Exorcist*.

The second class is *evocation*, which involves calling forth or summoning a spiritual entity to appear outside oneself. In magical practice, evocation techniques are often performed within a boundary, like a pentagram or circle, which is intended to provide safety and control over the process. Evocation is used when the practitioner seeks to communicate with or negotiate an agreement with an entity.

The third class is *conjuring*, which bears some similarity to evocation except in it the magician literally creates an entity by intention, rather than calling upon something that is assumed to already exist. Traditionally such entities have many names, like servitor, golem, or tulpa, according to culture.[2] As the magician Peter Carroll has put it, referring in general to the concept of entities or spirits, "The gods and goddesses exist as *thought forms of our own creation* and that in magical evocation you basically create 'spirits' as servitors."[3]

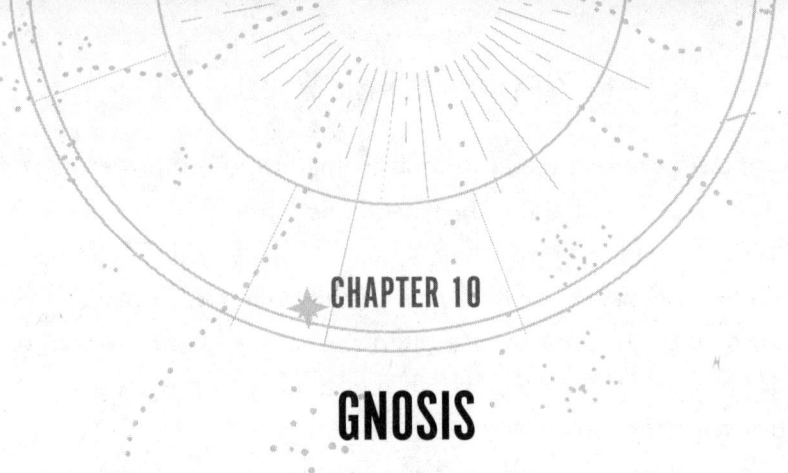

CHAPTER 10

GNOSIS

As we grow in our consciousness, there will be more compassion
and more love, and then the barriers between people, between
religions, between nations will begin to fall.

—RAM DASS

The state of *gnosis* is a profound, intuitive understanding or direct
knowledge of reality. It's what a yogi would call samadhi, a mystic
might describe as a mystical vision, and what scientists have called
noetic.[1] Derived from the Greek word for knowledge, *noēsis*, such
states were defined by William James in 1902, in his delightfully or-
nate prose, as "states of insight into depths of truth unplumbed by the
discursive intellect. They are illuminations, revelations, full of significance and importance, all inarticulate though they remain; and as a
rule they carry with them a curious sense of authority."[2]

Achieving gnosis is one of the goals of meditation, contemplative
prayer, ascetic practices, rituals, and the use of psychedelics in the
context of a spiritually oriented ceremony. It is associated with the
journey of self-realization and enlightenment, and many traditions
consider the guidance of an experienced teacher, guide, or guru to be
essential. This is less important today for those seeking an introduction to meditation, because of the endless array of meditation training
smartphone apps and YouTube courses. Still, for deepening one's

practice, a wise teacher who knows what they're doing is recommended.

The state of gnosis is not easily described. Indeed, it is often described as indescribable—beyond words—because it embodies a transformative shift in consciousness that offers a glimpse into the nature of naked existence, which some might call the divine. That headspace is so different from the everyday commonsense understanding of the world that despite millions of words being written about it, there are no words to actually describe it.

A WAY TO ACHIEVE GNOSIS

Short of spending years in deep, disciplined meditation, magical ritual work, or psychedelic therapy, how can a fledgling magician achieve gnosis? Those with natural talent can easily learn to dive into that state. Sometimes the very first time a person is taught how to meditate they end up there. That's annoying because most of us can't do that. We have to work at it.

I recommend a simple method that you can perform anywhere and anytime when you have a few minutes to just sit still. You can even do it with your eyes open, as long as you're not engaged in other work. It would be just as effective in a quiet cave or ashram as on a subway or airplane.

I learned this technique from my colleague Arnaud Delorme, a neuroscientist who has conducted extensive scientific studies of mind-wandering.[3] The method would also be a useful tuner for experienced meditators and magicians. Like many mindfulness meditation techniques, it involves counting ten breaths. But it includes a little twist that I've found to be useful.

Here's the first exercise:

> 1. As you sit quietly, on the first out-breath, progressively relax your mind and body. During the entire exhalation, say to

yourself, like a slow mantra, *Tennnnnn*. By a mantra, I don't mean to repeat this number, but rather keep the *nnnnn* humming along, silently and slowly.

2. When you reach the bottom of the out-breath, keep the mantra going for a few beats, but with increasing subtlety, until the mantra and your thoughts go completely silent.

3. On the next in-breath, again think *Tennnnnn*, but now more "loudly" in your mind, like a slow, incoming mantra.

4. When you switch to the next out-breath, slowly exhale *Ninennnnn*. At the bottom of the breath, keep that mantra going, quietly. Then on the in-breath keep it going but increase the mental "volume."

5. And so on for each successive out- and in-breath. Keep the number count going with different internal "volumes," and keep reducing the number count with each breath until you reach zero.

Don't cheat and go on to the next count if you don't clearly remember your number. This is not a competition. No one is watching except you. If you can't remember the next count, then just start over again at ten. If you keep getting stuck before you reach zero, try using your fingers to keep track of the current number. It gets easier with practice.

At first, this ten-count process will take anywhere from a minute to a few minutes to perform, depending on how fast you're breathing. If you're doing it right, your breathing will begin to slow down, a lot, as you progress.

When you can do this without forgetting the number count, congratulations! You've achieved step one toward gnosis. Celebrate with a delicious piece of pie, or alternatively a high fiber, sugar-free confection with a low glycemic index. If you forget the count, don't worry about it. Just start over at ten with the next out-breath. The first time I tried this, even with years of experience practicing different forms of meditation, I got to seven, then forgot what I was supposed to be doing. I do recall that I suddenly and oddly craved a piece of pie, but I was disciplined and completed the exercise before the pie.

When you've got the first exercise down pat and can reliably repeat it, try the second exercise:

> 1. On the first out-breath, as before, say to yourself during the entire exhalation *Tennnnnn*, like a very slow mantra. At the bottom of the exhale, think nothing at all. Empty your mind, just for a second or two.
>
> 2. Then, during the entire inhalation, continue to maintain no thoughts. Not blank like a void, but *vibrant awareness*, a state of pure crystalline awareness, without thoughts.
>
> 3. During the next out-breath, exhale *Ninennnnn* like a slow mantra. At the bottom of the breath, maintain only vibrant awareness.
>
> 4. And so on for each successive out- and in-breath. Keep reducing the number count until you reach zero.

This is more difficult than the first exercise because during the inhalation, you should have no thoughts, just awareness. When you first encounter this "empty" state, it's very easy to forget the count. If you do, no problem. Just repeat the process, counting backward from ten, until you can reliably reach a zero count.

To enter a state of gnosis, you may need to increase this second exercise to a count of one hundred before you can successfully enter and maintain clear awareness at will. If you can manage to do this reliably, you will have achieved a level of mental control enjoyed by very few people. Most dedicated meditators will eventually experience this state of clarity. Such experiences can be transformative, and within those states, the existence of psi and magic will be blazingly obvious.

Other approaches used to achieve gnosis are "screaming at fire" and psychedelics. The former is how I refer to extreme sports, where absolute mental clarity and presence are essential to be able to free climb a sheer rock face a thousand feet high, ski downhill at 150 miles per hour, or engage in prolonged or outrageously intense sexual activity. Those mental states are as far away from ordinary consciousness as what a lifelong monk achieves in a profoundly calm state. For those who prefer the path of the psychonaut and can inhale a full dose of 5MeO-DMT without fear, that too is a viable approach.

I prefer the calm approach to gnosis because magic requires focused intention. If you're engaged in the equivalent of skiing downhill backward at breakneck speed, you may not have the time or inclination to deflect your attention or intention to also perform a magical act.

Disclaimer: I am absolutely not recommending that anyone, at any age, smoke toad (5MeO-DMT) or any other psychedelic drug. Nor do I condone skydiving nude, BASE jumping off cliffs while blindfolded, or engaging in any activity that anyone anywhere has ever considered to be possibly dangerous or uncomfortable in any way. I only endorse calm, quiet, perfectly safe methods of achieving gnosis.

CHAPTER 11

TESTING MAGIC

Those who don't believe in magic will never find it.

—ROALD DAHL

The varieties of magic and the many ways it can be expressed make personal experimentation not just a good idea but essential for gaining magical skill. Besides recording each of your magical efforts, here are some simple experiments you can try.

DREAM PRECOGNITION

Keep a dream journal beside your bed. Every morning upon waking, and before getting out of bed, immediately record any dreams or feelings you recall. Writing in detail is not necessary. Just record enough so you'll recall the dreams. During the day, pay attention to patterns, events, or synchronicities that match the content or feelings of your dreams. You may also review the dream journal periodically to see if your dreams forecast events that occurred days or even weeks later. Precognitive dreams are among the most commonly reported psychic phenomena. Experiments have been conducted under controlled conditions to test whether telepathy and precognition in fact occur in dreams. And they do.[1]

One of the most extensive investigations of dream precognition and telepathy was conducted at the Maimonides (Hospital) Dream Laboratory, in Brooklyn, New York, starting in 1964. The way the study worked was that before a participant (let's call her Sally) went to sleep, EEG and rapid eye movement (REM) electrodes were attached to her head and face. During the night, each time the REM electrodes signaled that Sally was dreaming (because our eyes move when we're sleeping), the experimenters were alerted, and as soon as the rapid eye movements began to subside, they woke her up and asked her to describe her dreams. In the morning, when Sally was fully awake, she was asked to provide her overall impressions about the likely target (usually a photograph), which for a telepathy experiment had been randomly selected and then telepathically sent toward Sally by a third party as she slept; or for a precognition experiment, the target image would be randomly selected from a large pool of possible images after Sally's impressions were already recorded. Everything she said was captured on audiotape and then transcribed.

After many such nightly tests, and with transcripts in hand, judges who were not otherwise involved in these experiments were asked to try to match the transcripts with the actual targets used in each nightly experiment. Judges were usually asked to rank each picture. So for, say, a pool of eight pictures, the picture with the highest correspondence to the transcript would be ranked 1, and the picture with the least correspondence would be ranked 8. If the judges ranked the actual target picture in the top half of the pool, meaning ranks 1 through 4, that was considered a hit; otherwise it was a miss. This reduced each nightly test into a single datapoint, where the chance hit rate was 50 percent.

Here's an example of one dream telepathy session. The target image was Max Beckmann's painting *Descent from the Cross*.[2] It depicts Christ being taken down from the cross. The image may be described as follows:

A dramatic and somber scene with a group of figures gathered around a central figure being lowered from a cross. The composition is densely packed, with angular, elongated bodies and expressive, contorted faces. The colors are dark and muted, with deep reds, blues, and grays. The background shows a fragmented landscape with abstract shapes and shadowy structures. The lighting is harsh and dramatic, casting stark contrasts and emphasizing the emotional intensity of the moment. The overall style is expressionistic, conveying the anguish and suffering of the scene.

The telepathic sender was given this randomly selected image, and to further motivate him to get emotionally involved with the task, he was also given a small wooden crucifix, a Jesus doll, some nails, and a red marker. He was invited to nail the Jesus doll to the crucifix, then use the red marker to color his body with blood.

Two of the participant's dreams that night involved speeches by Winston Churchill and a Native ceremonial sacrifice. The dreams were described as follows:

In the Churchill thing there was a ceremonial thing going on, and in the native dream there was a type of ceremony going on . . . leading to whatever the ceremony would be to sacrificing two victims. . . . I would say the sacrifice feeling in the native dream . . . would be more like the primitive trying to destroy the civilized. . . . It believed in the god-authority . . . no god was speaking. It was the use of the fear of this, or the awe of god idea, that was to bring about the control.[3]

Based on those impressions, the judges correctly selected the *Descent from the Cross* painting, out of a total of eight possible images, as being most like the target that was telepathically sent. So that session was designated a hit. A total of 450 dream-telepathy sessions like this were reported from 1966 to 1973. The overall hit rate was 65 percent, leading to odds against chance of 10 billion to 1. An updated meta-analysis of dream-ESP studies by the psychologist Lance Storm and his colleagues reevaluated this line of research through 2016. The studies conducted at Maimonides Hospital were compared to similar experiments conducted later, and no difference was found, indicating that these dream psi results were independently repeatable. Storm's conclusion: "The combined effect sizes for both Maimonides and post-Maimonides studies suggest that judges may be able to use dream mentations [that is, spoken descriptions of dream imagery] to identify target materials correctly more often than would be expected by chance."[4]

So yes, telepathy and precognition do happen while dreaming, even in the laboratory.

EVOKING A SYNCHRONICITY

Set an intention to see a certain type and color of automobile, or an animal or bird. Make this target object something that you haven't seen in a while. Record your intention. Over the next few days, remain attentive and see if your intended object appears. We are constantly immersed in a huge array of objects and events, most of which go unnoticed. But by slightly tuning your attention with a specific intention, you may be surprised how often you can *evoke* what seems like a spontaneous synchronicity.

I've tried this with objects like large black ravens and super-expensive sports cars, neither of which I encounter very often. But when I set the intention, it seems that over the next few days the world is suddenly permeated with such objects. Does noticing *make* these objects appear, or were they here all along? To find out, first select an object that you think you are likely to observe, and then record over the next day or week how many of those objects you observe. Keep at this game for, say, ten objects, where each object is less likely to be observed than the previous one. By the end of the ten-object sequence, where the last object is very unlikely to spontaneously appear by chance, assess your synchronicity "hit rate."

FLAME MAGIC

Light a small candle in a dimly lit room and sit comfortably in front of it. Gaze at the flame, allowing your thoughts to dance freely as the flame wavers. When your thoughts subside and you become calm and clear, focus on the flame to see if you can mentally cause subtle changes in its height, flickering speed, or movements in one direction or another. Prevent your breath or ambient air currents from influencing the flame by placing the candle inside a glass box or vase, open at the top.

If you believe you can influence the flame, make a video where you announce that you are going to affect the flame and then later carefully analyze the video to see if you really could influence it, or if you only imagined it. This type of test can be further refined to turn it into a properly controlled scientific experiment.

As described in Chapter 2, a colleague and I conducted a similar test using an inexpensive eight-inch-diameter electrical plasma ball, the kind that's sold as a science toy or a night-light.[5] The experiment showed that intention focused toward the plasma ball influenced the movements of the electrical arcs inside the ball, even when it was located inside a two-thousand-pound, eight-foot-cubed, solid steel, double-walled, electromagnetically shielded chamber, and the participants were ten feet away and outside that chamber.

PLANT ENHANCEMENT

Begin with a small selection of seeds or plants of the same species and size. Flip a coin to randomly separate the seeds or plants into two sets. They should be located near each other, positioned to receive the same amount of light and water. Then flip the coin again to assign one set to receive positive, healthy, or loving intentions, while the other will receive neutral or no intentions at all. Observe the growth and health of both plants over a few weeks or months to notice any differences. Experiments like this have been successfully conducted for many years. A variation on this experiment is to use the same setup but intentionally "bless" water that is used to hydrate the seeds or plants, and use water from the same source, but not blessed, for the controls. This too has been successful.

SCRYING

Arrange a mirror in front of you that is angled slightly upward, so the reflection looks over your head. When you gaze at the mirror, you should see a blank wall or the ceiling. Dim the lighting in the room to the point where you cannot clearly see anything in the mirror. While seated in a comfortable position, and with your eyes soft, gaze at the mirror calmly while holding the expectation that you will see something appear.

After a few minutes, many people report that the mirror begins to look like a window, as though you're seeing through a portal into some other time or place. Then swirling, foglike motions will appear in the mirror, then shapes and colors. With practice, through this method, you can externalize your mental imagery.

The ancient art of scrying involves gazing into a crystal ball, a deep pool of water, or a "witch's mirror," which is a mirror made with a dark or black reflective surface. In modern terms, the psychiatrist Raymond Moody called this technique a "psychomanteum" (theater of the mind), and research using it has shown that for some people who are seeking to connect with departed loved ones, it's a highly effective way to experience reunions with the dead.[6] In more general terms, it appears to be a way to consciously experience, and to observe, what is otherwise floating dreamlike, just below conscious awareness. For a small percentage of people, the images will begin to look like a moving, colorful, three-dimensional scene, and that scene may even appear to emerge from the mirror. I was startled to personally experience the first stages of this phenomenon—a scene emerging from a swirling fog—in a psychomanteum I built for an experiment.[7]

TECH MAGIC

On the "Experiments" tab of my website, DeanRadin.com, I've listed commercial electronic devices and apps that are available (as of the date of the webpage) for testing and training enhancement (PK) and divination (ESP).

CHAPTER 12

BEYOND MAGIC

It's the best possible time to be alive, when almost everything you thought you knew is wrong.

—TOM STOPPARD

Based on a wealth of repeatable laboratory evidence published in peer-reviewed scientific journals, we've learned that psi phenomena are quite real. The evidence has gone through a century of severe scrutiny, and the most sophisticated criticism offered today by leading skeptics is that psi is impossible, so the evidence be damned. Willful ignorance is the last resort when you realize to your dismay that a debate is lost.

We've also learned that psi and magic are the same phenomenon viewed from different historical and practical perspectives. Psi research is the scientific and theoretical approach, and magic is the practical approach. These commonly reported phenomena have been deeply suppressed for centuries by religious and scientific authorities. The suppression has given rise to skeptical memes and stigmas that have been enormously successful in preventing the academic and scientific worlds from taking these phenomena seriously.

Another reason for the continuing skepticism is the way these phenomena are portrayed in entertainment. Sometimes I'm asked in interviews to describe "the most amazing psychic thing I've ever seen." I know that the interviewer wants to hear marvelous tales about levitation, teleportation, and phantastic ghosts. But what I sometimes say if I want to end an interview quickly is this: "There was this one time when we ran an experiment and we got a p-value of point zero zero zero one, and holy smoke, we were stunned!" At that point there's an uncomfortable period of dead air, and then the interview hastily wraps up.

This is not to say that I haven't witnessed some amazing psychic things, but I tend not to dwell on them because real psi and real magic are nowhere near as robust as the fantasies portrayed in fiction. "Real" and "huge" are often confounded in the public's mind, and that's unfortunate because we can know with high confidence that something *exists*, even if its magnitude is teeny-tiny. For example, we know that the charge on the electron is a mere $-1.602176634 \times 10^{-19}$ coulombs. That's 0.00000000016 coulombs, where a coulomb is a measure of charge (named after the eighteenth-century French physicist Charles-Augustin de Coulomb). To start up an internal combustion engine in an automobile takes about 1,000 coulombs, or roughly 200 amps of electrical current for five seconds. We don't have an equivalent yet for "magical charge," but one day I suspect we will. What sort of marvelous engine will 1,000 "magics" fire up?

Why are psi and magic generally so weak?

Because they're mental skills, and most people don't have the talent or the motivation to devote years of diligent practice to get these particular skills under control. That said, a growing number of people have had many decades of meditation practice, and they often do encounter experiences described as psi and magical.[1] They just don't talk about them much in public.

If magic is so weak, then what's it good for?

It may help to optimize your life. Or amplify your luck. Or accelerate healing. But if an invading army is heading your way, could we use magic to stop it? We might be able to mentally nudge the invading commander to become confused or to change his mind. But whenever lots of highly charged motivations are involved, "mental space" becomes exceedingly chaotic and magical influences tend to be washed out. This is one reason why sorcerers traditionally keep their magical acts and even their identities and locations strictly secret. You don't want others' attention or intentions to interfere. In addition, because gnosis and effortless striving are important factors in optimizing magic, it's not easy to achieve those refined states when bombs are falling. Even in fiction, Merlin and Gandalf can only shape destiny to a degree.

Magic in movies is almost always presented as scary or evil, so isn't it dangerous to teach people magic?

The idea of powerful magicians among us can be frightening, because we'd naturally worry what they can do to us. In some quarters of the world, fear of witches is still intensely alive, and if you're accused as a witch, you're in serious danger. Fortunately, the advanced mental practices that encourage the state of gnosis generally lead to kinder, more pleasant, more compassionate people. This means the magicians who are already among us are for the most part nice and quiet, and they don't want to have anything to do with you.

Can I win the lottery with magic?

In principle, yes. But keep in mind that lotteries with big payouts have odds against chance of, say, 200 million to 1. With magic, you might reduce that by a factor of 10, but you'd still face odds of 20 million to 1. It would be more efficient to aim for a "pick three" lottery, where you could potentially reduce the odds from a thousand to a hundred to one. And better still, get clarity on *why* you want to win the lottery in the first place. Use magic to aim for that goal instead of cash.

If I do a magical act for two hours instead of one, will that boost my results by a factor of two?

No, because magic is not an ordinary causal force that operates in a predictable, linear fashion. It operates outside of ordinary space-time, so it's not helpful to think about this in such simple terms. Just seek to optimize the factors known to modulate magical efficacy. Also, remember to practice, try different magical methods, and record what works for you and what doesn't.

Why should anyone care if magic is real?

I'm sure we'd all like to win a billion-dollar lottery and own a couple of private islands. On second thought, if everyone was a magician, then your take on a winning lottery would be less than the cost of a single ticket, and there are only so many islands to go around. So these sorts of typical desires might end up becoming the magical equivalent of gridlock. *Hey, that's my island. Oh yeah?* Combat magic ensues.

Perhaps the cognoscenti suppressed magic for millennia because of the unhappy prospect of accidentally unleashing combat magic. They knew what would happen if you gave an adolescent a nuclear bomb with a blinking red button on it labeled DO NOT PRESS THIS BUTTON. In any case, even with the wise use of magic, the fabric of reality may be flexible only to a limited extent, so if there were a sudden explosion of magic, it might end up rending the fabric of reality. Ripped Reality might be a great name for a rock band or a gym specializing in body building, but not for a place where you'd want to live.

Thus, rolling magic out slowly and carefully may be the way to go. That means we need to learn much more about what magic is, how it works, and what are its potential risks and benefits. I believe we have the competency to do this, and we've already seen that the scientific worldview is beginning to embrace philosophies that are increasingly compatible with magic. But whether *politics* has the competency to deal with magic, well, that's another matter.

When will modern and ancient paths to magical knowledge converge?

Here too the answer depends more on politics than on science.

Major advances in scientific knowledge are largely supported by federal grants because research is expensive. The annual US science budget was nearly $900 billion in 2022; worldwide it is estimated to be $2.5 trillion.[2] Of that impressive budget, exactly zero dollars was allocated for public research on psi or magic. How much might be allocated in secret is unknown, but I would be very surprised if it was zero.

Worldwide funding for research on these topics does exist, but it's almost entirely dependent on a few private foundations and wealthy individuals. Optimistically it amounts to perhaps $15 million a year, with a sizable percentage of that generously provided by the Bial Foundation in Portugal. This means that global funding for research on psi and magic is about 0.0004 percent of what we collectively spend each year on other scientific research. And yet a majority of the world's population is perennially interested in these topics. What's wrong with this picture?

Recent surveys have shown growing discontent with the state of everyday life. Perhaps this is due to extreme weather caused by climate change, or maybe the sun ate a sour asteroid and has the solar equivalent of a bellyache. Whatever the cause, if you mix widespread gloominess with fears about witchcraft, progress in understanding psi and magic can easily stall.[3]

If that happens, it would be a pity because gaining a better understanding of consciousness, psi, and magic could offer an enormous boon to humanity. As we learn more about the transformative power of seeing reality with naked awareness, whether that happens through a meditation practice, a spontaneous gnosis or noetic experience, a psychedelic trip, an NDE or OBE, a psychic, mystical, or spiritual experience, or any number of other paths, the effect in most cases is the same: *a major, positive shift in personality.* Having such experiences results in greater compassion, empathy, tolerance, gratefulness, optimism, and, in general, "prosocial" behavior.[4]

There's another reason for gaining a better understanding of consciousness. As an analogy, say you're walking in the woods with some friends, and you come upon a stream. To everyone's horror, you see dozens of crying babies floating down the stream. The natural impulse is to dive in and rescue as many of them as you can. That's what most of your friends will do. But while you're drying off the babies as they're brought ashore, you're thinking, what are all these babies doing in the stream in the first place? They just keep on coming, and we can't keep this up forever. So you decide that in the long run, it's more efficient to go upstream to discover the cause of this unfolding tragedy.

Likewise, to help solve all sorts of global existential crises, we need to go upstream and better understand the causes of these problems, many of which can be traced to our individual and collective understanding about who and what we are. This is a problem of *consciousness*.

A cynic might say this sounds like toxic positivity; it's unrealistic because the world is "red in tooth and claw," to use Alfred Lord Tennyson's dramatic phrase. But does it have to be that way? Are aggression and survival of the fittest the only way to live? Would an improved understanding of consciousness and its capacities lead toward a more life-affirming existence and guide us away from endless chest-beating, nihilism, and extinction? Why are noetic experiences so positively transformative? Are we mature enough as a species to safely and effectively provide magical experiences to anyone who wants them?

We won't know until we make it a societal priority to find out. To move things along, I'd propose that we devote one hundredth of one percent (0.01 percent) of the worldwide annual science budget toward the serious exploration of these questions. That would leave fully intact 99.99 percent of existing projects, but it would also provide about $250 million a year for the serious exploration of *inner space*. Would the knowledge we gain transform the world into a kinder and more compassionate place? I don't know, but I'm optimistic that such a moonshot would be well worth it to find out.

ACKNOWLEDGMENTS

I am grateful to the many foundations and individuals who have supported my research. They include the Bial Foundation (Portugal), the Research Network for the Study of Esoteric Practices (UK), the Subtle Energy Funders Collective, the Federico and Elvia Faggin Foundation, the Fetzer Institute, the Mental Insight Foundation, the Samueli Institute, the Parapsychological Foundation, the Bigelow Foundation, Harvard University's Richard Hodgson Memorial Fund, the Swedish Society for Psychical Research, the Norwegian Parapsychological Society, the Society for Psychical Research (England), the Institut für Grenzgebiete der Psychologie und Psychohygiene (Germany), the John B. Huntington Foundation, the Hittman Family Foundation, Jeff Parrett, Richard and Connie Adams, Klee Irwin, Claire Russell, Steve Curtis, and Ron Cline.

I am also indebted to my charming colleagues at the Institute of Noetic Sciences; to magician Peter J. Carroll and mystic G. M. Wolf for our enlightening discussions; to Robert Morris, Robert Jahn, Brenda Dunne, and Donald Baepler, who somehow bewitched university administrators to allow me to pursue psi research in academia; to Major General Alan Salisbury (retired) and David Liddle, who were fascinated enough by psi to allow me to conduct "blue sky" research projects in their industrial labs; to Edwin May, Russell Targ, and Hal Puthoff, who were my role models for how to conduct rigorous science in a perpetually controversial and captivating field; to my many magical friends and colleagues around the world, too numerous to mention; and to Donna Loffredo, my enchanting editor at Penguin Random House.

NOTES

PREFACE

1. Aakanksha Sharma, "Books That Will Change the Way You Look at the Universe," *Times of India*, April 4, 2024, timesofindia.indiatimes.com/life-style/books/web-stories/books-that-will-change-the-way-you-look-at-the-universe/photostory/109040037.cms.

2. John A. Wheeler, *At Home in the Universe* (American Institute of Physics, 1997).

3. Alexander Blum and Stefano Furlan, "How John Wheeler Lost His Faith in the Law," in *Rethinking the Concept of Law of Nature: Natural Order in the Light of Contemporary Science*, ed. Yemima Ben-Menahem, 283–322 (Springer International Publishing, 2022), doi.org/10.1007/978-3-030-96775-8_11.

CHAPTER 1: INTRODUCTION

1. Jagdish Mehra, ed. *The Physicist's Conception of Nature* (D. Reidel Publishing Company, 1973).

2. The list includes Max Planck, Erwin Schrödinger, Werner Heisenberg, Wolfgang Pauli, Arthur Eddington, John von Neumann, and many more.

3. Lynn Thorndike, *A History of Magic and Experimental Science* (Columbia University Press, 1923); DK, *A History of Magic, Witchcraft and the Occult* (DK, 2020).

4. James R. Doty, *Mind Magic: The Neuroscience of Manifestation and How It Changes Everything* (Avery, 2024); Jesper Sørensen, *A Cognitive Theory of Magic*, annotated ed. (Rowman Altamira, 2007); Matt Kaplan, *Science of the Magical: From the Holy Grail to Love Potions to Superpowers* (Scribner, 2015).

5. Dean Radin, *Real Magic: Ancient Wisdom, Modern Science, and a Guide to the Secret Power of the Universe* (Harmony, 2018); Serena Roney-Dougal, *Where Science and Magic Meet: A Convincing Explanation of Why Magical Things Can and Do Happen*, 3rd ed. (New Page Books, 2010); William A. Tiller, Walter Dibble, and J. Gregory Fandel, *Some Science Adventures with Real Magic* (Pavior, 2005).

6. Peter Vickers, "Should We Really Believe Scientific Facts Will Last Forever When History Is Full of Revolutions in Thinking?" *Conversation*, September 14, 2022, theconversation.com/should-we-really-believe-scientific-facts-will-last-forever-when-history-is-full-of-revolutions-in-thinking-190277.

7. Steven L. Goldman, *Science in the Twentieth Century: A Social-Intellectual Survey* (Teaching Company, 2004).

8. Zeng-Bing Chen, "Quantum Entanglement Dynamics of Spacetime and Matter," *Fundamental Research*, October 29, 2023, doi.org/10.1016/j.fmre.2023.10.004; Yasunori Nomura, Nico Salzetta, Fabio Sanches, and Sean J. Weinberg, "Spacetime Equals Entanglement," *Physics Letters B* 763, no. 10 (2016): 370–74, doi.org/10.1016/j.physletb.2016.10.045.

9. Swami Bhaskarananda, *Journey from Many to One: Essentials of Advaita Vedanta* (Viveka Press, 2009); Bernardo Kastrup, *The Idea of the World* (Iff Books, 2019); Donald D. Hoffman, *The Case Against Reality: Why Evolution Hid the Truth from Our Eyes* (W.W. Norton, 2019); Robert Lanza, Matej Pavšič, and Bob Berman, *The Grand Biocentric Design: How Life Creates Reality* (BenBella Books, 2020); Federico Faggin, *Irreducible: Consciousness, Life, Computers, and Human Nature* (Essentia Books, 2024).

10. N. David Mermin, "Is the Moon There When Nobody Looks? Reality and the Quantum Theory," *Physics Today* (1985): 38–47, lilith.fisica.ufmg.br/~fqii/Mermin-PhysToday85.pdf.

11. Christof Koch, *Then I Am Myself the World: What Consciousness Is and How to Expand It* (Basic Books, 2024).

12. "Richard Dawkins: Evolution, Intelligence, Simulation, and Memes," Lex Fridman Podcast no. 87 (c. 2020), youtu.be/5f-JlzBuUUU?si=mbl6bJitvaKKX7JS.

13. David Chalmers, "Idealism and the Mind-Body Problem," in *The Routledge Handbook of Panpsychism*, ed. William Seager (Routledge, 2020), 353.

14. Seth, Jane Roberts, and Robert F. Butts, *The Magical Approach: Seth Speaks About the Art of Creative Living* (Amber-Allen, 1995).

15. Isaac Bonewits, *Real Magic: An Introductory Treatise on the Basic Principles of Yellow Magic*, rev. ed. (Red Wheel/Weiser, 1989).

16. Peter J. Carroll, *Liber Kaos: Chaos Magic for the Pandaemonaeon*, rev. ed. (Weiser Books, 2023).

17. Peter J. Carroll and Ian Blumberg-Enge, *Interview with a Wizard* (Mandrake of Oxford, 2022), 80.

18. Julian Vayne, *Magick Works: Stories in Occultism in Theory and Practice* (Mandrake, 2020).

19. J. Finley Hurley, *Sorcery* (Routledge & Kegan Paul, 1985).

20. Jan Ehrenwald, *The ESP Experience: A Psychiatric Validation* (Basic Books, 1978).

21. Napoleon Hill, *Think and Grow Rich*, rev. ed. (TarcherPerigee, 2007).

22. Claude M. Bristol and Mitch Horowitz, *The Magic of Believing* (G&D Media, 2019).

23. Neville Goddard, *Imagination* (Andura, 2020).

CHAPTER 2: SCIENCE OF ENCHANTMENT

1. Joseph G. Pratt et al., *Extra-Sensory Perception After Sixty Years; A Critical Appraisal of the Research in Extra-Sensory Perception* (Henry Holt, 1940).

2. D. Johnson, "Platonic Parapsychology," *Daily Illini*, November 19, 1977, 2.

3. Arthur I. Miller, *Jung, Pauli, and the Pursuit of a Scientific Obsession* (W.W. Norton, 2010), 137.

4. Dean Radin and Jessica Utts, "Experiments Investigating the Influence of Intention on Random and Pseudorandom Events," *Journal of Scientific Exploration* 3, no. 1 (1989): 65–79, citeseerx.ist.psu.edu/document?repid=rep1&type=pdf&doi=81a1347a92eee99f2de3872ccc28135858345f73.

5. Dean Radin, "Evaluating Geometric Distance Scores in a Perceptual Task," in *Research in Parapsychology 1981*, ed. Robert L. Morris (Scarecrow Press, 1982).

6. Eben Alexander, *Proof of Heaven: A Neurosurgeon's Journey into the Afterlife* (Simon & Schuster, 2012); Jeffrey J. Kripal, *The Flip: Epiphanies of Mind and the Future of Knowledge* (Bellevue, 2019); E. L. Mayer, *Extraordinary Knowing: Science, Skepticism, and the Inexplicable Powers of the Human Mind* (Bantam, 2008); Mona Sobhani, *Proof of Spiritual Phenomena: A Neuroscientist's Discovery of the Ineffable Mysteries of the Universe* (Park Street Press, 2022);

Marjorie Woollacott, David Lorimer, and Gary E. Schwartz, *The Playful Universe: Synchronicity and the Nature of Consciousness* (Academy for the Advancement of Postmaterialist Sciences, 2024).

7. K. Walsh and Garret Moddel, "Effect of Belief on Psi Performance in a Card Guessing Task," *Journal of Scientific Exploration* 21, no. 3 (2007): 501–10.

8. Lance Storm and Patrizio Tressoldi, "Gathering in More Sheep and Goats: A Meta-Analysis of Forced-Choice Sheep-Goat ESP Studies, 1994–2015," *Journal of the Society for Psychical Research* 81, no. 2 (2017): 79.

9. František Bartoš et al., "Fair Coins Tend to Land on the Same Side They Started: Evidence from 350,757 Flips," arXiv:2310.04153, *arXiv*, June 2, 2024, doi.org/10.48550/arXiv.2310.04153.

10. Riccardo Boscariol and Patrizio Tressoldi, "From Ordinary to ExtraOrdinary: The Role of Placebo Effect on Intuitive Guessing," *PsyARXiv*, May 19, 2024, doi.org/10.31234/osf.io/c73ej.

11. Willis Harman, *Global Mind Change: The Promise of the 21st Century* (Institute of Noetic Sciences, 1998).

12. Brendan O'Regan and Caryle Hirshberg, *Spontaneous Remission: An Annotated Bibliography* (Institute of Noetic Sciences, 1993).

13. "IONS50 Series: Spontaneous Remission," IONS, March 18, 2024, noetic.org/blog/ions50-spontaneous-remission/.

14. Gudapureddy Radha and Manu Lopus, "The Spontaneous Remission of Cancer: Current Insights and Therapeutic Significance," *Translational Oncology* 14, no. 9 (2021): 101166, doi.org/10.1016/j.tranon.2021.101166.

15. Kelly A. Turner, *Radical Remission: Surviving Cancer Against All Odds* (HarperOne, 2014).

16. Joseph G. Pratt, "The Case for Psychokinesis," *Journal of Parapsychology* 14, no. 3 (1960): 171–88.

17. M. Bell, "Francis Bacon: Pioneer in Parapsychology," *International Journal of Parapsychology* 6, no. 2 (1964): 199–208.

18. Diane C. Ferrari, "Effects of Consciousness on the Fall of Dice: A Meta-Analysis," *Journal of Scientific Exploration* 5, no. 1 (1991): 61–83.

19. R. G. Jahn, "The Persistent Paradox of Psychic Phenomena: An Engineering Perspective," *Proceedings of the IEEE* 70, no. 2 (1982): 136–70, doi.org/10.1109/PROC.1982.12260.

20. Dean I. Radin and Roger D. Nelson, "Evidence for Consciousness-Related Anomalies in Random Physical Systems," *Foundations of Physics* 19, no. 12 (1989): 1499–514, doi.org/10.1007/BF00732509; Dean Radin, *Entangled Minds: Extrasensory Experiences in a Quantum Reality* (Simon & Schuster, 2006); Holger Bösch, Fiona Steinkamp, and Emil Boller, "Examining Psychokinesis: The Interaction of Human Intention with Random Number Generators— A Meta-Analysis," *Psychological Bulletin* 132, no. 4 (2006): 497–523, doi.org/10 .1037/0033-2909.132.4.497; Dean Radin, Roger Nelson, York Dobyns, and Joop Houtkooper, "Reexamining Psychokinesis: Commentary on the Bösch, Steinkamp and Boller Meta-Analysis," *Psychological Bulletin* 132, no. 4 (2006): 529–32, doi.org/10.1037/0033-2909.132.4.529.

21. Johanna A. Damen et al., "Indicators of Questionable Research Practices Were Identified in 163,129 Randomized Controlled Trials," *Journal of Clinical Epidemiology* 154 (2023): 23–32, doi.org/10.1016/j.jclinepi.2022.11.020.

22. Peter A. Bancel, "Simulating Questionable Research Practices," ResearchGate, June 2018, doi.org/10.13140/RG.2.2.12941.64487.

23. Bryan J. Williams, "Minding the Matter of Psychokinesis: A Review of Proof- and Process-Oriented Experimental Findings Related to Mental Influence on Random Number Generators," *Journal of Scientific Exploration* 35, no. 4 (2022): 829–932, doi.org/10.31275/20212359.

24. Helmut Schmidt, "The Strange Properties of Psychokinesis," *Journal of Scientific Exploration* 1, no. 2 (1987): 103–18.

25. Morris Freedman et al., "Mind–Matter Interactions and the Frontal Lobes of the Brain: A Novel Neurobiological Model of Psi Inhibition," *Explore* 14, no. 1 (2018): 76–85, doi.org/10.1016/j.explore.2017.08.003.

26. Morris Freedman et al., "Enhanced Mind-Matter Interactions Following rTMS Induced Frontal Lobe Inhibition," *Cortex* 172 (2024): 222–33, doi.org/10 .1016/j.cortex.2023.10.016.

27. Gabriel Guerrer, "Consciousness-Related Interactions in a Double-Slit Optical System," OSF, April 22, 2019, doi.org/10.17605/OSF.IO/QDKVX; Michael Ibison and Stanley Jeffers, "A Double-Slit Diffraction Experiment to Investigate Claims of Consciousness-Related Anomalies," *Journal of Scientific Exploration* 12, no. 4 (1998): 543–50, citeseerx.ist.psu.edu/document?repid= rep1&type=pdf&doi=bb426f89414dfc4d3e3beafe4d0d3ce39e75a47c; Andreja Vujanac et al., "Quantum Nature of Consciousness—Double Slit Diffraction Experiment in Medicine," *Medical Hypotheses* 133 (2019): 109382, doi.org/10

.1016/j.mehy.2019.109382; Dean Radin et al., "Consciousness and the Double-Slit Interference Pattern: Six Experiments," *Physics Essays* 25, no. 2 (2012): 157–71, doi.org/10.4006/0836-1398-25.2.157; Dean Radin, Leena Michel, and Arnaud Delorme, "Psychophysical Modulation of Fringe Visibility in a Distant Double-Slit Optical System," *Physics Essays* 29, no. 1 (2016): 14–22, physicsessays.org/browse-journal-2/product/1424-4-dean-radin-leena-michel-and -arnaud-delorme-psychophysical-modulation-of-fringe-visibility-in-a-distant -double-slit-optical-system.html; Dean Radin, Leena Michel, A. Pierce, and Arnaud Delorme, "Psychophysical Interactions with a Single-Photon Double-Slit Optical System," *Quantum Biosystems* 6, no. 1 (2015): 82–98.

28. To be more precise, these odds against chance were based on two-tailed p-values, i.e., bidirectional outcomes.

29. Teodora Milojević and Mark A. Elliott, "Chapter 1—The Causal Influence of Conscious Engagement on Photonic Behavior: A Review of the Mind-Matter Interaction," in *Neurophysiology of Silence Part B: Theory and Review*, ed. Tal Dotan Ben-Soussan, Joseph Glicksohn, and Narayanan Srinivasan, vol. 280 of *Progress in Brain Research* (Elsevier, 2023), doi.org/10.1016/bs.pbr.2023.03.005.

30. The term *cause* implies a force-like influence, portrayed in comic books like beams of lightning shooting out of a superhero's eyes. That's almost certainly not what we're dealing with here, but it's the closest analogy we have. Aristotle's notion of "final cause" is probably closer. See Dean Radin, Helané Wahbeh, Leena Michel, and Arnaud Delorme, "Psychophysical Interactions with a Double-Slit Interference Pattern: Exploratory Evidence of a Causal Influence," *Physics Essays* 34, no. 1 (2021): 79–88, dx.doi.org/10.4006/0836-1398-34.1.79.

31. But again, it is not like any ordinary causal force currently understood in physics. See David J. Chalmers and Kelvin J. McQueen, "Consciousness and the Collapse of the Wave Function," in *Consciousness and Quantum Mechanics*, ed. Shan Gao (Oxford University Press, 2022), doi.org/10.1093/oso/9780197501665.003.0002.

32. Loren Carpenter, Cédric Cannard, Helané Wahbeh, and Dean Radin, "Psychophysical Interactions with Photons: Three Exploratory Studies with Unexpected Results," *Journal of the Society for Psychical Research* 85, no. 1 (2021): 31–48, doi.org/10.31234/osf.io/bq7ne.

33. Katherine Howard and Cansu Okan, "Tacit and Explicit Knowledge," *Encyclopedia of Libraries, Librarianship, and Information Science* 2 (2025): 171–78, doi.org/10.1016/B978-0-323-95689-5.00271-6.

34. Richard Wiseman and Marilyn Schlitz, "Experimenter Effects and the Remote Detection of Staring," *Journal of Parapsychology* 61, no. 3 (1997): 197–208.

35. Dean Radin, "Observer Influence on Quantum Interference: Testing the von Neumann–Wigner Consciousness-Collapse Theory," *Physics Essays* (Volume 38 (2025), 64–80, physicsessays.org/browse-journal-2/product/2120-9-dean-radin -observer-influence-on.html. March 2025).

36. Michael White, *Isaac Newton: The Last Sorcerer* (Basic Books, 1997).

37. Dean Radin, Peter A. Bancel, and Arnaud Delorme, "Psychophysical Interactions with Entangled Photons: Five Exploratory Studies," *Journal of Anomalous Experience and Cognition* 1, no. 1–2 (2021), doi.org/10.31156/jaex .23392.

38. "quEDU: The Science Kit for Quantum Education," QuTools, n.d., qutools .com/quedu/.

39. William Crookes, "On a Fourth State of Matter," *Journal of the Franklin Institute* 110, no. 2 (1880): 117–20, doi.org/10.1016/0016-0032(80)90072-1.

40. Cutler J. Cleveland and Christopher Morris, *Chronologies, Top Ten Lists, and Word Clouds* vol. 2 of *Handbook of Energy* (Elsevier, 2014), 353–80, doi.org/ 10.1016/B978-0-12-417013-1.00021-2.

41. Project Hessdalen, Norway, www.hessdalen.org.

42. Carlos S. Alvarado, "Musings on Materializations: Eric J. Dingwall on 'The Plasma Theory,'" *Journal of Scientific Exploration* 33, no. 1 (2019): 73–113; J. D. Frodsham, "A Note on a Luminous Phenomenon," *Journal of the Society for Psychical Research* 49, no. 776 (1978): 852–54; Trevor Hall, "The Cock Lane Ghost: A Historical Note," *International Journal of Parapsychology* 4, no. 1 (1962): 71–87.

43. Robert A. Charman, review of *The Hyperspace of Consciousness* by Massimo Teodorani, *Journal of the Society for Psychical Research* 80, no. 2 (2016), www.spr .ac.uk/book-review/hyperspace-consciousness-massimo-teodorani; Massimo Teodorani, *The Hyperspace of Consciousness* (Elementà, 2015).

44. H. W. Phillips, "Tesla Talks and Confirms His Astounding Story," *Criterion*, November 19, 1898, reprinted in Tesla Collection, teslacollection.com/tesla_articles/ 1898/criterion/h_w_phillips/tesla_talks_and_confirms_his_astounding_story.

45. William A. Tiller, "A Gas Discharge Device for Investigating Focused Human Attention," *Journal of Scientific Exploration* 4, no. 2 (1990): 255–71.

46. Gary E. Schwartz, "A Computer-Automated, Multi-Center, Multi-Blinded, Randomized Control Trial Evaluating Hypothesized Spirit Presence and Communication," *Explore* 17, no. 4 (2021): 351–59, doi.org/10.1016/j.explore .2019.11.007.

47. Dean Radin and Joyce Anastasia, "Psychophysical Interactions with Electrical Plasma: Three Exploratory Experiments," *Journal of the Society for Psychical Research* 87, no. 4 (2022): 226–43, doi.org/10.31234/osf.io/tqwb3.

48. Ian Thompson, "How the Non-Physical Influences Physics and Physiology: A Proposal," *Dualism Review* 3 (2021): 1–13, philarchive.org/archive/THOHTN-3.

49. Masaru Emoto, *The Hidden Messages in Water* (Atria Books, 2005).

50. Dean Radin, Gail Hayssen, Masaru Emoto, and Takashige Kizu, "Double-Blind Test of the Effects of Distant Intention on Water Crystal Formation," *Explore* 2, no. 5 (2006): 408–11, doi.org/10.1016/j.explore.2006.06.004; Dean Radin, Nancy Lund, Masaru Emoto, and Takashige Kizu, "Effects of Distant Intention on Water Crystal Formation: A Triple-Blind Replication," *Journal of Scientific Exploration* 12, no. 4 (2008): 481–93.

51. Dean Radin, Gail Hayssen, and J. Walsh, "Effects of Intentionally Enhanced Chocolate on Mood," *Explore* 3, no. 5 (2007): 485–92, doi.org/10.1016/j.explore .2007.06.004.

52. Yung-Jong Shiah and Dean Radin, "Metaphysics of the Tea Ceremony: A Randomized Trial Investigating the Roles of Intention and Belief on Mood While Drinking Tea," *Explore* 9, no. 6 (2013): 355–60, doi.org/10.1016/j.explore .2013.08.005.

53. Yung-Jong Shiah, Hsu-Liang Hsieh, Huai-Ju Chen, and Dean Radin, "Effects of Intentionally Treated Water on Growth of *Arabidopsis thaliana* Seeds with Cryptochrome Mutations," *Explore* 13, no. 6 (2017): 371–78, doi.org/10 .1016/j.explore.2017.05.001.

54. Yung-Jong Shiah, Hsu-Liang Hsieh, Huai-Ju Chen, and Dean I. Radin, "Effects of Intentionally Treated Water and Seeds on the Growth of *Arabidopsis thaliana*," *Explore* 17, no. 1 (2021): 55–59, doi.org/10.1016/j.explore.2020.04.006.

55. Zoë Schlanger, "The Mysteries of Plant 'Intelligence,'" *Atlantic*, May 1, 2024, www.theatlantic.com/magazine/archive/2024/06/plant-consciousness -intelligence-light-eaters/678207/.

56. Yung-Jong Shiah, Liang Shan, Dean I. Radin, and George T.-J. Huang, "Effects of Intentionally Treated Water on the Growth of Mesenchymal Stem

Cells: An Exploratory Study," *Explore* 18, no. 6 (2022): 663–69, doi.org/10.1016/j.explore.2021.11.007.

57. Dean Radin, "Special Issue on Energy Medicine," *Explore* 17, no. 1 (2021): 9–10, doi.org/10.1016/j.explore.2020.10.011.

58. William F. Bengston and Sylvia Fraser, *The Energy Cure: Unraveling The Mystery of Hands-On Healing* (Sounds True, 2010).

59. William F. Bengston and David Krinsley, "The Effect of the 'Laying On of Hands' on Transplanted Breast Cancer in Mice," *Journal of Scientific Exploration* 14, no. 3 (2000): 353–64, www.fourmilab.ch/documents/gtpp/Documents/jse_14_3_bengston.pdf.

60. Bengston Research, bengstonresearch.com.

61. Dawson Church, *The EFT Manual*, 4th ed. (Energy Psychology Press, 2018).

62. Bernard Grad, "A Telekinetic Effect on Plant Growth: II. Experiments Involving Treatment of Saline in Stoppered Bottles," *International Journal of Parapsychology* 6, no. 4 (1964): 473–98; Bernard Grad, "Some Biological Effects of the 'Laying on of Hands': A Review of Experiments with Animals and Plants," *Journal of the American Society for Psychical Research* 59, no. 2 (1965): 95–127; Bernard Grad et al., "An Unorthodox Method of Treatment on Wound Healing in Mice," *International Journal of Parapsychology* 3, no. 2 (1961): 5–24.

63. Sarah Beseme et al., "Transcriptional Changes in Cancer Cells Induced by Exposure to a Healing Method," *Dose-Response* 16, no. 3 (2018), doi.org/10.1177/1559325818782843; Sarah Beseme et al., "Effects Induced in Vivo by Exposure to Magnetic Signals Derived from a Healing Technique," *Dose-Response* 18, no. 1 (2020), doi.org/10.1177/1559325820907741.

64. Garret Yount et al., "Energy Medicine Treatments for Hand and Wrist Pain: A Pilot Study," *Explore* 17, no. 1 (2021): 11–21, doi.org/10.1016/j.explore.2020.10.015.

65. Dean Radin et al., "Spectroscopic Analysis of Water Treated By and In Proximity to Energy Medicine Practitioners: An Exploratory Study," *Explore* 17, no. 1 (2021): 27–31, doi.org/10.1016/j.explore.2020.10.005.

66. Stephan A. Schwartz, Randall J. De Mattei, Edward G. Brame, Jr., and S. James P. Spottiswoode, "Infrared Spectra Alteration in Water Proximate to the Palms of Therapeutic Practitioners," *Explore* 11, no. 2 (2015): 143–55, doi.org/10.1016/j.explore.2014.12.008.

67. Wayne B. Jonas and Cincy C. Crawford, "The Healing Presence: Can It Be Reliably Measured?" *Journal of Alternative and Complementary Medicine* 10, no. 5 (2004): 751–56, doi.org/10.1089/acm.2004.10.751.

68. Loren Carpenter et al., "Possible Negentropic Effects Observed During Energy Medicine Sessions," *Explore* 17, no. 1 (2020): 45–49, doi.org/10.1016/j.explore.2020.09.003.

69. Dean Radin and Garret Yount, "Effects of Healing Intention on Cultured Cells and Truly Random Events," *Journal of Alternative and Complementary Medicine* 10, no. 1 (2004): 103–12, doi.org/10.1089/107555304322849020.

70. O. Costa de Beauregard, "Macroscopic Retrocausation," *Foundations of Physics Letters* 8 (1995): 287–91, doi.org/10.1007/BF02187352; Yoon-Ho Kim et al., "Delayed 'Choice' Quantum Eraser," *Physical Review Letters* 84, no. 1 (2000): 1–5, doi.org/10.1103/PhysRevLett.84.1; Daniel P. Sheehan, ed., *Frontiers of Time: Retrocausation Experiment and Theory: AIP Conference Proceedings* 863 (American Institute of Physics, 2006); Daniel P. Sheehan, "Remembrance of Things Future: A Case for Retrocausation and Precognition," in *Extrasensory Perception: Support, Skepticism, and Science*, ed. Edwin C. May and Sonali B. Marwaha (Praeger/ABC-CLIO, 2015).

71. Gustav Theodor Fechner, *The Little Book of Life and After Death* (Little, Brown, 1905).

72. I. J. Good, "Letter to the Editor," *Journal of Parapsychology* 25 (1961): 58.

73. Julia Mossbridge, Patrizio Tressoldi, and Jessica Utts, "Predictive Physiological Anticipation Preceding Seemingly Unpredictable Stimuli: A Meta-Analysis," *Frontiers in Psychology* 3 (2012), doi.org/10.3389/fpsyg.2012.00390.

74. Michael Duggan and Patrizio Tressoldi, "Predictive Physiological Anticipatory Activity Preceding Seemingly Unpredictable Stimuli: An Update of Mossbridge et al.'s Meta-Analysis," *F1000Research* 7 (2018): 407, doi.org/10.12688/f1000research.14330.2.

75. Leonard D. van Brussel, Maarten A. S. Boksem, Roeland C. Dietvorst, and Ale Smidts, "Brain Activity of Professional Investors Signals Future Stock Performance," *Proceedings of the National Academy of Sciences* 121, no. 16 (2024) doi.org/10.1073/pnas.2307982121.

76. Debra Lynne Katz and Jon Knowles, *Associative Remote Viewing: The Art and Science of Predicting Outcomes for Sports, Politics, Finances and the Lottery* (Living Dreams Press, 2021).

77. Dick Bierman and Thomas Rabeyron, "Can Psi Research Sponsor Itself? Simulations and Results of an Automated ARV-Casino Experiment," presentation to the 56th Annual Convention of the Parapsychological Association, Viterbo, Italy, August 2013.

78. Greg Kolodziejzyk, "Greg Kolodziejzyk's 13-Year Associated Remote Viewing Experiment Results," *Journal of Parapsychology* 76, no. 2 (2012): 349–68.

79. Collection of Mediumistic Art, mediumistic.art/about.

80. Rex G. Stanford, T. A. Zenhausern, and M. A. Dwyer, "Psychokinesis as Psi-Mediated Instrumental Response," *Journal of the American Society for Psychical Research* 69, no. 2 (1975): 127–33.

81. Elmar Gruber, "PK Effects on Pre-recorded Group Behavior of Living Systems," *European Journal of Parapsychology* 3 (1980): 167–75.

82. William Braud, "Wellness Implications of Retroactive Intentional Influence: Exploring an Outrageous Hypothesis," *Alternative Therapies in Health and Medicine* 6, no. 1 (2000): 37–48.

83. Helmut Schmidt, "PK Effect on Pre-Recorded Targets," *Journal of the American Society for Psychical Research* 70, no. 3 (1976): 267–91.

84. Helmut Schmidt, "Addition Effect for PK on Prerecorded Targets," *Journal of Parapsychology* 49, no. 3 (1985b): 229–44; Helmut Schmidt, R. Morris, and L. Rudolph, "Channeling Evidence for a PK Effect to Independent Observers," *Journal of Parapsychology* 50, no. 1 (1986): 1–15.

85. Dick Bierman, "Do Psi Phenomena Suggest Radical Dualism?" in *Toward a Science of Consciousness II: The Second Tucson Discussions and Debates*, ed. S. R. Hameroff, A. W. Kazniak, and A. C. Scott (Bradford/MIT Press, 1998).

86. Williams, "Minding the Matter of Psychokinesis."

87. C. Helfrich-Förster et al., "Women Temporarily Synchronize Their Menstrual Cycles With the Luminance and Gravimetric Cycles of the Moon," *Science Advances* 7, no. 5 (2021), doi.org/10.1126/sciadv.abe1358.

88. Julia Mossbridge and Daryl Bem, "Reproductive Hormonal Status as a Predictor of Precognition" (2016), www.koestler-parapsychology.psy.ed.ac.uk/Documents/KPU_1043_Results.pdf.

89. William G. Braud, *Distant Mental Influence: Its Contributions to Science, Healing, and Human Interactions* (Hampton Roads, 2003).

90. D. Millett, "Hans Berger: From Psychic Energy to the EEG," *Perspectives in Biology and Medicine* 44, no. 4 (2001): 522–42, doi.org/10.1353/pbm.2001.0070.

91. Rupert Sheldrake, Hugo Godwin, and Simon Rockell, "A Filmed Experiment on Telephone Telepathy with the Nolan Sisters," *Journal of the Society for Psychical Research* 68 (2004): 168–72; Rupert Sheldrake and Pamela Smart, "Videotaped Experiments on Telephone Telepathy," *Journal of Parapsychology* 67, no. 1 (2003): 187–206; Rupert Sheldrake and Tom Stedall, "A Comparison of Four New Automated Tests for Telephone Telepathy," *Journal of Anomalous Experience and Cognition* 4, no. 1 (2024), doi.org/10.31156/jaex.25250.

92. Patrizio Tressoldi and Lance Storm, "Stage 2 Registered Report: Anomalous Perception in a Ganzfeld Condition—A Meta-Analysis of More than 40 Years Investigation," *F1000Research* (2024), doi.org/10.12688/f1000research.51746.3.

93. Steven J. Haggbloom et al., "The 100 Most Eminent Psychologists of the Twentieth Century," *Review of General Psychology* 6, no. 2 (2002): 139–52, doi.org/10.1037/1089-2680.6.2.139.

94. Etzel Cardeña, "In Memoriam: Robert Rosenthal (1933–2024): Affable Giant of Psychology and Champion of Honest Science," *Journal of Anomalous Experience and Cognition* 4, no. 1 (2024), doi.org/10.31156/jaex.26221.

95. Dean Radin, *The Conscious Universe: The Scientific Truth of Psychic Phenomena* (HarperOne, 1997).

96. Monya Baker, "1,500 Scientists Lift the Lid on Reproducibility," *Nature* 533, no. 7604 (2016): 452–54, doi.org/10.1038/533452a.

97. Karmela Padavic-Callaghan, "Physicists Are Grappling with Their Own Reproducibility Crisis," *NewScientist*, May 17, 2024, www.newscientist.com/article/2431927-physicists-are-grappling-with-their-own-reproducibility-crisis/.

98. Harry M. Collins and Trevor Pinch, *The Golem: What You Should Know About Science*, 2nd ed. (Cambridge University Press, 2012).

99. Harry M. Collins, "The TEA Set: Tacit Knowledge and Scientific Networks," *Science Studies* 4, no. 2 (1974): 165–86, doi.org/10.1177/030631277400400203.

100. Dean Radin and A. Pierce, "Psi and Psychophysiology," in *Parapsychology: A Handbook for the 21st Century*, ed. Etzel Cardeña, John Palmer, and David Marcusson-Clavertz (McFarland & Co., 2015), psycnet.apa.org/record/2015-48721-017.

101. Thomas D. Duane and Thomas Behrendt, "Extrasensory Electroencephalographic Induction Between Identical Twins," *Science* 150, no. 3694 (1965): 367, doi.org/10.1126/science.150.3694.367.

102. Tolga E. Özkurt, "Revisiting the Earliest Hyperscanning Study: Power and Functional Connectivity in the Alpha Band May Link Brains Far Apart," *Frontiers in Human Neuroscience* 18 (2024), doi.org/10.3389/fnhum.2024.1476944.

103. Göran Brusewitz and Adrian Parker, "An Experiment with Three Studies of Physiological Connectedness Amongst Twins and Its Possible Relationship to Attachment," *Explore* 20, no. 5 (2024), doi.org/10.1016/j.explore.2024.01.008; Christian G. Jensen and Adrian Parker, "Entangled in the Womb? A Pilot Study on the Possible Physiological Connectedness Between Identical Twins with Different Embryonic Backgrounds," *Explore* 8, no. 6 (2012): 339–47, doi.org/10.1016/j.explore.2012.08.001; Adrian Parker and Christian Jensen, "Further Possible Physiological Connectedness Between Identical Twins: The London Study," *Explore* 9, no. 1 (2013): 26–31, doi.org/10.1016/j.explore.2012.10.001.

104. To list just a few of about two dozen such studies: Jeanne Achterberg et al., "Evidence for Correlations Between Distant Intentionality and Brain Function in Recipients: A Functional Magnetic Resonance Imaging Analysis," *Journal of Alternative and Complementary Medicine* 11, no. 6 (2005): 965–71, doi.org/10.1089/acm.2005.11.965; Efstratios Karavasilis et al., "Functional MRI Study to Examine Possible Emotional Connectedness in Identical Twins: A Case Study," *Explore* 14, no. 1 (2018): 86–91, doi.org/10.1016/j.explore.2017.06.008; Todd L. Richards, Leila Kozak, L. Clark Johnson, and Leanna J. Standish, "Replicable Functional Magnetic Resonance Imaging Evidence of Correlated Brain Signals Between Physically and Sensory Isolated Subjects," *Journal of Alternative and Complementary Medicine* 11, no. 6 (2005): 955–63, doi.org/10.1089/acm.2005.11.955; Leanna J. Standish, L. Clark Johnson, Leila Kozak, and Todd Richards, "Evidence of Correlated Functional Magnetic Resonance Imaging Signals Between Distant Human Brains," *Alternative Therapies in Health and Medicine* 9, no. 1 (2003): 122–25.

105. Richard B. Silberstein and Felicity J. Bigelow, "Brain Functional Connectivity Correlates of Anomalous Interaction Between Sensorily Isolated Monozygotic Twins," *Frontiers in Human Neuroscience* 18 (2024), doi.org/10.3389/fnhum.2024.1388049.

106. Stefan Schmidt, Rainer Scheider, Jessica Utts, and Harald Walach, "Distant Intentionality and the Feeling of Being Stared At: Two Meta-Analyses," *British Journal of Psychology* 95 (2004): 235–47, doi.org/10.1348/000712604773952449.

107. John S. Hagelin et al., "Effects of Group Practice of the Transcendental Meditation Program on Preventing Violent Crime in Washington, D.C.: Results of the National Demonstration Project, June–July 1993," *Social Indicators Research* 47, no. 2 (1999): 153–201; David W. Orme-Johnson, "Preventing Crime Through the Maharishi Effect," *Journal of Offender Rehabilitation* 36, no. 1–4 (2003): 257–81, doi.org/10.1300/J076v36n01_12.

108. Global Consciousness Project 2.0, gcp2.net.

109. Roger D. Nelson, "Implicit Physical Psi: The Global Consciousness Project," in *Parapsychology: A Handbook for the 21st Century*, ed. Etzel Cardeña, John Palmer, and David Marcusson-Clavertz (McFarland & Co., 2015); Roger D. Nelson et al., "Field REG Anomalies in Group Situations," *Journal of Scientific Exploration* 10, no. 1 (1996): 111–41.

110. I put the word *cause* in quotes because it isn't clear that the underlying mechanisms are causal in the usual sense of that term. What we see are unexpected correlations, but why these correlations appear may not be due to any of the known four forces in physics.

111. Peter A. Bancel, "Searching for Global Consciousness: A 17-Year Exploration," *Explore* 13, no. 2 (2017): 94–101, doi.org/10.1016/j.explore.2016.12.003.

112. Dean Radin, "Effects of Global Consciousness on New Year's Eve: A Study in Experimental Metaphysics," *Journal of Scientific Exploration* (forthcoming, 2025).

113. Dean Radin, "Sentiment and Presentiment in Twitter: Do Trends in Collective Mood 'Feel the Future'?" *World Futures* 79, no. 5 (2023): 525–35, doi.org/10.1080/02604027.2023.2216629.

CHAPTER 3: SCIENCE OF DIVINATION

1. Edwin C. May and Sonali B. Marwaha, eds., *Remote Viewing, 1972–1984*, vol. 1 of *The Star Gate Archives: Reports of the United States Government Sponsored Psi Program, 1972–1995* (McFarland & Co., 2018).

2. International Remote Viewing Association, www.irva.org.

3. Patrizio Tressoldi and Lance Storm, "Anomalous Cognition: An Umbrella Review of the Meta-Analytic Evidence," *PsyArXiv* (2021), doi.org/10.31234/osf.io/5gwqb.

4. Danny Penman, "Could There Be Proof to the Theory That We're ALL Psychic?" *Daily Mail*, January 29, 2008, www.dailymail.co.uk/news/article-510762/Could-proof-theory-ALL-psychic.html.

5. Patrizio Tressoldi and Debra Katz, "Remote Viewing: A 1974–2022 Systematic Review and Meta-Analysis," *Journal of Scientific Exploration* 37, no. 3 (2023), doi.org/10.31275/20232931.

6. "Ask Molly: Did CIA Really Study Psychic Powers?" CIA, October 27, 2021, www.cia.gov/stories/story/ask-molly-did-cia-really-study-psychic-powers/; Sarah Pruitt, "The CIA Recruited 'Mind Readers' to Spy on the Soviets in the 1970s," History, October 17, 2018, www.history.com/news/cia-esp-espionage-soviet-union-cold-war.

7. John Greenewald, "DoD Releases 'KONA BLUE' Documents," Black Vault, April 16, 2024, www.theblackvault.com/documentarchive/dod-releases-kona-blue-documents/.

8. Edith Olmsted, "U.S. Eyed Program on Mind Reading and Reverse-Engineering UFOs," *Daily Beast*, March 8, 2024, www.thedailybeast.com/new-report-reveals-us-eyed-program-on-mind-reading-and-reverse-engineering-ufos.

9. Luis Elizondo, *Imminent: Inside the Pentagon's Hunt for UFOs* (William Morrow, 2024).

CHAPTER 4: SCIENCE OF THEURGY

1. Albert Einstein, *Albert Einstein, The Human Side: Glimpses from His Archives*, ed. Helen Dukas and Banesh Hoffman, rev. ed. (Princeton University Press, 2013).

2. Eben Alexander III, "Extraordinary Cases of Miraculous Healing," *Explore* 13, no. 4 (2017): 257–58, doi.org/10.1016/j.explore.2017.04.006; Dirk J. Kruijthoff et al., "Can You Be Cured If the Doctor Disagrees? A Case Study of 27 Prayer Healing Reports Evaluated by a Medical Assessment Team in the Netherlands," *Explore* 19, no. 3 (2023): 376–82, doi.org/10.1016/j.explore.2022.07.008; George A. Mashour et al., "Paradoxical Lucidity: A Potential Paradigm Shift for the Neurobiology and Treatment of Severe Dementias," *Alzheimer's and Dementia* 15, no. 8 (2019): 1107–14, doi.org/10.1016/j.jalz.2019.04.002; Michael Nahm, Bruce Greyson, Emily W. Kelly, and Erlendur Haraldsson, "Terminal Lucidity: A Review and a Case Collection," *Archives of Gerontology and Geriatrics* 55, no. 1 (2012): 138–42, doi.org/10.1016/j.archger.2011.06.031; Michael Nahm and Bruce Greyson, "Terminal Lucidity in Patients with Chronic Schizophrenia and Dementia: A Survey of the Literature," *Journal of Nervous and Mental Disease* 197, no. 12 (2009): 942–44, doi.org/10.1097/NMD.0b013e3181c22583; Donna Thomas and Graeme O'Connor, "Exploring Near Death Experiences with Children Post Intensive Care: A Case Series," *Explore* 20, no. 3 (2024): 443–49, doi.org/10.1016/j.explore.2023.11.003.

3. Rachel Nuwer, "Lifting the Veil on Near-Death Experiences," *Scientific American*, May 14, 2024, www.scientificamerican.com/article/lifting-the-veil-on -near-death-experiences/.

4. William G. Roll, *The Poltergeist* (Doubleday, 1972).

5. Fred M. Wilcox, dir., *Forbidden Planet*, Metro-Goldwyn-Mayer, released June 13, 1956.

6. Arnaud Delorme et al., "Electrocortical Activity Associated with Subjective Communication with the Deceased," *Frontiers in Psychology* 4, no. 834 (2013), doi.org/10.3389/fpsyg.2013.00834; Arnaud Delorme, Cedric Cannard, Dean Radin, and Helané Wahbeh, "Accuracy and Neural Correlates of Blinded Mediumship Compared to Controls on an Image Classification Task," *Brain and Cognition* 146 (2020), doi.org/10.1016/j.bandc.2020.105638.

7. Matthew Sarraf, Michael A. Woodley, and Patrizio Tressoldi, "Anomalous Information Reception by Mediums: A Meta-Analysis of the Scientific Evidence," *Explore* 17, no. 5 (2021): 396–402, doi.org/10.1016/j.explore.2020.04 .002.

8. Iris M. Owen and Margaret Sparrow, *Conjuring Up Philip: An Adventure in Psychokinesis* (Fitzhenry & Whiteside, 1976); R. Reichbart, "Group Psi: Comments on the Recent Toronto PK Experiment as Recounted in *Conjuring Up Philip*," *Journal of the American Society for Psychical Research* 71, no. 2 (1977): 201–12.

9. "Life After Death Essay Contest Runners-Up," Bigelow Institute for Consciousness Studies, n.d., www.bigelowinstitute.org/index.php/bics-afterlife -proof/bics-essay-contest-winners-runners-up/.

10. Bernardo Kastrup, "A Rational, Empirical Case for Postmortem Survival Based Solely on Mainstream Science," Bigelow Institute for Consciousness Studies, www.bigelowinstitute.org/wp-content/uploads/2022/10/kastrup-empirical -postmortem-survival.pdf.

11. Ibid.

CHAPTER 5: TAKING MAGIC SERIOUSLY

1. Chris French, *The Science of Weird Shit: Why Our Minds Conjure the Paranormal* (MIT Press, 2025).

2. Helané Wahbeh et al., "Exceptional Experiences Reported by Scientists and Engineers," *Explore* 14, no. 5 (2018): 329–41, doi.org/10.1016/j.explore.2018.05 .002.

3. Andreas Sommer, "What Is the Best Available Evidence for the Survival of Human Consciousness after Permanent Bodily Death?," Bigelow Institute for Consciousness Studies, www.bigelowinstitute.org/wp-content/uploads/2022/10/sommer-best-evidence-survival.pdf.

4. Skeptical About Skeptics, skepticalaboutskeptics.org.

5. Harry M. Collins and Robert Evans, "The Third Wave of Science Studies: Studies of Expertise and Experience," *Social Studies of Science* 32, no. 2 (2002): 235–96 at 265, doi.org/10.1177/0306312702032002003.

6. Andreas Sommer, "Psychical Research in the History and Philosophy of Science. An Introduction and Review," *Studies in History and Philosophy of Science Part C: Studies in History and Philosophy of Biological and Biomedical Sciences* 48, pt. A (2014): 38–45, doi.org/10.1016/j.shpsc.2014.08.004.

7. Freeman Dyson, "One in a Million," *New York Review of Books*, March 25, 2004.

8. John Horgan, "Brilliant Scientists Are Open-Minded About Paranormal Stuff, So Why Not You?" *Scientific American*, July 20, 2012, www.scientificamerican.com/blog/cross-check/brilliant-scientists-are-open-minded-about-paranormal-stuff-so-why-not-you/.

9. Alan Turing, "Computing Machinery and Intelligence," *Mind* 49, no. 236 (1950): 433–60, doi.org/10.1093/mind/LIX.236.433.

10. Etzel Cardeña, "Eminent People Interested in Psi," *Psi Encyclopedia*, n.d., psi-encyclopedia.spr.ac.uk/articles/eminent-people-interested-psi.

11. Martin Gardner and John Archibald Wheeler, "Quantum Theory and Quack Theory," *New York Review of Books*, May 17, 1979, www.nybooks.com/articles/1979/05/17/quantum-theory-and-quack-theory/.

12. Sean Carroll, "Telekinesis and Quantum Field Theory," *Discover*, February 18, 2008, www.discovermagazine.com/the-sciences/telekinesis-and-quantum-field-theory.

13. Carl Sagan, "The Burden of Skepticism," *Skeptical Inquirer* 12, no. 1 (1987), 38–46.

14. Bertrand Russell, *Mortals and Others: Bertrand Russell's American Essays, 1931–1935* (Routledge, 1975).

15. Dean Radin, *The Conscious Universe: The Scientific Truth of Psychic Phenomena* (HarperOne, 1997).

16. "Skeptics Concede Evidence for Psi," Skeptical About Skeptics, n.d.,

skepticalaboutskeptics.org/examining-skeptics/editorial-skeptics-concede
-evidence-for-psi/.

17. Benoît Godin and Yves Gingras, "The Experimenters' Regress: From Skepticism to Argumentation," *Studies in History and Philosophy of Science Part A* 33, no. 1 (2002): 133–48, doi.org/10.1016/S0039-3681(01)00032-2.

18. Arthur S. Reber and James E. Alcock, "Searching for the Impossible: Parapsychology's Elusive Quest," *American Psychologist* 75, no. 3 (2019): 391–99, doi.org/10.1037/amp0000486.

19. Kok-Wei Bong et al., "A Strong No-Go Theorem on the Wigner's Friend Paradox," *Nature Physics* 16, no. 12 (2020): 1199–205, https://doi.org/10.1038/s41567-020-0990-x; S. Friederich and P. W. Evans, "Retrocausality in Quantum Mechanics," in *The Stanford Encyclopedia of Philosophy*, ed. Edward N. Zalta and Uri Nodelman (Metaphysics Research Lab, Stanford University, 2023), plato.stanford.edu/archives/win2023/entries/qm-retrocausality/; Matthew S. Leifer and Matthew F. Pusey, "Is a Time Symmetric Interpretation of Quantum Theory Possible Without Retrocausality?" *Proceedings of the Royal Society A: Mathematical, Physical and Engineering Sciences* 473, no. 2202 (2017): 20160607, doi.org/10.1098/rspa.2016.0607; Adrian Cho, "Quantum Experiment in Space Confirms That Reality Is What You Make It," *Science*, October 27, 2017, www.science.org/content/article/quantum-experiment-space-confirms -reality-what-you-make-it-0; Sangbae Kim and Byoung S. Ham, "Observations of the Delayed-Choice Quantum Eraser Using Coherent Photons," *Scientific Reports* 13, no. 9758 (2023), www.nature.com/articles/s41598-023-36590-7.

20. Matt Swayne, "Quantum Fiber Optics in the Brain Enhance Processing, May Protect Against Degenerative Diseases," *Quantum Insider*, May 13, 2024, thequantuminsider.com/2024/05/13/quantum-fiber-optics-in-the-brain-enhance -processing-may-protect-against-degenerative-diseases/.

21. Jennifer C. Brookes, "Quantum Effects in Biology: Golden Rule in Enzymes, Olfaction, Photosynthesis and Magnetodetection," *Proceedings of the Royal Society A: Mathematical, Physical and Engineering Sciences* 473, no. 2201 (2017): 20160822, doi.org/10.1098/rspa.2016.0822.

22. N. S. Babcock et al., "Ultraviolet Superradiance from Mega-Networks of Tryptophan in Biological Architectures," *Journal of Physical Chemistry B: Biophysical and Biochemical Systems and Processes* 128, no. 17 (2024): 4035–46, doi.org/10.1021/acs.jpcb.3c07936; Christian M. Kerskens and David L. Pérez, "Experimental Indications of Non-Classical Brain Functions," *Journal of Physics Communications* 6, no. 10 (2022): 105001, doi.org/10.1088/2399-6528/ac94be.

23. E. H. Walker, "Quantum Mechanics/Psi Phenomena: The Theory and Suggestions for New Experiments," *Journal of Research in Psi Phenomena* 1, no. 1 (1976): 38–52.

24. Dean Radin, Gail Hayssen, and James Walsh, "Effects of Intentionally Enhanced Chocolate on Mood," *Explore* 3, no. 5 (2007): 485–92, doi.org/10 .1016/j.explore.2007.06.004.

25. Edwin C. May and Sonali B. Marwaha, eds., *Extrasensory Perception: Support, Skepticism, and Science*, 2 vols. (Praeger/ABC-CLIO, 2015).

26. Carlos M. N. Eire, *They Flew: A History of the Impossible* (Yale University Press, 2023), xiii.

27. Ibid., 374.

28. Etzel Cardeña,"The Experimental Evidence for Parapsychological Phenomena: A Review," *American Psychologist* 73, no. 5 (2018): 663–77, doi.org/ 10.1037/amp0000236.

29. Arthur S. Reber and James E. Alcock, "Searching for the Impossible: Parapsychology's Elusive Quest," *American Psychologist* 75, no. 3 (2019), doi.org/ 10.1037/amp0000486.

30. David W. Moore, "Three in Four Americans Believe in Paranormal: Little Change from Similar Results in 2001," Gallup, June 16, 2005, www.gallup.com/ poll/16915/three-four-americansbelieve-paranormal.aspx; Tom W. Rice, "Believe It or Not: Religious and Other Paranormal Beliefs in the United States," *Journal for the Scientific Study of Religion* 42, no. 1 (2003): 95–106, doi.org/10.1111/ 1468-5906.00163; Wahbeh et al., "Exceptional Experiences."

31. Jibum Kim et al., "Paranormal Beliefs: Using Survey Trends from the USA to Suggest a New Area of Research in Asia," *Asian Journal for Public Opinion Research* 2, no. 4 (2015): 279–306, doi.org/10.15206/ajpor.2015.2.4.279.

32. Yoshimasa Majima, Alexander C. Walker, Martin H. Turpin, and Jonathan A. Fugelsang, "Culture as a Moderator of Epistemically Suspect Beliefs," *Frontiers in Psychology* 13 (2022), doi.org/10.3389/fpsyg.2022.745580.

33. Most of these are in the United Kingdom, largely due to the legacy of the Koestler Chair of Parapsychology at the University of Edinburgh, which was established in 1985 as a bequest of the author Arthur Koestler and his wife, Cynthia. Since then, doctorates who graduated from that program have held appointments at the University of Northampton, Bucks New University, University of Greenwich, University of Derby, Manchester Metropolitan

University, Northumbria University Newcastle, University of York, Nottingham Trent University, Leeds Beckett University, Robert Gordon University, University of Buckingham, Birmingham City University, Canterbury Christ Church University, Staffordshire University, University of Chester, Open University, Coventry University, University of the West of England, University of Central Lancashire, University of Hertfordshire, University of Wales Trinity Saint David, and so on.

34. Michael Shermer, *Why People Believe Weird Things: Pseudoscience, Superstition, and Other Confusions of Our Time*, rev. ed. (Henry Holt, 2002).

35. Jenny Gross, "A U.K. University Will Confer a New Title: A Master's Degree in the Occult," *New York Times*, October 13, 2024.

36. Jessica Bennett, "When Did Everybody Become a Witch?" *New York Times*, October 24, 2019.

37. Egil Asprem, "The Society for Psychical Research," in *The Occult World*, ed. Christopher Partridge (Routledge, 2015); Alan Gauld, *The Founders of Psychical Research* (Routledge, 2019), 387, doi.org/10.4324/9780429060526.

38. Kenneth G. Drinkwater, Neil Dagnall, Andrew Denovan, and Christopher Williams, "Paranormal Belief, Thinking Style and Delusion Formation: A Latent Profile Analysis of Within-Individual Variations in Experience-Based Paranormal Facets," *Frontiers in Psychology* 12 (2021), doi.org/10.3389/fpsyg.2021.670959; José M. Pérez Navarro and Xana M. Martínez Guerra, "Personality, Cognition, and Morbidity in the Understanding of Paranormal Belief," *PsyCh Journal* 9, no. 1 (2020): 118–31, doi.org/10.1002/pchj.295; Frederik Schwerter and Florian Zimmermann, "Determinants of Trust: The Role of Personal Experiences," *Games and Economic Behavior* 122 (2020): 413–25, doi.org/10.1016/j.geb.2020.05.002.

39. Tess Armstrong, Matthew Rockloff, Matthew Browne, and Alexander Blaszczynski, "Encouraging Gamblers to Think Critically Using Generalised Analytical Priming Is Ineffective at Reducing Gambling Biases," *Journal of Gambling Studies* 36, no. 3 (2020): 851–69, doi.org/10.1007/s10899-019-09910-8; Toby Prike, Michelle M. Arnold, and Paul Williamson, "The Relationship Between Anomalistic Belief, Misperception of Chance and the Base Rate Fallacy," *Thinking and Reasoning* 26, no. 3 (2019): 447–77, doi.org/10.1080/13546783.2019.1653371.

40. Olival Freire, Jr., "Quantum Dissidents: Research on the Foundations of Quantum Theory Circa 1970," *Studies in History and Philosophy of Science Part*

B: Studies in History and Philosophy of Modern Physics 40, no. 4 (2009): 280–89, doi.org/10.1016/j.shpsb.2009.09.002; Bruce Rosenblum and Fred Kuttner, *Quantum Enigma: Physics Encounters Consciousness* (Oxford University Press, 2006).

41. Bernardo Kastrup, *Why Materialism Is Baloney: How True Skeptics Know There Is No Death and Fathom Answers to Life, the Universe, and Everything* (Iff Books, 2014); Bernardo Kastrup, *The Idea of the World: A Multi-Disciplinary Argument for the Mental Nature of Reality* (Iff Books, 2019); Brentyn Ramm, "Panpsychism and the First-Person Perspective: The Case for Panpsychist Idealism," *Mind and Matter* 19, no. 1 (2021): 75–106; Leopold Stubenberg, "Neutral Monism," in *The Stanford Encyclopedia of Philosophy*, ed. Edward N. Zalta (Metaphysics Research Lab, Stanford University, 2018), plato.stanford .edu/archives/fall2018/entries/neutral-monism/; Giulio Tononi and Christof Koch, "Consciousness: Here, There and Everywhere?" *Philosophical Transactions of the Royal Society B: Biological Sciences* 370, no. 1668 (2015), doi .org/10.1098/rstb.2014.0167.

42. Ralph Blumenthal and Leslie Kean, "No Longer in Shadows, Pentagon's U.F.O. Unit Will Make Some Findings Public," *New York Times*, July 23, 2020, www.nytimes.com/2020/07/23/us/politics/pentagon-ufo-harry-reid-navy.html.

43. Marieta Pehlivanova, Marina Weiler, and Bruce Greyson, "Cognitive Styles and Psi: Psi Researchers Are More Similar to Skeptics Than to Lay Believers," *Frontiers in Psychology* 15 (2024), doi.org/10.3389/fpsyg.2024.1398121.

44. Sommer, "Psychical Research."

45. Samuel K. Cohn, Jr., "The Black Death: End of a Paradigm," *American Historical Review* 107, no. 3 (2002): 703–38, doi.org/10.1086/ahr/107.3.703.

46. Roderick Main, *Breaking the Spell of Disenchantment: Mystery, Meaning, and Metaphysics in the Work of C. G. Jung* (Chiron, 2022), 24.

47. Patrick McNamara, William Newsome, Brie Linkenhoker, and Jordan Grafman, "Neuroscientists Must Not Be Afraid to Study Religion," *Nature* 631, no. 8019 (2024): 25–27, doi.org/10.1038/d41586-024-02153-7.

48. John Palmer, "Hansel's Ghost: Resurrection of the Experimenter Fraud Hypothesis in Parapsychology," *Journal of Parapsychology* 80, no. 1 (2016): 5–16.

49. Sommer, "Psychical Research."

50. Ibid., 42.

51. Robert L. Kuhn, "A Landscape of Consciousness: Toward a Taxonomy of

Explanations and Implications," *Progress in Biophysics and Molecular Biology* 190 (2024): 28–169, doi.org/10.1016/j.pbiomolbio.2023.12.003.

52. Ulrich A. K. Betz et al., "Game Changers in Science and Technology—Now and Beyond," *Technological Forecasting and Social Change* 193 (2023): 122588, doi.org/10.1016/j.techfore.2023.122588.

53. Michael Dickson, "Intellectual Humility Is a Key Ingredient for Scientific Progress," *The Conversation*, December 6, 2023, theconversation.com/intellectual-humility-is-a-key-ingredient-for-scientific-progress-211410.

54. Lord Kelvin, "Nineteenth Century Clouds Over the Dynamical Theory of Heat and Light," *London, Edinburgh, and Dublin Philosophical Magazine and Journal of Science* 1, no. 7 (1901): 1–40, doi.org/10.1080/14786440109462664.

55. Patricia S. Churchland, *Neurophilosophy: Toward a Unified Science of the Mind-Brain* (MIT Press, 1986); Francis Crick, *The Astonishing Hypothesis: The Scientific Search for the Soul* (Simon & Schuster, 1994).

56. Max Tegmark, *Our Mathematical Universe: My Quest for the Ultimate Nature of Reality* (Knopf, 2014).

57. Maximilian Schlosshauer, *Decoherence and the Quantum-to-Classical Transition* (Springer, 2007).

58. Edward F. Kelly and Emily W. Kelly, *Irreducible Mind: Toward a Psychology for the 21st Century* (Rowman & Littlefield, 2007); Stephan A. Schwartz, "Nonlocality and Exceptional Experiences: A Study of Genius, Religious Epiphany, and the Psychic," *Explore* 6, no. 4 (2010): 227–36, doi.org/10.1016/j.explore.2010.04.008.

CHAPTER 6: THEORIES OF MAGIC

1. Gerhard Mayer, "Magic and Its Evaluation—Reports and Views of Practitioners," *Journal of Parapsychology* (in press).

2. I thank G. M. Wolf for clarifying the distinction between *want* and *need*.

3. Mayer, "Magic and Its Evaluation."

4. Thomas Cleary, trans., *The Secret of the Golden Flower* (HarperOne, 1991).

5. Frater U.D., *High Magic: Theory and Practice* (Llewellyn, 2005).

6. Peter J. Carroll, *Liber Kaos: Chaos Magic for the Pandaemonaeon*, rev. ed. (Weiser Books, 2023).

7. Isaac Bonewits, "The Laws of Magic," in *Authentic Thaumaturgy* (Steve Jackson Games, 1988), www.neopagan.net/AT_Laws.html.

8. Isaac Bonewits, *Real Magic: An Introductory Treatise on the Basic Principles of Yellow Magic*, rev. ed. (Red Wheel/Weiser, 1989).

9. Peter Ayton, Leonardo Weiss-Cohen, and Matthew Barson, "Magical Contagion and Commemorative Plaques: Effects of Celebrity Occupancy on Property Values," *Journal of Environmental Psychology* 79 (2022): 101723, doi .org/10.1016/j.jenvp.2021.101723.

10. Karl S. Rosengren, Carl N. Johnson, and Paul L. Harris, eds., *Imagining the Impossible: Magical, Scientific, and Religious Thinking in Children* (Cambridge University Press, 2000), doi.org/10.1017/CBO9780511571381.

11. Joshua Howgego, "The Universe Is Built a Lot Like a Giant Brain—So Is It Conscious?" *NewScientist*, June 25, 2024, www.newscientist.com/article/ mg26234971-200-the-universe-is-built-a-lot-like-a-giant-brain-so-is-it-conscious/.

12. Sharon Begley, *Train Your Mind, Change Your Brain: How a New Science Reveals Our Extraordinary Potential to Transform Ourselves* (Ballantine, 2007); Francis Crick, *The Astonishing Hypothesis: The Scientific Search for the Soul* (Simon & Schuster, 1994); Adam Garfinkle, "Scott Adams' Moist Robots," Law & Liberty, lawliberty.org/scott-adams-moist-robots/. The phrase "meat machine" is attributed to MIT's Marvin Minsky.

13. Neuralink, neuralink.com.

14. Jerry Fodor, "The Big Idea: Can There Be a Science of Mind?" *Times Literary Supplement*, July 3, 1992, 5–7.

15. Pallab Ghosh, "Are Animals Conscious? Some Scientists Now Think They Are," BBC, June 15, 2024, www.bbc.com/news/articles/cv223z15mpmo; Natalie Lawrence, "The Radical New Experiments That Hint at Plant Consciousness," *New Scientist*, August 24, 2022, www.newscientist.com/article/mg25534012-800 -the-radical-new-experiments-that-hint-at-plant-consciousness/; Dan Falk, "Insects and Other Animals Have Consciousness, Experts Declare," *Quanta Magazine*, April 19, 2024, www.quantamagazine.org/insects-and-other-animals -have-consciousness-experts-declare-20240419.

16. Marcus H. Mast, "Claims of Anomalously Long Fasting: An Assessment of the Evidence from Investigated Cases," *Explore* 16, no. 5 (2020): 287–96, doi .org/10.1016/j.explore.2020.05.015.

17. "Alexandrina Maria da Costa (1904–1955)," Vatican, n.d., www.vatican.va/ news_services/liturgy/saints/ns_lit_doc_20040425_da-costa_en.html.

18. Francis Johnston, *Alexandrina: The Agony and the Glory* (1979; reprint TAN Books, 2015).

19. Harald Atmanspacher and Dean Rickles, *Dual-Aspect Monism and the Deep Structure of Meaning* (Routledge, 2022).

20. Marcus E. Raichle, "The Brain's Dark Energy," *Scientific American*, March 1, 2010, www.scientificamerican.com/article/the-brains-dark-energy/.

21. Herbert van Erkelens, *Science and Religion: One World—Changing Perspectives on Reality*, ed. J. W. Fennema and Paul Iain (Springer Netherlands, 1990), 201ff, doi.org/10.1007/978-94-009-2021-7_21.

22. Dennis William Hauck, "In the Mind of the Universe: The Monad and You," Monad Manifesto, n.d., monadmanifesto.com.

23. Harald Atmanspacher, "Synchronicity and the Experience of Psychophysical Correlations," in *Research in Analytical Psychology*, ed. Christian Roesler (Routledge, 2018).

24. Bernard Beitman, *Meaningful Coincidences: How and Why Synchronicity and Serendipity Happen* (Park Street Press, 2022); Squire D. Rushnell, *When God Winks: How the Power of Coincidence Guides Your Life* (Howard Books, 2018).

25. Pamela Rae Heath, *Mind-Matter Interaction: A Review of Historical Reports, Theory and Research* (McFarland & Co., 2011).

26. Research Network for the Study of Esoteric Practices, www.rensep.org.

27. Anil Ananthaswamy, "Can AI Save Schrödinger's Cat?" *Scientific American*, July 1, 2024, www.scientificamerican.com/article/can-ai-save-schroedingers-cat/.

28. Joop M. Houtkooper, "Arguing for an Observational Theory of Paranormal Phenomena," *Journal of Scientific Exploration* 16, no. 2 (2002): 171–85; Brian Millar, "The Observational Theories: A Primer," *European Journal of Parapsychology* 1, no. 2–3 (1978): 304–32.

29. Philip Ball, "Two Slits and One Hell of a Quantum Conundrum," *Nature*, August 7, 2018, www.nature.com/articles/d41586-018-05892-6.

30. Helmut Schmidt, "Comparison of a Teleological Model with a Quantum Collapse Model of Psi," *Journal of Parapsychology* 48, no. 4 (1984): 261–76; Helmut Schmidt, "Addition Effect for PK on Prerecorded Targets," *Journal of Parapsychology* 49, no. 3 (1985): 229–44.

31. Ball, "Two Slits."

32. Juan Miguel Marin, "'Mysticism' in Quantum Mechanics: The Forgotten Controversy," *European Journal of Physics* 30, no. 4 (2009): 807–22, doi.org/10.1088/0143-0807/30/4/014.

33. Ken Wilber and Fredrick M. Stein, eds., *Quantum Questions: Mystical Writings of the World's Great Physicists* (Shambhala, 1984), reviewed by Frederick M. Stein in *American Journal of Physics* 53, no. 6 (1985): 601.

34. Arthur I. Miller, *Jung, Pauli, and the Pursuit of a Scientific Obsession* (W.W. Norton, 2010), 249.

35. Marin, "'Mysticism' in Quantum Mechanics."

36. Ball, "Two Slits," 40.

37. John Archibald Wheeler, *Geons, Black Holes and Quantum Foam: A Life in Physics* (W.W. Norton, 1998), 191.

38. Philip Ball, *Beyond Weird: Why Everything You Thought You Knew about Quantum Physics Is Different* (Vintage, 2019), 89.

39. Ibid. 118.

40. Paul Levy, *Quantum Revelation: A Radical Synthesis of Science and Spirituality* (SelectBooks, 2018).

41. Donald D. Hoffman, *The Case Against Reality: Why Evolution Hid the Truth from Our Eyes* (W.W. Norton, 2019), 101.

42. Ball, *Beyond Weird*, 347.

43. Henry P. Stapp, *Mindful Universe: Quantum Mechanics and the Participating Observer* (Springer, 2009); John C. Eccles, *How the Self Controls Its Brain* (Springer, 1986); Evan Harris Walker, "The Nature of Consciousness: A Hypothesis," *Mathematical Biosciences* 7, no. 1–2 (1970): 131–78; Stuart R. Hameroff and Roger Penrose, "Consciousness in the Universe: A Review of the 'Orch OR' Theory," *Physics of Life Reviews* 11, no. 1 (2014): 39–78, doi.org/10.1016/j.plrev.2013.08.002.

44. Michael Duggan, "Walter von Lucadou," *Psi Encyclopedia*, psi-encyclopedia.spr.ac.uk/articles/walter-von-lucadou.

45. Katrin Becker, Melanie Becker, and John H. Schwarz, *String Theory and M-Theory: A Modern Introduction* (Cambridge University Press, 2007).

46. Vernon M. Neppe and Edward R. Close, *Reality Begins with Consciousness: A Paradigm Shift that Works* (BrainVoyage.com, 2012), brainvoyage.com/RBC/perspective.php; Bernard Carr, "Worlds Apart? Can Psychical Research Bridge the Gulf Between Matter and Mind?" *Proceedings of the Society for Psychical Research* 59 (2008): 1–96; John R. Smythies, *The Walls of Plato's Cave* (Avebury Press, 2003); Johann K. F. Zöllner, *Transcendental Physics* (1878).

47. Rupert Sheldrake, *A New Science of Life: The Hypothesis of Morphic Resonance* (Tarcher, 1981); "Morphic Resonance: Research and Papers," Rupert Sheldrake, n.d., sheldrake.org/research/morphic-resonance.

48. Richard Shoup and Thomas Etter, "Can Causal Influence Propagate Backwards in Time? A Simple Experiment in Markov Chains and Causality" (Boundary Institute, 2002), www.scribd.com/document/78366752/Richard-Shoup -and-Thomas-Etter-Can-Causal-Influence-Propagate-Backwards-in-Time-a-Simple -Experiment-in-Markov-Chains-and-Causality; Richard Shoup, "Anomalies and Constraints: Can Clairvoyance, Precognition, and Psychokinesis Be Accommodated within Known Physics?" *Journal of Scientific Exploration* 16, no. 1 (2002): 3–18; Richard Shoup, "Physics Without Causality—Theory and Evidence," in Daniel P. Sheehan, ed., *Frontiers of Time: Retrocausation Experiment and Theory: AIP Conference Proceedings* 863 (American Institute of Physics, 2006), doi.org/10.1063/1.2388754; Richard Shoup, "Understanding Retrocausality—Can a Message Be Sent to the Past?" in *Quantum Retrocausation: Theory and Experiment: AIP Conference Proceedings*, ed. Daniel P. Sheehan (American Institute of Physics, 2011), doi.org/10.1063/1.3663728.

49. Edwin C. May and Sonali B. Marwaha, eds., *Extrasensory Perception: Support, Skepticism, and Science*, 2 vols. (Praeger/ABC-CLIO, 2015).

50. J. B. Rhine, ed., *Parapsychology from Duke to FRMN* (Parapsychology Press, 1965), 106.

51. Rex G. Stanford, "An Experimentally Testable Model for Spontaneous Psi Events II. Psychokinetic Events," *Journal of the American Society for Psychical Research* 68, no. 4 (1974): 321–56; Rex G. Stanford, "Psychological Concepts of Psi Function: A Review and Constructive Critique," in *Parapsychology: A Handbook for the 21st Century*, ed. Etzel Cardeña, John Palmer, and David Marcusson-Clavertz (McFarland & Co., 2015).

52. Lance C. Storm, "Parapsychological Investigation of the Theory of Psychopraxia: Experimental and Theoretical Researches into an Alternative Theory Explaining Normal and Paranormal Phenomena," PhD thesis, University of Adelaide, 2001.

53. James C. Carpenter, *First Sight: ESP and Parapsychology in Everyday Life* (Rowman & Littlefield, 2015).

54. Edwin C. May, Jessica Utts, and S. James P. Spottiswoode, "Decision Augmentation Theory: Toward a Model of Anomalous Mental Phenomena," *Journal of Parapsychology* 59 (1995): 195–220.

55. David Luke, "The Science of Magic: A Parapsychological Model of Psychic Ability in the Context of Magical Will," *Journal for the Academic Study of Magic* 4 (2007): 90–119.

56. David Luke, "Psi-verts and Psychic Piracy: The Future of Parapsychology?" in *Exploring the Edge Realms of Consciousness: Liminal Zones, Psychic Science, and Hidden Dimensions of the Mind,* ed. Daniel Pinchbeck and Ken Jordan (North Atlantic Books, 2012), gala.gre.ac.uk/id/eprint/11585/.

CHAPTER 7: DOING MAGIC

1. Alan Chapman, *Advanced Magick for Beginners* (Aeon Books, 2008), 16.

2. Roald Dahl, *The Wonderful Story of Henry Sugar* (1977; reprint Viking Books for Young Readers, 2000).

3. Donald M. Kraig, *Modern Magick: Twelve Lessons in the High Magickal Arts,* rev. ed. (Llewellyn, 2010), 41.

4. Robert Falconer, *The Others Within Us: Internal Family Systems, Porous Mind, and Spirit Possession* (Great Mystery Press, 2023); Kenaz Filan and Raven Kaldera, *Drawing Down the Spirits: The Traditions and Techniques of Spirit Possession* (Destiny Books, 2009).

5. Chapman, *Advanced Magick,* 21.

CHAPTER 8: ENCHANTMENT

1. Dean Radin and Jannine M. Rebman, "Seeking Psi in the Casino," *Journal of the Society for Psychical Research* 62, no. 850 (1998): 193–219; "Does the Moon Effect Our Ability to Make Decisions?" Adventures of Greg, April 19, 2020, adventuresofgreg.com/blog/2020/04/19/does-the-moon-effect-our-ability-to-make-decisions/.

2. Alan Chapman, *Advanced Magick for Beginners* (Aeon Books, 2008), 37.

3. Lynne Thorndike, *A History of Magic and Experimental Science* (Columbia University Press, 1958).

4. Bruno Bettelheim, *The Uses of Enchantment: The Meaning and Importance of Fairy Tales* (Thames & Hudson, 1976).

5. David Thompson, *Hidden in Plain Sight: The Art and Creation of Sigils* (n.p., 2023), 17.

CHAPTER 9: DIVINATION AND THEURGY

1. Amar Annus, ed., *Divination and Interpretation of Signs in the Ancient World* (University of Chicago, 2010); P. D. Newman, *Theurgy: Theory and Practice: The Mysteries of the Ascent to the Divine* (Simon & Schuster, 2023).

2. John Kreiter, "Create a Servitor: Harness the Power of Thought Forms," John Kreiter, 2014, www.johnkreiter.com.

3. Peter J. Carroll and Ian Blumberg-Enge, *Interview with a Wizard* (Mandrake of Oxford, 2022).

CHAPTER 10: GNOSIS

1. Samuel Aun Weor, *Introduction to Gnosis: Gnostic Methods for Today's World* (1961; Glorian, 2009); Dean Radin, *Supernormal: Science, Yoga, and the Evidence for Extraordinary Psychic Abilities* (Deepak Chopra Books/Random House, 2013).

2. Cassandra Vieten, "What Are Noetic Sciences?" *Psychology Today*, May 10, 2011.

3. Arnaud Delorme, *Why Our Minds Wander: Understand the Science and Learn How to Focus Your Thoughts* (Welbeck Balance, 2024).

CHAPTER 11: TESTING MAGIC

1. Dale E. Graff, *Tracks in the Psychic Wilderness: An Exploration of Remote Viewing, ESP, Precognitive Dreaming, and Synchronicity* (Element Books, 1998).

2. Montague Ullman, Stanley Krippner, and Alan Vaughan, *Dream Telepathy: The Landmark ESP Experiments* (Afterworlds Press, 2023).

3. Dean Radin, *The Conscious Universe: The Scientific Truth of Psychic Phenomena* (HarperOne, 1997), 107.

4. Lance Storm et al., "On the Correspondence Between Dream Content and Target Material Under Laboratory Conditions: A Meta-Analysis of Dream-ESP Studies, 1966–2016," *International Journal of Dream Research* 10, no. 2 (2017): 120–40, doi.org/10.11588/ijodr.2017.2.34888.

5. Dean Radin and Joyce Anastasia, "Psychophysical Interactions with Electrical Plasma: Three Exploratory Experiments," *Journal of the Society for Psychical Research* 87, no. 4 (2022): 226–43, doi.org/10.31234/osf.io/tqwb3.

6. Raymond Moody, *Reunions: Visionary Encounters with Departed Loved Ones* (Villard, 1993); Raymond Moody, "Family Reunions: Visionary Encounters with

the Departed in a Modern-Day Psychomanteum," *Journal of Near-Death Studies* 11, no. 2 (1992): 83–121, doi.org/10.1007/BF01074301.

7. Dean Radin and Jannine M. Rebman, "Are Phantasms Fact or Fantasy? A Preliminary Investigation of Apparitions Evoked in the Laboratory," *Journal of the Society for Psychical Research* 61, no. 843 (1996): 65–87.

CHAPTER 12: BEYOND MAGIC

1. M. D. S. Brewer and A. Judson, "Advanced Meditation Alters Consciousness and Our Basic Sense of Self," *Scientific American*, June 25, 2024, www .scientificamerican.com/article/advanced-meditation-alters-consciousness-and -our-basic-sense-of-self/; Cassandra Vieten et al., "Future Directions in Meditation Research: Recommendations for Expanding the Field of Contemplative Science," *PLOS One* 13, no. 11 (2018): e0205740, doi.org/10 .1371/journal.pone.0205740. .

2. S. Galan, "Research and Development Worldwide—Statistics and Facts," Statista, January 22, 2025, www.statista.com/topics/6737/research-and -development-worldwide/.

3. Agence France-Presse, "Witch-Hunt Murders Surge in Democratic Republic of Congo," *Guardian*, September 28, 2021, www.theguardian.com/world/2021/ sep/28/witch-hunt-murders-surge-democratic-republic-congo-women-south-kivu -province; Matt Siegel, "Papua New Guinea Considers Repealing Sorcery Law," *New York Times*, April 12, 2013.

4. Marilyn Schlitz, Cassandra Vieten, and Tina Amorok, *Living Deeply: The Art and Science of Transformation in Everyday Life* (New Harbinger, 2008).

INDEX

ABOUT THE AUTHOR

DEAN RADIN, PHD, is Chief Scientist at the Institute of Noetic Sciences (IONS), Associated Distinguished Professor at the California Institute of Integral Studies, and co-founder and chairman of the biotech company Cognigenics. He earned an MS (electrical engineering) and a PhD (psychology) from the University of Illinois, Urbana-Champaign, and in 2022 he was awarded an Honorary DSc from the Swami Vivekananda University in Bangalore, India. He is the author or co-author of some three hundred scientific and popular articles, four dozen book chapters, and nine books, four of which have been translated into fifteen foreign languages: *The Conscious Universe* (1997), *Entangled Minds* (2006), *Supernormal* (2013), and *Real Magic* (2018).